Language, Educ
Neoliberalism

FSC
www.fsc.org
MIX
Paper from
responsible sources
FSC® C014540

CRITICAL LANGUAGE AND LITERACY STUDIES

Series Editors: Professor Alastair Pennycook (*University of Technology, Sydney, Australia*) and **Professor Brian Morgan** (*Glendon College/York University, Toronto, Canada*) and **Professor Ryuko Kubota** (*University of British Columbia, Vancouver, Canada*)

Critical Language and Literacy Studies is an international series that encourages monographs directly addressing issues of power (its flows, inequities, distributions, trajectories) in a variety of language- and literacy-related realms. The aim with this series is twofold: (1) to cultivate scholarship that openly engages with social, political, and historical dimensions in language and literacy studies, and (2) to widen disciplinary horizons by encouraging new work on topics that have received little focus (see below for partial list of subject areas) and that use innovative theoretical frameworks.

Full details of all the books in this series and of all our other publications can be found on http://www.multilingual-matters.com, or by writing to Multilingual Matters, St Nicholas House, 31-34 High Street, Bristol BS1 2AW, UK.

Other books in the series

Gendered Identities and Immigrant Language Learning
Julia Menard-Warwick
China and English: Globalisation and the Dilemmas of Identity
Joseph Lo Bianco, Jane Orton and Gao Yihong (eds)
Language and HIV/AIDS
Christina Higgins and Bonny Norton (eds)
Hybrid Identities and Adolescent Girls: Being 'Half' in Japan
Laurel D. Kamada
Decolonizing Literacy: Mexican Lives in the Era of Global Capitalism
Gregorio Hernandez-Zamora
Contending with Globalization in World Englishes
Mukul Saxena and Tope Omoniyi (eds)
ELT, Gender and International Development: Myths of Progress in a Neocolonial World
Roslyn Appleby
Examining Education, Media, and Dialogue under Occupation: The Case of Palestine and Israel
Ilham Nasser, Lawrence N. Berlin and Shelley Wong (eds)
The Struggle for Legitimacy: Indigenized Englishes in Settler Schools
Andrea Sterzuk
Style, Identity and Literacy: English in Singapore
Christopher Stroud and Lionel Wee
Language and Mobility: Unexpected Places
Alastair Pennycook
Talk, Text and Technology: Literacy and Social Practice in a Remote Indigenous Community
Inge Kral
Language Learning, Gender and Desire: Japanese Women on the Move
Kimie Takahashi
English and Development: Policy, Pedagogy and Globalization
Elizabeth J. Erling and Philip Seargeant (eds)
Ethnography, Superdiversity and Linguistic Landscapes: Chronicles of Complexity
Jan Blommaert
Power and Meaning Making in an EAP Classroom - Engaging with the Everyday
Christian W. Chun
Local Languaging, Literacy and Multilingualism in a West African Society
Kasper Juffermans
English Teaching and Evangelical Mission - The Case of Lighthouse School
Bill Johnston
Race and Ethnicity in English Language Teaching
Christopher Joseph Jenks

CRITICAL LANGUAGE AND LITERACY STUDIES: 23

Language, Education and Neoliberalism

Critical Studies in Sociolinguistics

Edited by
Mi-Cha Flubacher and Alfonso Del Percio

MULTILINGUAL MATTERS
Bristol • Blue Ridge Summit

DOI 10.21832/FLUBAC8682

Library of Congress Cataloging in Publication Data
A catalog record for this book is available from the Library of Congress.
Names: Flubacher, Mi-Cha, editor. | Percio, Alfonso Del, editor.
Title: Language, Education and Neoliberalism: Critical Studies in Sociolinguistics/Edited by
  Mi-Cha Flubacher and Alfonso Del Percio.
Description: Bristol, UK; Blue Ridge Summit, PA: Multilingual Matters, [2017] | Series:
  Critical Language and Literacy Studies: 23 | Includes bibliographical references and
  index.
Identifiers: LCCN 2017014936| ISBN 9781783098682 (hardcover : acid-free paper) | ISBN
  9781783098675 (softcover : acid-free paper) | ISBN 9781783098699 (pdf) | ISBN
  9781783098705 (epub) | ISBN 9781783098712 (kindle)
Subjects: LCSH: Language and education–Social aspects. | Neoliberalism–Social aspects. |
  Sociolinguistics.
Classification: LCC P40.8 .L3669 2017 | DDC 306.44–dc23 LC record available at https://
  lccn.loc.gov/2017014936

British Library Cataloguing in Publication Data
A catalogue entry for this book is available from the British Library.

ISBN-13: 978-1-78309-868-2 (hbk)
ISBN-13: 978-1-78309-867-5 (pbk)

Multilingual Matters
UK: St Nicholas House, 31-34 High Street, Bristol BS1 2AW, UK.
USA: NBN, Blue Ridge Summit, PA, USA.

Website: www.multilingual-matters.com
Twitter: Multi_Ling_Mat
Facebook: https://www.facebook.com/multilingualmatters
Blog: www.channelviewpublications.wordpress.com

The policy of Multilingual Matters/Channel View Publications is to use papers that are natural, renewable and recyclable products, made from wood grown in sustainable forests. In the
manufacturing process of our books, and to further support our policy, preference is given to
printers that have FSC and PEFC Chain of Custody certification. The FSC and/or PEFC logos
will appear on those books where full certification has been granted to the printer concerned.

Typeset by Deanta Global Publishing Services Limited.
Printed and bound in the UK by Short Run Press Ltd.
Printed and bound in the US by Edwards Brothers Malloy, Inc.

Contents

Contributors

Alfonso Del Percio is lecturer of applied linguistics at UCL Institute of Education, University College London. His research focuses on language, work and inequality; language, migration and governmentality; multilingualism and nationalism; language, branding and the nation state; language and political economy. His recent publications include 'Discourses of Diversity' (*Language and Communication*, 2016, co-edited with Zorana Sokolovska), 'A Semiotics of Nation Branding' (*Signs and Society*, 2016) and *Language and Political Economy*, with Mi-Cha Flubacher and Alexandre Duchêne (Oxford University Press, 2016).

Haley De Korne conducts research and advocacy in relation to minoritized language communities, multilingual education, and language politics. She has participated in Indigenous language education projects as a linguist and educational consultant in a variety of contexts, in particular in Oaxaca, Mexico. She is a postdoctoral fellow at the Center for Multilingualism in Society across the Lifespan at the University of Oslo, Norway, and gratefully acknowledges the support of a predoctoral fellowship in anthropology from the Smithsonian Institute which enabled the research presented in Chapter 3.

Nelson Flores is an assistant professor of educational linguistics at the University of Pennsylvania Graduate School of Education. His research seeks to denaturalize raciolinguistic ideologies that inform current conceptualizations of language education. This entails both historical analysis of the origins of contemporary raciolinguistic ideologies and contemporary analysis examining how current language education policies and practices reproduce these ideologies. His work has appeared in scholarly journals such as *Critical Inquiry in Language Studies, Linguistics and Education, TESOL Quarterly* and *Harvard Educational Review*.

Mi-Cha Flubacher is a postdoctoral assistant in applied linguistics at the Department of Linguistics, University of Vienna, Austria. Collaborating in various research projects, she has gained extensive research experience on questions of multilingualism policies as well as multilingual practices and their consequences, e.g. in the workplace, as her publications attest. Her research interests include ethnographic approaches to the economic commodification of language and multilingualism, to language as a site of the reproduction of social inequality and to questions of language and race/ethnicity in the process of exoticization.

Shuang Gao is a sociolinguist working at the Department of English, University of Liverpool, UK. Her research interests include language and identity, ethnography, language ideology, language and globalization. She has published in the *Journal of Sociolinguistics*, *Language in Society* and others.

Gregory Hadley is a professor of applied linguistics and cultural studies in the Department of Humanities at Niigata University, Japan, and a visiting fellow at Kellogg College, The University of Oxford. He received his PhD from the University of Birmingham, UK. His most recent work is *English for Academic Purposes in Neoliberal Universities: A Critical Grounded Theory* (Springer, 2015).

Jill Koyama, an anthropologist, is associate professor in educational policy studies and practice and teaching learning and sociocultural studies. She is also affiliated with graduate interdisciplinary programs in social, cultural and critical theory, the Institute for LGBT Studies and second language acquisition and teaching. Her work is situated across three strands of inquiry: the productive social assemblage of policy, the controversies of globalizing educational policy and the politics of immigrant and refugee education. Her work has appeared in the *American Journal of Education*, *Anthropology and Education Quarterly*, *British Journal of Sociology of Education*, *Educational Policy*, *Educational Researcher* and *Journal of Education Policy*.

Beatriz Lorente is a lecturer at the Department of English of the University of Basel and a postdoctoral fellow at the Institute of Multilingualism of the University of Fribourg. Her research interests are in language and globalization, language and migration and language policy.

Jonathan Luke is a PhD student in the graduate program in linguistics and applied linguistics at York University in Toronto, Canada. His research interests include language policy and planning, the global position and function of English and critical English for academic purposes. He is currently completing his dissertation research project involving international students, English language learning and language policies in higher education.

Mary McGroarty, professor emerita in the applied linguistics program of the English Department at Northern Arizona University, Flagstaff, has taught courses in language policy and pedagogy for more than three decades in Arizona and California. She has trained teachers in China, Hungary, Morocco, Peru, Tunisia and Venezuela as well as the US. A past president of the American Association for Applied Linguistics, she has served on several editorial advisory boards in the US, the UK and Canada and has published in *Applied Linguistics, Canadian Modern Language Review, Language Policy, Language Learning, TESOL Quarterly* and in many edited collections.

Joseph Sung-Yul Park is associate professor in the Department of English Language and Literature at the National University of Singapore. His work focuses on the intersection of language and globalization, particularly the politics of language and neoliberalism, the discursive processes of transnationalism and English as a global language in an Asian context. He is the author of *The Local Construction of a Global Language: Ideologies of English in South Korea* (Mouton de Gruyter, 2009) and *Markets of English: Linguistic Capital and Language Ideology in a Globalizing World* (co-authored with Lionel Wee, Routledge, 2012).

Honey B. Tabiola is instructor in education at Father Saturnino Urios University, Philippines. He has a master's degree in English language and literature teaching from the Ateneo de Manila University and was a graduate student research fellow at the Asia Research Institute at the National University of Singapore in 2013. His research sits at the intersections of English language teaching, critical social thought in education and democratic citizenship.

Sarah Van Hoof is assistant professor of Dutch and multilingual communication at Ghent University. Her research focuses on language ideologies, institutional language policies and multilingualism in Flanders (Belgium). Her work has been published in *Tijdschrift voor Nederlandse Taal- en Letterkunde, Pragmatics* and *Journal of Germanic Linguistics* and in several edited volumes. She currently supervises the research project

'Language and employability', envisaging a sociolinguistic ethnographic investigation of the activation of migrant job seekers in Flanders (Flemish Research Foundation [FWO] and Ghent University Special Research Fund, 2017–2021).

Martina Zimmermann holds a PhD from the University of Fribourg. In her sociolinguistic dissertation supervised by Alexandre Duchêne, she analyzed discourses and practices of (im-)mobility in higher education across linguistic borders in Switzerland. She works as a lecturer in the field of foreign languages at the University of Teacher Education Lucerne. Her main research interests include language and inequality, language and mobility, education, ethnographic research, discourse analysis and contemporary as well as historic perspectives on language in society.

Series Editors' Preface

Neoliberalism can best be described as a unifying or umbrella term to address a broad range of social, cultural and political transformations that reflect the priorities and values of a market-based economy, increasingly global in reach and integration, yet local and often personal in its workings. The current and extensive popularity of the neoliberal label reflects its explanatory value for prevailing insecurities and the relative powerlessness and anxiety increasingly felt by individuals and communities, urged to become more competitive, more efficient, more flexible, and always more productive in this new entrepreneurial order.

Neoliberalism is not merely a glorification of the market: it is more than the expansion of the commodity sphere and capital accumulation, more than the curtailment of rights and liberties. Neoliberalism also has to be understood as a form of *governmentality* (Foucault, 2008), as a means by which social relations, ways of living and subjectivities are *produced*: it enjoins us all, from wage-earners to professionals, to operate in competition with each other, aligning the social world with the logic of the market, promoting and validating increased inequality, and pushing individuals to operate as enterprises themselves (Dardot & Laval, 2009). Holborow's (2015) critical examination of the language of neoliberalism – '*Mission* has replaced policy, *entrepreneurial* has become the most prized social trait, *valued customers* are what we are and *competitive* and *market efficient* what we could be' (2015: 1) – gives us a useful handle on the effects of such discourse on daily practice.

Given such presence, neoliberalism is a term whose growing application risks over-use and ambiguity, and perhaps even a bit of intellectual fatigue for over-exposed readers. In academic circles, we use the word 'neoliberal' as a catch-all derogatory descriptor to critique anything from our own compliance-obsessed managers to the current sorry state of global politics. Quantifiable evidence – the gold standard of audit cultures – suggests that *neoliberalism* is now widely used to explain many forms of social and cultural change. Michelle Brady (2014), for example, identifies 'a third of articles in cultural anthropology and sociology employing this term to label, explain and critique transformations in social and political life' (2014: 12). As she further notes, it is a research trend with remarkable exponential growth (e.g. 'from a handful of articles a year to around a thousand a year between 2002 and 2005. ... [plus] a nine-fold increase in the use of the term in the Google book collection between 1990 and 2009', 2014: fn. 2, p. 12).

Part of the ambiguity that sometimes surrounds the term may be terminological in that contemporary liberalism is equated – and often pejoratively in North America – with increased state intervention through progressive forms of taxation and investments in social welfare as tools to alleviate inequality (see McGroarty, this volume). Such priorities bear little resemblance to the liberalism of the 18th century and notions of *laissez-faire*, *homo economicus*, and Adam Smith's 'invisible hand' of supply and demand (the myth of self-regulating markets), which provided the philosophical rationale for the reorganization of society in the service of industrial capitalism in England (cf. Birth of the Liberal Creed, in Polanyi, 2001).

It is worth considering other descriptors that have been used to examine similar or parallel socio-economic developments: notions such as *market-place utility* (Corson, 2002; Morgan, 2015), *corporatism* (Luke *et al.*, 2007) or *managerialism* (Klikauer, 2013), as a few examples. Are such terms interchangeable within the purview of a neoliberal framework? Or, do they foreground (semi) autonomous domains (histories, rationalities, epistemologies, rituals, etc.) and institutional power relations that precede or exceed neoliberal analyses weighted down by more doctrinaire forms of ideological critique (i.e. classical Marxism, dialectical materialism) or traditional class-based analyses less applicable to contemporary flows of global capital (Pennycook, 2015) and the growing non-materiality (i.e. financialization) of current economic activity (cf. neoliberalism as culture, Hilgers, 2011)? Perhaps more relevant, do these nuanced differences in terms and conceptual frames bear consequences for the strategies of resistance we might imagine and act upon in institutional settings in which language and education are primary activities increasingly subject to neoliberal measures?

Such concerns inform the rich collection of chapters in this new contribution to the Critical Language and Literacy series. Co-edited by Mi-Cha Flubacher and Alfonso Del Percio, *Language, Education and Neoliberalism: Critical Studies in Sociolinguistics*, is an important book for the series and for language educators and researchers carefully walking the tightrope of conformity/resistance in the face of increasing bureaucratic incursion and market-oriented 'reforms'. The editors have brought together an impressive group of emerging and established applied linguists and sociolinguists, whose work across a remarkably diverse set of national and educational settings (primary to tertiary, private language institutes, international development projects) serves to highlight specific realizations and articulations of neoliberal language practices and their normalizing effects on identity formation (e.g. as human capital, entrepreneurial selves, or capital ability machines, cf. Tadiar in Tabiola & Lorente, this volume).

Across chapters, we also gain new insights into the notion of language as commodity (see Gao, this volume) – arguably, a concept as flexibly applied as neoliberalism in the research literature (Block, 2014). As well, we learn about the specific ways in which language can be objectified, standardized and quantified in the service of misguided political agendas for English Language Learners (i.e. No Child Left Behind [NCLB] in the US; Koyama, this volume) or perceived, naively, as merely a 'conduit' to be easily and quickly acquired to facilitate the goals of the Ciência sem Fronteiras (Science without Borders) program developed in Brazil (see Luke, this volume). Also, following recent debates regarding the multi/pluri turn (Kubota, 2014; Flores, 2013), we witness the appropriation of diversity in the superficial marketing of Italian language services and programming in a predominantly Swiss-German university eager to recruit students from the minority region of Ticino (see Zimmermann & Flubacher, this volume). Linguistic diversity is similarly appropriated in what Flores (this volume) describes as the Coke-ification of bilingual education for Latino students in the US, a development that illuminates race and racialization as foundational to neoliberal processes (see also, Jenks, 2017).

Yet we also see cases of linguistic homogenization at work in this volume: in Mindanao, the aggressive promotion of universalized, pragmatic discourse norms for the global call center industry as implemented through a USAID project (i.e. the Job Enabling English Proficiency, or JEEP project; see Tabiola & Lorente, this volume); and in Italy, we learn about the SOFIIA project, similarly engaged in advancing generic entrepreneurial literacies and skills deemed necessary for the integration and employability of migrant agricultural workers (Del Percio & Van Hoof, this volume). Such processes of appropriating diversity and promoting standardization are two sides of the same coin. The focus on diversity can be understood not only as a means to co-opt difference as part of a neoliberal agenda, but also as a *neohumanist capitalist* focus on the universality of free-market operations (Pennycook, 2018). That is to say, neoliberalism co-opts discourses of diversity through, for example, the Coke-ification of bilingual education (Flores, this volume), and simultaneously provides support for standardized forms of scripted servitude (Tabiola & Lorente, this volume; Lorente, in press) as part of a unifying logic in pursuit of a unified global market. In short, neoliberal strategies of marketization, dispossession and accumulation are remarkably flexible in respect to the localized, value-adding options that language can provide.

It is at this more localized level where language professionals and their allies can begin to challenge the sense of powerlessness conveyed through dominant discourses of universality, inevitability and progress that naturalize neoliberal agendas in society. And it is at this more local level where language professionals are well placed to act upon opportunities to subvert and/or alleviate neoliberal practices, a standpoint of particular strength in this collection. We have, for example, Koyama's chapter in which she describes the mobilization of workers and parents against the dehumanizing 'qualculation' of refugee students under NCLB-designed curricula. Equally inspiring is De Korne's (this volume) discussion of the local initiatives to revalue the indigenous language of Diidxazá in Oaxaca. Park's chapter addresses a problem common across international tertiary education: the global hegemony of English and its growing presence in both outer and expanding circle countries for recruitment, income generation, and enhanced global university rankings (see also Gao; Hadley; Luke, this volume). In the context of Korean universities, he describes an ulterior purpose to English Medium of Instruction policies, which serve to prepare neoliberal subjects for lifelong 'self-improvement' by reinforcing native-speaker ideologies and the self-perceptions of Korean students that 'proper' English is a permanent yet unattainable goal. For Park, subjectivity, the inner-world of the learner/citizen (e.g. an ideology of self-deprecation), becomes a key site to subvert neoliberal ideologies, a strategic perspective that references recent research examining the intersections of language, emotions and neoliberalism in applied linguistics (see Benesch, 2017; Clarke, 2014; Motha & Lin, 2013).

Language, Education and Neoliberalism: Critical Studies in Sociolinguistics is a most welcome addition to this series. It builds on innovative applied linguistic research already undertaken (see e.g. Del Percio & Flubacher's excellent introduction and references; also see Chun, 2015; Miller, 2016; Shin & Park, 2016) and extends our theoretical and pedagogical understanding in unique, field-internal ways that suggest transgressive insights and strategies more specific to language work in neoliberal times. As language educators we need to be able to do more than label particular regimes as neoliberal, do more than bemoan the regimes of compliance in which we now work, do more than merely critique the current world order and the ways languages have been deployed within it. We also need strategies of resistance where language and education play a major role. We are indebted to the editors and contributors for the critical possibilities that distinguish this important book.

Brian Morgan, Alastair Pennycook, Ryuko Kubota

References

Benesch, S. (2017) *Emotions and English Language Teaching.* New York: Routledge.

Block, D. (2014) *Social Class in Applied Linguistics.* London: Routledge.

Chun, C. (2015) *Power and Meaning Making in an EAP Classroom: Engaging with the Everyday.* Bristol: Multilingual Matters.

Clarke, M. (2014) The sublime objects of education policy: Quality, equity and ideology *Discourse: Studies in the Cultural Politics of Education* 35, 584–598.

Corson, D. (2002) Teaching and learning for market-place utility. *International Journal of Leadership in Education* 1, 1–13.

Brady, M. (2014) Ethnographies of neoliberal governmentalities: From the neoliberal apparatus to neoliberalism and governmental assemblages. *Foucault Studies* 18, 11–33.

Dardot, P. and Laval, C. (2009) *La nouvelle raison du monde: Essai sur la société néolibérale.* Paris: Éditions La Découverte.

Flores, N. (2013) The unexamined relationship between neoliberalism and plurilingualism: A cautionary tale. *TESOL Quarterly* 47 (3), 500–520.

Foucault, M. (2008) *The birth of biopolitics: Lectures at the Collège de France* (trans. G. Burchell). New York: Palgrave MacMillan.

Hilgers, M. (2011) The three anthropological approaches to neoliberalism. *International Social Science Journal* 61, 351–364.

Holborow, M. (2015) *The Language of Neoliberalism.* London: Routledge.

Jenks, C.J. (2017) *Race and Ethnicity in English Language Teaching: Korea in Focus.* Bristol: Multilingual Matters.

Klikauer, T. (2013) *Managerialism: A Critique of an Ideology.* New York: Palgrave Macmillan.

Kubota, R. (2016) The multi/plural turn, postcolonial theory, and neoliberal multiculturalism: Complicities and implications for applied linguistics. *Applied Linguistics* 37, 474–494.

Lorente, B. (in press) *Scripts of Servitude: Language, Labor Migration and Transnational Domestic Work.* Bristol: Multilingual Matters.

Luke, A., Luke, C. and Graham, P. (2007) Globalization, corporatism, and critical language education. *International Multilingual Research Journal* 1 (1), 1–13.

Miller, E.R. (2016) The ideology of learner agency and the neoliberal self. *International Journal of Applied Linguistics* 26 (3), 348–365.

Morgan, B. (2015) Teaching for market-place utility: Language teacher identity and the certification of adult ESL teachers in Ontario. In Y.L. Cheung, S.B. Said and K. Park (eds) *Advances and Current Trends in Language Teacher Identity Research* (pp. 235–249). New York: Routledge.

Motha, S. and Lin, A. (2013) 'Non-coercive Rearrangements': Theorizing desire in TESOL. *TESOL Quarterly* 48, 331–359.

Pennycook, A. (2015) Class is out: Erasing social class in applied linguistics. Review Essay of D. Block: *Social Class in Applied Linguistics, 2014. Applied Linguistics* 36, 270–277.

Pennycook, A. (2018) *Posthumanist applied linguistics*. London: Routledge.

Polanyi, K. (2001) *The Great Transformation: The Political and Economic Origins of Our Time*. Boston: Beacon Press.

Shin, H. and Park, J.S. (2016) (eds) Researching language and neoliberalism. *Journal of Multilingual and Multicultural Development* 37 (5), 443–522.

1 Language, Education and Neoliberalism

Alfonso Del Percio and Mi-Cha Flubacher

Introduction

On May 3, 1981, *The Sunday Times* published an exclusive interview with Prime Minister Margaret Thatcher in which she was asked to elaborate on the measures taken by her cabinet to counter the economic recession. Competitiveness, she argued, was the key to economic recovery and job creation. To take advantage of expanding world trade, Thatcher noted, national industries needed to boost productivity and become more flexible. Then, it would be important to appraise and pay labor based on output. Moreover, workers should be liberated from the unionist structures and their feelings of loyalty to their employers fostered, while their cooperation with, and sense of responsibility to, their own companies should be promoted. Instead of blaming the government for increasing unemployment rates, Thatcher claimed that individuals needed to make the best of what technological change and industrial restructuration had to offer. She made an argument for a more effective and less monopolistic and bureaucratic state apparatus capable of supporting the British industry in transforming into a flourishing, efficient state able to compete with any other company across the globe. 'Economics', she concluded, 'are [just] the method. The object is to change the heart and soul of the nation' (Butt, 1981).

Language and education played a major role in the societal transformations that the British prime minister had in mind. In order to get at the 'heart and soul of the nation', i.e. to promote an ideological reorientation of the British public and to change people's attitudes and behaviors, Thatcher launched educational reforms that would produce the type of self-responsible, flexible and productive citizens needed for economic recovery. Pupils, especially, had to make headway in mathematics and science while also improving their English skills – i.e. in written and spoken English as well as in knowledge of literature. British schoolchildren should learn to articulate well, to give their thoughts and views appropriate expression, to develop the specific communicative qualities that would make them desirable for employment in local businesses and industries and, finally, to prepare themselves for technological change (Keay, 1987). Thatcher's educational reform also encompassed a redefinition of the privileges traditionally enjoyed by the 'educational establishment' in terms of unionism, salaries, training and performance assessment as well as the application of market logics to every domain of Britain's educational apparatus (Edwards, 1989; Wilby, 2013).

The social and economic changes promoted by Thatcher were informed by *neoliberalism*, a political economic philosophy developed and promoted by a 'thought collective' that has been traced by historians to the networks of intellectuals in Europe and North America after World War I (Mirowski & Plehwe, 2009). These intellectuals aimed to oppose the rising tide of collectivism, state-centered planning, and socialism that, in their view, had caused the Great War (Lemke, 2001). In order to counter the dominance of Keynesian politics and to avoid the dangers of alternative paradigms propagated by the Soviet Union, this group of intellectuals argued for the institutionalization of neoliberalism, i.e. they envisioned a society based on a political economic philosophy that preserves individual freedom through the protection of private property and that posits a competitive market as the key logic underpinning every domain of social life (Plehwe, 2009). Indeed, private property was considered the prerequisite for decentralized power and individual freedom. Freedom of choice – on the part of the producer, worker and consumer but also in terms of every individual's capacity to choose and plan their own lives independently – was therefore also seen as a source of democracy and an imperative for the efficient and satisfactory production of goods and services. Moreover, proponents of neoliberalism believed a stable and predictable legal and institutional state apparatus, i.e. the 'rule of law' (cf. von Hayek, 1944), constitutes an integral component in ensuring an effective competitive order (Ganti, 2014; Lemke, 2001; Plehwe, 2009). If these intellectuals shared *classical liberalism*'s belief in the regulatory forces of the market, one of the main ways their philosophy differed from the older ideology was the assumption that a 'good' and 'just' society does not occur naturally, but instead requires an organized political effort (Rose & Miller, 2008), i.e. a redefined mode of governmentality that – by extending and disseminating market values to all institutions and social actions – reorganizes the relationship between the state, capital, property and individuals and that has as its main goal the maintenance of 'freedom' and competition (Brown, 2015).

Thatcher was not the only politician influenced by neoliberal philosophy. Neoliberal ideas are believed to be at the root of several reform agendas that, with the support of persuasive economic advisors as well as bastions of neoliberalism such as the International Monetary Fund (IMF), the Organisation for Economic Co-operation and Development (OECD) or the World Trade Organization (WTO), have been implemented since the late 1970s by various governments around the world (Harvey, 2005). For instance, neoliberalism has been argued to be the main motor in propelling the transition from a so-called 'socialist economy' to a 'market economy' (e.g. in Eastern Europe, South America and Asia) (Hemment, 2012; Kalb, 2009; Musaraj, 2011) and has also contributed to reforms of education systems in a variety of national contexts. In turn, these education reforms were put in place by neoliberal governments to cope with economic recessions, inflation and unemployment (Dunk, 2002; Morgen, 2001). Neoliberal ideas were furthermore implemented to fight the causes and effects of various financial crises (Mercille & Murphy, 2015; Streeck, 2013) and to manage societal demands for social justice, cultural and economic revitalization as well as for empowerment and redistribution (Berrey, 2015; Muehlmann, 2009). Finally, investments in neoliberalism have also been enacted by non-governmental organizations, public institutions and stakeholders in civil society who have recognized in neoliberal ideas a powerful mode of thinking that facilitates access to forms of capital such as visibility, prestige and recognition and that, in certain cases, has even opened the door for challenging positions of marginality and systems of exclusion (Kamat, 2004).

Studying Neoliberalism

Since the end of the 1990s, neoliberalism has represented one of the core themes of social scientific research around the world. Scholars from different fields and disciplines have employed the concept to respond to the social and political need to better understand the rapid changes that, in recent decades, have affected individuals and societies in many countries and in various political contexts. Yet, and despite its tremendous popularity in explaining the push and pull factors of a transforming world, neoliberalism as a concept seems to mean different things to different scholars; as a result, research on neoliberalism has taken many different directions (Allan & McElhinny, 2017; Chun, 2016; Ganti, 2014; Ong, 2006; cf. the discussion by McGroarty, this volume).

When surveying the body of work that references neoliberalism, Ganti (2014), for instance, identifies four major lines of investigation. First, neoliberalism is viewed as a set of economic reform policies that are concerned with the deregulation of the economy, trade and industry as well as with the privatization of state-owned assets (Harvey, 2005). Second, neoliberalism is seen as an economic development model that defines different roles for labor, capital and the state with powerful economic, social and political repercussions (Boas & Gans-Morse, 2009). Third, the concept is construed as a discourse, or an ideology, that values market exchange as an ethic in itself and that informs the choices and actions of individual, state and corporate actors (Bourdieu, 1984, 1998; Treanor, 2005). Fourth, neoliberalism is regarded as a technology of governance that extends and disseminates market values to all institutions and social activities, and that influences individual conduct by interpellating each member of society as an entrepreneurial self in every sphere of life (Brown, 2014; Foucault, 1980; Gershon, 2011; Rose & Miller, 2010).

By engaging with and responding to this critical scholarship of neoliberalism, this edited volume aims to produce an empirically grounded account of the ways in which neoliberal ideas – as a mobile, transnationally circulating logic or body of knowledge (Ong, 2006) – are selectively adopted on the ground by different actors in different educational settings and national contexts. It furthermore examines how these ideas affect organizational structures, actions, processes and individual behavior, and demonstrates how they challenge (or sometimes reproduce) the dynamics of inequality and exclusion.

This book focuses on language and education, as both factors play a crucial role in forms of change that people and institutions want to induce when they invest in, implement and enact neoliberal ideas. At issue is an examination of language and education both as objects of neoliberalization and as powerful tools and sites through which neoliberal societies and economies are (re)produced and maintained. The overall aim of the publication is to take into account changes and continuities in how neoliberal modes of reasoning conceptualize, invest in and govern language and multilingual selves. Consequently, this volume aims to produce a complex understanding of how neoliberal rationalities are articulated within locally anchored and historical regimes of knowledge on language, education and society. In addition to Foucault's (1977, cf. also Martin Rojo, 2016) understanding of knowledge formation as productive and, at the same time, constraining, this book discusses the multiple, disparate and sometimes contradictory social and political tactics, strategies and projects that neoliberal ideas serve. It also presents an empirical analysis of how neoliberal thinking influences the unequal access people have to valued resources and how it affects the maintenance (or contestation) of legitimacies, inequalities and relations of domination.

The Resignification of Language, Education and the Self

This edited volume unites 10 original contributions in the field of language, education and neoliberalism that document a range of educational sites in different national and regional contexts (Brazil, Canada, China, Italy, Japan, Korea, Mexico, the Philippines, Switzerland, the UK and the US). The chapters span governmental, non-governmental and corporate settings, secondary schools, vocational education, higher education and corporate education service providers. Despite using different terms to designate neoliberalism – for some, neoliberalism is an 'ideology', an 'order' or a 'discourse' while others prefer to call it 'politics' or a 'policy' and still others call it a 'logic', a 'turn', a 'philosophy', a 'force' or, as in this introduction, a 'rationale', a set of 'ideas', a 'theory' or a 'mode of governmentality' – that stand for different epistemological lines of thinking about and discussing neoliberalism (for a discussion of the different approaches to neoliberalism adopted in this volume cf. McGroarty, this volume), the various contributions in this book share an interest in the multiple circumstances under which neoliberal rationales are tied to educational apparatuses and that therefore affect the way people make sense of, and invest in, language and multilingualism.

The resignification of education

Some of the activities and practices documented in the chapters intersect with current restructuring efforts in education that are expressed via processes of the marketization and internationalization of higher education, via changing modes of governmentality of professional routines and practices of language instruction and via the commodification of language and multilingualism. Other contributions focus on how the neoliberalization of language and education correlates to histories of nationalism, imperialism and (post)coloniality as well as to histories of political activism and social mobility, while also demonstrating how language and education become entrenched in processes of disciplining and regulating the multilingual self.

From an analytical standpoint, the authors of the various contributions explore the empirically observable processes through which neoliberal ideas affect language and education. This focus involves locating the documented investments in, and effects of, neoliberalism in specific circumstances, agendas and strategies that are enacted by specific persons or institutional stakeholders occupying unequally valued positions in society.

Addressing the processual nature of neoliberalism also implies challenging perhaps too-readily made assumptions about the status of neoliberalism in current societies and its inevitable colonization of language and education. Moreover, this approach involves a commitment to a nuanced account of the complex and sometimes unexpected links between language, education and neoliberalism on the one hand and, on the other, the consequences that neoliberal rationales have on freedom, equality and emancipation.

One of the processes carefully documented in the different chapters in this volume concerns the ways in which neoliberal rationales have been employed in different national contexts to govern, organize and justify the reform of *educational settings* according to maxims of competitiveness, efficiency and profitability. Along the lines of critical scholarship in applied linguistics (Block et al., 2012; Holborow, 2015) and linguistic anthropology (Allan & McElhinny, 2017; Urciuoli, 2009) but also in the sociology of education (Peters et al., 2009; Saunders, 2010; Wilkins, 2010), authors in this volume have noted that educational institutions located in varying national contexts have become increasingly subjected to processes of internationalization, privatization and financialization, exposed to the logics of the free market and to the commodification of their services (Gao, this volume), and regulated by a so-called audit culture that imposes a logic of numbers and control on every activity (Hadley, this volume).

These changes have brought about not only a precarization of labor for employees in education, including teachers, curriculum coordinators and administrators who are asked to produce and guarantee quality and excellence under increasingly unstable and fluctuating work conditions (Luke, this volume). The neoliberalization of education has also raised issues about who (and under which conditions) can gain access to education. In certain cases, this has led to a de-responsibilization of the state for education (Zimmermann & Flubacher, this volume).

Neoliberal education reforms furthermore affect the objectives and structures of educational programs. The authors in this book argue that educational institutions – while intrinsically dedicated to the creation of equality and progress – are increasingly expected to shape (future) workers to meet the demands of the globalized, neoliberal order (Tabiola & Lorente, this volume), which further implies a (trans)nationally mobile and interchangeable labor force. This narrowed agenda has led to the development of standardized curricula, learning objectives and assessment tools that aim to transform every acquired competence into a quantifiable skill and render workers comparable within and across national economies (Koyama, this volume).

Moreover, the authors in this volume argue that the deregulation and resulting precarization of labor, which characterize a neoliberal economy, have necessitated the development of an educational infrastructure that will ensure the employability of workers within a capitalist society undergoing fluctuations and restructuring. For instance, educational curricula must be designed to address the tension of continually changing technological and professional demands of the employing industries (Del Percio & Van Hoof, this volume). Or, the principle of lifelong learning is employed to motivate employees to rise to the challenges of the modern workplace and to constantly develop and diversify their professional skills, thereby ensuring that they can be relocated to new economic sectors or professional positions, if necessary (Luke, this volume). Finally, education programs per se have become more flexible and thus increasingly able to accommodate individuals who have unstable work conditions and who cannot attend classes at regular hours; programs are offered on- or offline and allow participants to choose learning modules that address their needs (Tabiola & Lorente, this volume).

The resignification of language

The second process that is transversally analyzed in this edited volume is the resignification of *language* in accordance with neoliberal rationales. In line with current critical scholarship on language and education (Flores, 2013; Kubota, 2015; Martin Rojo, 2016; Park & Wee, 2012; Tupas, 2015; Urciuoli & LaDousa, 2013), the authors in this volume argue that adapting education to the changing demands of capitalism has also become a factor in the conceptualization of language and multilingualism in education (Flores, this volume). For example, it is noted that the technologization, digitalization, and automatization of production processes have forced employees to acquire new linguistic competences. Contributors to this volume argue that language and communication are conceptualized as skills that stand for forms of expertise and professionalism and that, according to neoliberal principles of competitiveness and distinction, are imagined to raise the value of individuals in the various neoliberal workplaces (Luke, this volume). Education programs therefore increasingly put training in language and communication at the core of their agenda (Tabiola & Lorente, this volume). This holds true not only for the service economy or for administrative domains in which language and communication have historically played a key role as a resource for production, but also for job trainings in the primary and secondary sectors, which traditionally have been conceptualized as only marginally 'languagy' (Del Percio & Van Hoof, this volume). Within such a context, language itself becomes a commodity (cf. Heller [2010] and Heller & Duchêne [2016] for an elaboration of how language is resignified as a commodity), i.e. a resource that can be bought and appropriated by those employees who can afford to pay for trainings and forms of 'self-skilling' that are sold by a language training industry (Gao, this volume).

The international expansion of economic activities has further led to the implementation of education programs that focus on multilingualism and the teaching of commonly spoken languages (Park, this volume). English, in particular, is resignified by institutions of higher education as a key resource that stands for internationalism, progress and modernity as well as for high quality, economic prosperity and development (Luke, this volume). Both instructors and students are asked to internalize English in order to attract national and international capital in the form of grants or investors and to gain prestige, visibility and recognition (Hadley, this volume). English skills are thus resignified as a key precondition for national and international mobility, both social and geographic (Gao, this volume). In addition, contributors note that principles of competitiveness, excellence and quality in the education sector go hand in hand with a celebration of diversity and multilingualism, thus setting the stage for a valorization of educational infrastructures for linguistic, cultural and racial minorities and laying the groundwork to create consent for the social consequences of neoliberalism in education (Flores, this volume).

In a related area, contributors in this volume argue that the neoliberal resignification of language as a factor of competitiveness and distinction does not stand in opposition to existing ideologies that link language to questions of territoriality, community and identity. If the commodification of language instruction by specific language industries has enabled a softening of standardized ideologies of languages and speakers (Gao, this volume), the neoliberalization of language and multilingualism remains highly entrenched with assumptions of nativeness and purity that continue to produce and legitimize hierarchies and forms of difference (Park, this volume). In addition, contributors note that, despite the dominance of neoliberal ideas in education, these ideas do not seem to be omnipresent, at least not in all social settings and national contexts. To the contrary, when valuating or investing in language and multilingualism, speakers continue to draw on preexisting logics – such as genealogy, kinship or identity – that coexist with, but do not depend on, neoliberal rationales (De Korne, this volume).

The resignification of the self

Finally, several chapters in this volume also explore the processes in which neoliberal rationales are extended to individual conduct and in which individuals are posited as entrepreneurial *selves*, i.e. as rational members of society who are asked to make a certain number of investments in their selves for their own well-being and for the good of society at large. In particular, the authors demonstrate that – given the central role ascribed to language and communication by neoliberal rationales – language plays a key role in the self-disciplining of individuals. Language is therefore a strategic tool through which an idealized mode of conduct and thinking is communicated to people and inculcated in their minds (Flores, this volume). At the same time, language and more particularly communicative conduct is one of the principle aspects of individual behavior that is subjected to regulation and disciplining. In line with Fraser (2003) and Sennett (1998), the authors in this volume demonstrate that a constant investment in the acquisition of communicative competence and the monitoring of an individual's own communicative conduct and modes of thinking are constructed by educational actors as the only viable ways for an individual to remain competitive in an unstable and precarious labor market (Del Percio & Van Hoof, this volume; McGroarty, this volume) and, consequently, to gain access to social and economic emancipation. Accordingly, individuals are asked to constantly invest in language learning and multilingualism and to improve their capacity to speak and communicate across social, professional and geographic borders (Park, this volume). Such linguistic competence is construed not only as capable of raising an individual's competitiveness on the labor market (Zimmermann & Flubacher, this volume), but also as capable of promoting prosperity and security in the societies and nations they inhabit (Tabiola & Lorente, this volume).

Contributors to this volume thus demonstrate that, although certain individuals appropriate this neoliberal rationale and willingly work on their communicative conduct in order to gain access to social and professional mobility, the likelihood of converting the acquired communicative competence into forms of symbolic or monetary recognition neither correlates with their motivation to invest in language learning nor with the quality of their communicative achievements (Luke, this volume). It rather appears that the desired conversion is mainly dependent on local historical epistemologies of personhood that affect the ways in which individuals and their languages are valued (Park, this volume). With reference to critical scholarship on language in society (cf. McElhinny, 2016, for a review), the thoughts presented in this volume also demonstrate that the valuation of language and speakers is entrenched with histories of dispossession, imperialism and subalternity that tend to naturalize and trivialize the connecting cultural and racial features among groups of speakers with unequally valued positions in social structure (Flores, this volume).

Finally, this volume also shows that, despite the extension of neoliberal rationales to all domains of social life, certain individuals are able to enact alternative subjectivities and pursue life projects that involve divergent conceptualizations and uses of language and communication (Koyama, this volume). Solidarity, loyalty and social change remain factors that motivate people to make sense of their own and others' linguistic selves and language choices and to coexist with neoliberal logics of capital accumulation. In this sense, the authors argue that neoliberalism is far from being a totalizing rationale; rather, it is locally contested and challenged by logics and modes of reasoning that preexist neoliberalism and that will probably continue to exist (De Korne, this volume).

Chapter Breakdown

In the following, we present the structure of this volume and discuss how the single contributions promote an understanding of the relationship between language, education and neoliberalism. The chapter by Shuang Gao (Chapter 2) explores shifting conceptions of language and presents the circumstances and modalities through which Mandarin and English are caught up in the neoliberalization of the Chinese economy. She focuses on the divergent ways that Mandarin and English are commercialized by an emerging Chinese-language teaching industry and sheds light on the dynamic nature of neoliberalism, while also revealing the complex ways linguistic authenticity and authority are calibrated for commodification under neoliberal globalization. In doing so, she argues that underlying the apparent coherence of neoliberal practice (such as the commodification of language) is, in reality, a fluid process wherein languages are evaluated, managed and commodified in various ways in different language industries in that neoliberalism perpetually reinvents itself by recalibrating the relationships between state and market, individual and society and nation-state and global geopolitics.

Haley De Korne (Chapter 3) brings us to Mexico and draws on a single example of a localized minority language (in this case Isthmus Zapotec in Mexico) that has undergone valuation and devaluation processes fraught with tension and interrelated with multi-scalar transformations of the political economy and language hierarchies. De Korne describes how both neoliberal influences and non-neoliberal ideologies of genealogy, historicity and place shape the subjectivities and practices around Isthmus Zapotec. For example, by embedding her trajectory in diversity politics, one speaker of Isthmus Zapotec in De Korne's study evoked her status as a heritage speaker of this minority language in the interest of enhancing her application to a university in the US while simultaneously emphasizing that the main value of the language lies in family and community connections. This example, among others, is invoked by De Korne to depict the shifting valorization process of one specific language according to context and scale, thus reminding us of the power of language ideologies that can work both against (cf. Park, this volume) or for speakers of certain languages.

Nelson Flores (Chapter 4) also examines shifting understandings of languages and speakers. Taking two different Coke commercials as entry points, Flores discusses how the commodification of diversity has gradually shifted discourses around bilingual education in the US away from a perspective embedded in civil rights activism and community struggle toward a neoliberal, multicultural framing in which language is reconceptualized as a resource or an economic asset. Flores particularly argues that this reconceptualization of bilingual education has moved our understanding of racism away from the institutions creating and exacerbating racial inequalities toward a focus on individual prejudice. For this reason, Flores calls for a theory of socially transformative forms of bilingual education. Specifically, he calls for a move away from viewing language as a resource toward understanding language as a struggle, thus resituating bilingualism and bilingual education within anti-racist and anti-oppressive struggles led by language minority populations in the US and abroad. Understanding language as a struggle, he argues, leads to the recognition that social transformation can only develop through grassroots community efforts and not through what he calls the feel-good commodification of difference.

The neoliberal resignification of language and education in market-based terms also influences the ways in which learners make sense of their own languages and subjectivities. In his chapter on the promotion of English as a language of instruction in higher education in South Korea, Joseph Park (Chapter 5) documents the anxieties that characterize Korean students' relationship with English. These anxieties, Park argues, are the product of a socially shared way of positioning oneself as a particular subject, for instance, as a product of the 'ideology of self-deprecation' inculcated in Koreans through a common social and historical experience that assumes Koreans lack practical language skills despite the huge investments they make in English language learning. Park argues that this stance towards

English is the product of the colonial relations between the US and Korea and, more particularly, of the notion of the US as the unattainable Other representing the truly advanced world that a purportedly backward Korea apparently dreams of becoming, but can never quite achieve. This 'ideology of self-deprecation', as Park terms it, contributes to the naturalization of the neoliberal policies that underpin the Korean universities' push for English as a language of instruction.

In Chapter 6, Jonathan Luke examines the interconnections between neoliberal internationalization and economic development initiatives, life-aspirations of students and their subject positions in relation to English language learning policies. He particularly elaborates on 11 Brazilian students who went to English-speaking Canada on a national scholarship with the goal of improving their English skills to such a degree that they would be able to study science, technology, engineering and mathematics (the so-called STEM subjects) in Canada. It was also hoped that this investment in future STEM experts would result in boosting the Brazilian economy in the long term. Luke examines how these educational initiatives emerged and evolved for the students in this program, while also highlighting the neoliberal discourses that run through it. He also documents the shifting and sometimes contested status of English language learning for this cohort of scholarship recipients and examines the multiple ways these individuals make sense of the role of English for their life trajectories. In doing so, Luke argues that, despite the powerful nature and effects of neoliberal policies on the ways that individuals make sense of learning English and the significance that the English language has for socioeconomic mobility and professional integration, individuals such as those presented in his study are able to enact alternative modes of subjectification and rationalization of their languages and life perspectives.

In their contribution, Honey B. Tabiola and Beatriz Lorente (Chapter 7) also examine the interconnection between English and neoliberal projects of economic development; they argue that current English language teaching aid projects sponsored by the US in the Philippines are emblematic for the ways in which neoliberalism frames development aid. Investing time, money and energy in projects to promote English learning, the authors argue, is not a charitable endeavor on the part of US stakeholders wishing to shape employable selves in the Philippines; rather, it is a way to ensure that industries in the private sector remain competitive and attractive enough for local and foreign (often US) investors. According to this logic, Tabiola and Lorente argue that English becomes a 'speculative capital': both students and donors invest in English with the hope that this investment will bring future benefits. However, the likelihood that students can convert their acquired English skills into forms of labor remains questionable (especially in the highly fluctuating Filipino labor market). Nevertheless, for those stakeholders sponsoring the development aid projects as well as for the Filipino authorities, promoting the English language represents an investment in a nation of cheap, skilled and linguistically proficient employees, i.e. in a 'stock capital', which in the near future is imagined to be exchangeable with a return in terms of credit-worthiness, a transnational capital flow into the country and foreign investments in, for instance, the form of American call centers.

In Chapter 8, Alfonso Del Percio and Sarah Van Hoof examine the complex relationship between state-sponsored entrepreneurial education, neoliberal policies of economic development and the acquisition of communicational skills. The authors document a training organized by a social cooperative that addressed unemployed migrants in Italy with the aim of having them participate in an entrepreneurial activity in the agricultural sector. Particular attention is given to the status of specific entrepreneurial communicative registers that participants are asked to reproduce. Del Percio and Van Hoof discuss the multiple meanings of these trainings and anchor the meanings in the multiple, and often contradictory, logics, interests and rationales enacted by the governmental authorities and instructors investing in, organizing and conducting these trainings as well as by the migrants who consume them. In doing so, the authors point both to the neoliberal rationales and agendas that the Italian state promotes through its investment in these programs and to the multiple ways in which both social cooperatives and migrants themselves (fail to) appropriate these rationales and the resources offered in such trainings in order to pursue alternative projects that effectively lead to social inclusion and change.

In Chapter 9, Jill Koyama shifts our conversation to a middle school in the US to illustrate how language education policy has taken a neoliberal turn in US schooling and how these changes affect English language learners (ELL). She focuses on the controversies that emerged in an American school after the school direction announced the use of a pre-packaged curriculum and training program designed by a for-profit educational support company. The product was specifically aimed at the school's refugee and new students, who were deemed 'responsible' for the school's failure in meeting the adequate yearly progress (AYP) objectives in English Language Arts. In particular, Koyama documents the ways in which a handful of English as a second language (ESL) teachers, refugee parents, community activists and refugee caseworkers resisted the practices introduced by the authorized policy actors, while also demonstrating how these individuals pushed back against the numerical categories used to label and rate students according to their English proficiency levels. Koyama also examines the ways in which this group of people challenged and disrupted accepted notions of language learning by creating their own tutorial programs that do not follow the purchased curricula. In doing so, Koyama points to the changes that neoliberal rationales and tools introduce in US schooling routines and highlights the strategies invested in by individuals in order to navigate and challenge the constraining features of a changing educational apparatus.

Gregory Hadley (Chapter 10) documents how English for academic purpose (EAP) programs are affected by the neoliberal transformation of higher education. Taking the changing work conditions of university staff as the starting point for his analysis, Hadley demonstrates that EAP professionals play a central role in the enactment and implementation of the managerial regimes that are a driving force behind the neoliberalization and corporatization of universities. He notes that, in order to cope with the challenges faced in neoliberal universities, EAP professionals invest in what he calls 'resource leeching'. Resource leeching is a concept that describes the intentional exploitation of unremunerated resources of volunteers, co-workers, educators and students to realize innovative projects, reduce the weight of increased workloads, cut costs and improve the image of a given university or department. Hadley's study finds that EAP professionals – sandwiched between the managerial level and a simpler status as English language teachers – use resource leeching as a powerful technique to impress senior administrative officers with their managerial and strategic skills and to improve their own standing in a university context, which, due to decreases in public funding, hiring freezes and larger workloads, is increasingly affected by labor market flexibility and precarity.

In Chapter 11, Martina Zimmermann and Mi-Cha Flubacher focus on current changes in a small university located in German-speaking Switzerland to shed light on how neoliberal rationales are implemented in higher education settings. The two authors particularly document the circumstances in which language and multilingualism are used by the management of a small Swiss university in order to create distinction, i.e. to stage its capacity to accommodate a linguistically diverse group of students and to compete nationally with other universities for public funds and students. Zimmermann and Flubacher demonstrate that, if the provision of specific services in the language of the addressed students enables the university to attract students from other non-German-speaking Swiss regions, the thus marketized university falls short in executing its educational mandate and effectively hands over responsibility for education successes or failures to its multilingual students, who more often than not struggle with the linguistic challenges they encounter in their daily learning activities.

This edited volume is concluded with a discussion by Mary McGroarty, who presents three major transversal trends that have emerged in the contributions: (a) language as a recruiting tool; (b) the restructuring of language instruction; and (c) language learning as self-realization. Suggesting the need for future investigations of neoliberal reform in language education, McGroarty particularly calls for further research on the links between linguistic skills and earning power. In her view, additional findings are needed to gain a better understanding of the long-term effects of neoliberal projects and agendas and to allow greater insight into the circumstances that cause them to fail or succeed. Expanding on this line of thinking, McGroarty also says that greater attention must be given to the social and financial costs of neoliberal reforms in order to bring about a definition of new accountability criteria such as 'opportunity to learn' or 'distribution of resources' that contribute to the production of equality and inclusion. Finally, she argues that major attention must be given both to the locally and transnationally circulating political ideas and agendas that inform neoliberal reforms of education and to the personal interests and projects of both decision makers and language learners, which, in the end, result in the endorsement or rejection of neoliberal rationales.

In sum, this volume is the product of a larger transnational conversation conducted by scholars with different epistemological positions and disciplinary backgrounds, who also work in different educational settings. By presenting insights from educational practices in institutions and sites around the world, this collection of chapters and findings aims to contribute to the discipline's greater understanding of the resignification of language, education and the self occurring in the most recent decades and to furthermore link these transformations to processes that materialize in other domains of social life, including culture, citizenship, migration, economy and labor as well as in changing conditions of welfare, financial standing and industrial production. As such, we, the authors, join those scholars whose aim is to advance a critically engaged understanding of the political economic conditions of language and education.

Acknowledgments

We are indebted to a number of people without whom this edited volume would have not seen the light of day. First of all, we would like to thank the contributors and especially the two discussants, Aneta Pavlenko and Luisa Martin Rojo to our panel 'Neoliberalism linguistically applied', at the conference of the American Association of Applied Linguistics in Dallas in March 2013. It was in this context that the idea for an edited volume emerged, supported by Aneta Pavlenko, whom we would like to thank in particular. We are also thankful to Alexandre Duchêne and our other former colleagues at the Institute of Multilingualism, University of Fribourg, with whom we always so productively discussed theoretical ideas and/or methodological problems, also with regard to this volume. Of course, our thanks extend furthermore to the final contributors to this volume; we enjoyed pulling them together from different disciplines and regions and highly appreciate their valuable work beyond this volume. Furthermore, we are enormously grateful to the external reviewers of the contributions and the editors of the series, namely Alastair Pennycook, Brian Morgan and Ryuko Kubota. Last, but not least, we would like to express our gratitude to the supportive and patient folks at Multilingual Matters: Tommi Grover, Kim Eggleton and Anna Roderick.

References

Allan, K. and McElhinny, B. (2017) Neoliberalism, language and migration. In S. Canagarajah (ed.) *The Routledge Handbook on Language and Migration*. New York: Routledge.

Berrey, E. (2015) *The Enigma of Diversity*. Chicago, IL: Chicago University Press.

Block, D., Gray, J. and Holborow, M. (2012) *Neoliberalism and Applied Linguistics*. London: Routledge.

Boas, T. and Gans-Morse, J. (2009) Neoliberalism: From new liberal philosophy to anti-liberal slogan. *Studies in Comparative International Development* 44 (2), 137–161.

Bourdieu, P. (1984) *Homo Academicus*. Paris: Les Éditions de Minuit.

Bourdieu, P. (1998) What is neoliberalism? A programme for destroying collective structures which may impede the pure market logic. *Le Monde diplomatique* translated by Jeremy J. Shapiro, December 1998. See http://mondediplo.com/1998/12/08bourdieu& (accessed 12 August 2015).

Brown, W. (2014) *Walled States, Waning Sovereignty*. Cambridge, MA/London: MIT Press.

Brown, W. (2015) *Undoing the Demos*. Cambridge, MA/London: MIT Press.

Butt, R. (1981) Interview with Margaret Thatcher. *The Sunday Times*. See http://www.margaretthatcher.org/document/104475 (accessed 30 August 2016).

Chun, C. (2016) Exploring neoliberal language, discourses, and identities. In S. Preece (ed.) *Handbook of Language and Identity* (pp. 558–571). Abingdon/New York: Routledge.

Dunk, T. (2002) Remaking the working class: Experience, class consciousness, and the industrial adjustment process. *American Ethnologist* 29, 878–900.

Edwards, R. (1989) Margaret Thatcher, Thatcherism and education. *McGill Journal of Education* 24 (2), 203–214.

Flores, N. (2013) The unexamined relationship between neoliberalism and plurilingualism: A cautionary tale. *TESOL Quarterly* 47 (3), 500–520.

Foucault, M. (1977) *Discipline and Punish*. New York: Pantheon Books.

Foucault, M. (1980) *Power/Knowledge*. New York: Pantheon Books.

Fraser, N. (2003) From discipline to flexibilization? Rereading Foucault in the shadow of globalization. *Constellations* 10 (2), 160–171.

Ganti, T. (2014) Neoliberalism. *Annual Review of Anthropology* 43, 89–104.

Gershon, I. (2011) Neoliberal agency. *Current Anthropology* 52 (4), 527–555.

Harvey, D. (2005) *A Brief History of Neoliberalism*. Oxford: Oxford University Press.

Heller, M. (2010) The commodification of language. *Annual Review of Anthropology* 39, 101–114.

Heller, M. and Duchêne, A. (2016) Treating language as an economic resource: Discourse, data, debates. In N. Coupland (ed.) *Sociolinguistics: Theoretical Debates* (pp. 139–156). Cambridge: Cambridge University Press.

Hemment, J. (2012) Redefining need, reconfiguring expectations: The rise of state-run youth voluntarism programs in Russia. *Anthropological Quarterly* 85, 519–554.

Holborow, M. (2015) *Language and Neoliberalism*. Abingdon: Routledge.

Kalb, D. (2009) Conversations with a Polish populist: Tracing hidden histories of globalization, class, and dispossession in postsocialism (and beyond). *American Ethnologist* 36, 207–223.

Kamat, S. (2004) The privatization of public interest: Theorizing NGO discourse in a neoliberal era. *Review of International Political Economy* 11 (1), 155–176.

Keay, D. (1987) Interview with Margaret Thatcher. *Woman's Own*. See http://www.margaretthatcher.org/document/106689 (accessed 30 August 2016).

Kubota, R. (2015) Neoliberal paradoxes of language learning. *Journal of Multilingual and Multicultural Development* 37 (5), 467–480.

Lemke, T. (2001) The birth of bio-politics. *Economy and Society* 30 (2), 190–207.

Martin Rojo, L. (ed.) (2016) *Occupy. The Spatial Dynamics of Discourse in Global Protest Movements*. Amsterdam: Benjamins.

McElhinny, B. (2016) Reparations and racism, discourse and diversity: Neoliberal multiculturalism and the Canadian age of apologies. *Language and Communication* 51, 50–68.

Mercille, J. and Murphy, E. (2015) *Deepening Neoliberalism, Austerity, and Crises*. London: Palgrave Macmillan.

Mirowski, P. and Plehwe, D. (eds) (2009) *The Road from Mont Pèlerin: The Making of the Neoliberal Thought Collective*. Cambridge, MA: Harvard University Press.

Morgen, S. (2001) The agency of welfare workers: Negotiating devolution, privatization, and the meaning of self-sufficiency. *American Anthropologist* 103 (3), 747–761.

Muehlmann, S. (2009) How do real Indians fish? Neoliberal multiculturalism and contested indigeneities in the Colorado Delta. *American Anthropologist* 111 (4), 468–479.

Musaraj, S. (2011) Tales from Albarado: The materiality of pyramid schemes in postsocialist Albania. *Cultural Anthropology* 26, 84–110.

Ong, A. (2006) *Neoliberalism as Exception: Mutations in Citizenship and Sovereignty*. Durham, NC: Duke University Press.

Park, J. and Wee, L. (2012) *Linguistic Capital and Language Policy in a Globalizing World*. New York: Routledge.

Peters, M., Weber, S., Maurer, S., Olssen, M. and Belsey, A. (eds) (2009) *Governmentality Studies in Education*. Rotterdam/Boston, MA/Taipei: Sense Publishers.

Plehwe, D. (2009) Introduction. In P. Mirowski and D. Plehwe (eds) *The Road from Mont Pèlerin: The Making of the Neoliberal Thought Collective* (pp. 1–42). Cambridge, MA: Harvard University Press.

Rose, N. and Miller, P. (2008) *Governing the Present*. Laden: Polity Press.

Rose, N. and Miller, P. (2010) Political power beyond the State: Problematics of government. *The British Journal of Sociology* 61 (1), 271–303.

Saunders, D.B. (2010) Neoliberal ideology and public higher education in the United States. *Journal for Critical Education Policy Studies* 8 (1), 41–77.

Sennett, R. (1998) *The Corrosion of Character: The Personal Consequences of Work in the New Capitalism*. New York: W.W. Norton.

Streeck, W. (2013) The Politics of Public Debt. MPIfG Discussion Paper 13/7. See http://www.mpi-fg-koeln.mpg.de/pu/mpifg_dp/dp13-7.pdf (accessed 28 December 2016).

Treanor, P. (2005) Neoliberalism: Origins, theory, definition. See http://web.inter.nl.net/users/Paul.Treanor/neoliberalism.html (accessed 28 December 2016).

Tupas, R. (2015) *Unequal Englishes*. Amsterdam: Palgrave.

Urciuoli, B. (2009) Neoliberal education. In J. Greenhouse (ed.) *Ethnographies of Neoliberalism* (pp. 162–176). Philadelphia, PA: University of Pennsylvania.

Urciuoli, B. and LaDousa, C. (2013) Language management/labor. *Annual Review of Anthropology* 42, 175–190.

von Hayek, F.A. (1944) *The Road to Serfdom*. Chicago, IL: University of Chicago Press.

Wilby, P. (2013) Margaret Thatcher's education legacy is still with us – driven on by Gove. *The Guardian*, 15 April. See https://www.theguardian.com/education/2013/apr/15/margaret-thatcher-education-legacy-gove (accessed 17 August 2016).

Wilkins, A. (2010) Citizens and/or consumers: Mutations in the construction of concepts and practices of school choice. *Journal of Education Policy* 25 (2), 171–189.

2 The Commodification of Language in Neoliberalizing China: The Cases of English and Mandarin

Shuang Gao

Introduction

By opening itself up to the outside world and carrying out economic reforms from within, the past three decades have witnessed China's shift from central planning to a market economy as it attempts to revitalize its economy and boost productivity in the post-Mao era. This process is characterized by a multitude of societal transformations, including decentralization, privatization, increasing regional disparity, emergence of a middle class, re-management of human capital and changing conceptions of China's identity in the new world order. Such multifaceted social change, dubbed as neoliberalism with Chinese characteristics (Harvey, 2005), has its own peculiarities despite sharing parallels and similarities with what has been observed in other countries. This is because neoliberalism in practice is always contingent upon specific socio-historical contexts and 'defies schematic analysis' (Ong, 2007: 3; see also Harvey, 2005; Peck & Tickell, 2002). Our critique of neoliberalism therefore needs to be sensitive to social and geographical differentiation. Other scholars also caution against the totalizing tendency in research on neoliberalism (see Kipnis, 2007; Nonini, 2008), arguing that while China is arguably developing along the lines of neoliberalism, its neoliberalization process is not a coherent implementation of a neoliberal theory or policy but grounded in the particular socio-history of China, being contingent, experimental and full of tensions, contradictions and exceptions (see also Ong, 2007; Zhang, 2000).

In this chapter, I examine some of the recent changes in the language education industry in China, focusing in particular on how Mandarin and English, two key languages of great national importance, are embedded in and conducive to China's neoliberalization process. As the national language of China, Mandarin represents the Chinese identity on the global stage, whereas English constitutes an important foreign language for China's economic development under globalization. Given their different political-economic importance and status, they are bound to be caught up in different ways in the neoliberalization process. However, the two languages are illuminative not just because of their prominent socio-political significance but also because of the insights they could reveal about the nexus of language education, nation state and global geopolitics. As I will show, looking at how the two languages are implicated in the neoliberal globalization process reveals the complex ways that linguistic authenticity and authority are calibrated for commodification and marketization, and also sheds light on the dynamic, flexible and paradoxical nature of neoliberalization as a historical process. Specifically, I examine the historical conditions, institutional structures and economic processes through which the two languages become commodified and language education industrialized as (profitable) enterprises in national and global markets, that is, market-intervened language educational practices and enterprises.

Drawing upon multiple data sources (news reports, policy statements and published research), I focus on the expansion of the private English language education industry since the 1990s and the global promotion of Mandarin since the early 21st century, paying particular attention to the socio-political and economic conditions under which language gets 'produced, controlled, distributed, [and] valued' as a commodity (Heller, 2010: 108). The commodification of the two languages first started at different historical times amid different global geopolitical structures. As I will show, the commodification of English emerges against the background of a national craze toward English, a highly competed linguistic capital for upward social mobility and is most evidently shown in the fast expansion of English language education into a US$4.7 billion industry, as estimated in the year 2010 (Bolton & Graddol, 2012: 3). In the case of Mandarin, it is not just a marker of Chinese identity but represents China's attempt at establishing linguistic hegemony on the global stage, in particular via the establishment of Confucius Institutes worldwide since the early 2000s (Heller, 2010; Paradise, 2009; Zhou, 2015; Zhu & Li, 2014). The promotion of the two languages takes some parallel but also some different routes, and is illustrative of the interplay and tension between nation state and neoliberal globalization, or as I will elaborate later, the roll-back and roll-out processes of neoliberalization (Peck & Tickell, 2002). In discussing the commodification of two languages, I pay particular attention to (1) the often overlooked factor of nationalism and the role of the state in a neoliberal economy; (2) the dynamic, flexible and paradoxical nature of neoliberalism; (3) both local and translocal factors underlying neoliberal practices; and (4) the mutation of neoliberalism as a historically contingent process. Through examining the varied ways that Mandarin and English are caught up in the neoliberalization process, it is shown that underlying the apparent coherence of neoliberal practice (i.e. commodification of language) is actually a dynamic and flexible process wherein languages are evaluated, managed and commodified in varied ways at different historical times as neoliberalism constantly reinvents itself through recalibrating the relationship between state and market, individual and society, nation state and global geopolitics.

Market, State and Language Education in Neoliberalizing China

Neoliberalism as a political economic theory stipulates that state intervention should be kept to a minimum so that the principle of market saturates every aspect of society. Neoliberalism is therefore associated with the destruction of former institutional frameworks under embedded liberalism through deregulation, privatization and individual entrepreneurship (Harvey, 2005). Such unleashing of the force of market is rationalized and naturalized as the best way to achieve social welfare: 'the social good will be maximized by maximizing the reach and frequency of market transactions, and it seeks to bring all human action into the domain of the market' (Harvey, 2005: 3). Having established itself as a hegemonic economic doctrine, neoliberalism now constitutes a common-sense way of interpreting and inhabiting the world (Harvey, 2005: 3).

However, there are always disjunctures between neoliberalism as a utopian theory and neoliberalism in actual practice, which is arguably its 'most essential feature' (Brenner & Theodore, 2002: 353). The vitality of the neoliberal theory partly depends on its ability to constantly re-invent itself in practice, such that when principles of the neoliberal doctrine clash with the actual conditions of its implementation, it can be abandoned or even twisted to become unrecognizable (Harvey, 2005: 19). Neoliberalism in practice is therefore multifaceted and variegated. It can be contingently implemented and partially adopted (Ong, 2006) and therefore 'defies schematic analysis' (Ong, 2007: 3). Harvey (2005: 70) also cautions that 'any attempt to extract some composite picture of a typical neoliberal state from this unstable and volatile historical geography would seem to be a fool's errand'. In our critique of neoliberalism, therefore, we need to pay attention to 'the tension between the theory of neoliberalism and the actual pragmatics of neoliberalization' (Harvey, 2005: 21), in other words, its 'transformative and adaptive capacity' (Peck & Tickell, 2002: 380).

One useful way to reveal such tensions and contradictions, as proposed by Peck and Tickell (2002), is not to study neoliberalism in terms of its static characteristics and their corresponding manifestation, which might be misleading, but to adopt a historical and process-based approach to neoliberalization. This perspective has the benefits of capturing the contingent ways that neoliberalism unfolds in reality and revealing how particular neoliberal practices are actually embedded in local and extralocal relations. As they elaborate, we need to pay attention to

> how 'local' institutional forms of neoliberalism relate to its more general (ideological) character. This means walking a line of sorts between producing, on the one hand, overgeneralized accounts of a monolithic and omnipresent neoliberalism, which tend to be insufficiently sensitive to its local variability and complex internal constitution, and on the other hand, excessively concrete and contingent analyses of (local) neoliberal strategies, which are inadequately attentive to the substantial connections and necessary characteristics of neoliberalism as an extralocal project. (Peck & Tickell, 2002: 381–382)

In other words, 'neoliberalization should be understood as a process, not an end-state. ...Analyses of this process should therefore focus especially sharply on *change* – on shifts in systems and logics, dominant patterns of restructuring and so forth' (Peck & Tickell, 2002: 383, italics original).

It is this process-based historical perspective toward neoliberalism that I adopt here and I focus in particular on dynamic mutations of neoliberalism as shown in the commodification of Mandarin and English, exploring the discrepancies as well as the parallels in each case. As I will show, the commodification of each language indicates different phases of China's neoliberalization process, and is illuminative of what Peck and Tickell (2002) call the roll-back and roll-out process of neoliberalization. As they explain, while in the early phase of neoliberalization, there is 'the pattern of deregulation and dismantlement... which might be characterized as "roll-back neoliberalism"; in its more disguised form, there is an emergent phase of active state-building and regulatory reform – an ascendant moment of "roll-out neoliberalism"' (Peck & Tickell, 2002: 384):

in the course of this shift, the agenda has gradually moved from one preoccupied with the active *destruction and discreditation* of Keynesian-welfarist and social-collectivist institutions (broadly defined) to one focused on the purposeful *construction and consolidation* of neoliberalized state forms, modes of governance, and regulatory relations. It is this more recent pattern of institutional and regulatory restricting, which we characterize here as a radical, emergent combination of neoliberalized economic management and authoritarian state forms, that demands both analytical and political attention. This may represent a critical conjuncture, since it reflects *both* the contradictions/limitations of earlier forms of neoliberalization *and* the attainment of a more aggressive/proactive form of contemporary neoliberalization. (Peck & Tickell, 2002: 384, italics original)

And in this process, 'the neoliberal project itself gradually metamorphosed into more socially interventionist and ameliorative forms, ... This most recent phase might be portrayed as one of "roll-out" neoliberalism, underlining the sense in which new forms of institution-building and governmental intervention have been licensed with the (broadly defined) neoliberalized project' (Peck & Tickell, 2002: 389).

While the so-called roll-out neoliberalism might seem at first sight to be contradictory to the neoliberal template, it actually conforms to the neoliberal rule of competition. This is because, as Peck and Tickell (2002: 385) suggest, under neoliberalism, spatial relations are themselves neoliberalized: 'extralocal rule regimes at this time seemed critically to undermine the potential of non-neoliberal projects at the local scale, while engendering a lemming-like rush towards urban entrepreneurialism, which itself would only serve to facilitate, encourage, and even publicly subsidize the accelerated mobility of circulating capital and resources. As if to add insult to injury, regimes of public investment and finance, too, would increasingly come to mimic these marketized conditions'.

In other words, the state does not simply disappear under neoliberalism but functions in new ways. The competition between nation states intensifies in new ways amid changing global geopolitics, which makes state intervention inevitable in the interconnected global neoliberalization project. As Harvey (2005: 65) notes, 'the neoliberal state should persistently seek out internal reorganizations and new institutional arrangements that improve its competitive position as an entity *vis-à-vis* other states in the global market'. This inter-state competition is therefore closely related to the issue of nationalism under neoliberal globalization, as Harvey keenly observes:

nationalism has, of course, been a long-standing feature of the global economy and it would have been strange indeed if had sunk without trace as a result of neoliberal reforms; in fact it has revived to some degree in opposition to what neoliberalization has been about...The neoliberal state needs nationalism of a certain sort to survive... In China, the appeal to nationalist sentiment in the struggle to procure the state's position (if not hegemony) in the global economy is overt. (Harvey, 2005: 85)

Harvey, nevertheless, does not elaborate on how exactly nationalism becomes overt in China. As I will show below, the commodification of Mandarin can provide insights into this relationality between the state and neoliberalism. It is to this dual process of roll-back and roll-out neoliberalism that I will now turn to, examining how the commodification of English and Mandarin provides important insights into neoliberalism as a dynamic, flexible and historical process.

The Commodification of English Under the Market Economy

The English language was re-integrated into the national educational curriculum in 1978 when China made the transition from planned economy to market socialism after the Cultural Revolution (Pride & Liu, 1988). It is considered as an important language for China's economic development and engagement with the international world. In this section, I focus on two main ways through which the English language is incorporated into the neoliberal economy. First, I document how English language learning is tied to the cultivation of human capital as it becomes an important linguistic capital and a social stratification factor among Chinese nationals. Second, I look at enterprises of English language teaching and explore how the commodification of English is embedded in the changing ideologies of English and a new economic-political structure in China.

English, social stratification and the cultivation of human capital

Since the 1990s, under a more mature market economy, the educational system in China has undergone increasing decentralization (Mok & Lo, 2007). Regional economic disparities have emerged and enlarged under the market economy and the provision of educational resources has become very much dependent on the local authority and autonomy, especially due to the downsizing of public educational subsidies from the central government. The provision of English language education, accordingly, has become very much contingent upon specific local economic situations given the uneven economic development in different regions in China; English language educational resources are unequally distributed (Hu, 2005). Nevertheless, English constitutes one important compulsory subject from primary school to higher education and is even the medium of instruction in some elite schools (Sun *et al.*, 2016: 10). In other words, despite the uneven distribution of language educational resources, the importance of the English language remains unequivocal all over China. In this context, English language competence symbolizes a good educational background and a relatively high social status, and the active pursuit of English, though controversially debated in China, has become irreversible (Gao, 2012; Sun *et al.*, 2016). This valorization of English has provided a fertile ground for the emergence and rapid expansion of the industrialization of English education under a more mature market economy since the 1990s. Bilingual kindergartens and private schools with native English teachers emerged and started to gain popularity among parents who want to give their children a head start in English (Jin & Cortazzi, 2002: 55–56). The privatization and industrialization of English language education makes English a commodity, further perpetuating the unequal access to English which has become a marker of middle-class identity.

Notably, the pursuit of English has been intensifying since the late 1990s when market reform deepened and China sped up its globalization process, especially after it joined the World Trade Organization (Pang *et al.*, 2002) and successfully won the bid for the 2008 Olympic Games (Henry, 2010). Since then, English has become not just a social stratification factor within the educational system, but also in workplaces where English language mediates the competitive need for self-development under the neoliberal economy (Gao, 2016; Pang *et al.*, 2002). Such valorization of English means that it has become an integral part of the human capital which inevitably leads to investment in English as one tries hard to move up the social ladder.

Enterprises of English language education

Catering to the increasing demand for English, private English language training centers started to emerge and quickly expand under the market economy. It is difficult to provide a concise number of how many private language schools there are in China and how large the market is, but it is widely agreed that English language education is definitely a multibillion dollar industry in China (US$4.7 billion in 2010) (Bolton & Graddol, 2012: 3; see also Hu & McKay, 2012: 347; Wang, 2004). In this highly competitive industry of English language education, several established enterprises have achieved fame and hegemony in China. Looking at these enterprises can provide insights into how the industrialization of English education is linked to the neoliberalization process of China amid changing ideologies toward English and how the English education industry constitutes one of the new ways to achieve personal distinction and accumulate personal wealth.

Crazy English (see Bolton, 2003, for details) and New Oriental were among the earliest private language training centers that managed to establish themselves as renowned English education brands nationwide within a fairly short time. Crazy English was established by Li Yang, a former English–Chinese interpreter, in 1994, whereas New Oriental was opened in 1993 by Yu Minhong, a former college English teacher. Both were the first people in China to embrace English language education as a private enterprise during the early 1990s when the legitimacy of private economic forms first started to be acknowledged and encouraged in China. Neoliberalism, as Harvey (2005) observes, involves the re-stratification of class relations and new modes of capital accumulation emerge in this process. During China's transformation into a market economy, class re-stratification was shown more in terms of the creation of social hierarchies: the accumulation of personal wealth through capitalizing on the national craze for English emerged as a new economic practice. The founding of New Oriental by Yu Minhong is one prominent example of this.

Yu used to be an English teacher in a university in Beijing in the mid-1980s. Like many of his friends at that time, he was planning to go to the United States for his postgraduate studies; however, due to lack of scholarship, he had to subsidize himself financially. He started to teach students English in his spare time to earn some extra money but when the university found out, he was penalized and sacked. In 1993, having lost what could have been a permanent job, he decided to make a living by opening an English tutoring center which grew into what is now known as the New Oriental. The company expanded quickly from a local language training center in Beijing to one with several hundreds of branch schools all over China. In 2006, it was publicly listed on the New York Stock Exchange, and is estimated to have a market value of US$3 billion. New Oriental now claims to be the main place for preparing Chinese students for overseas studies. Each year, New Oriental makes a profit of hundreds of millions of Chinese yuan, with its businesses accounting for about 70% of China's educational market for studying abroad (Chen 2013).

On its 20th anniversary, New Oriental had about 16 million students in total (Chen, 2013). For this reason, Yu is known in China as the father of studying abroad (China.com, 2002).

The success of his business largely depends on the valorization of English among Chinese nationals which helps foster the commodification of English and the industrialization of the English language learning industry. The movie *American Dreams in China* (中国合伙人), based on Yu's life story, was released in 2013 and directed by the multiple award-winning Hong Kong-based director Peter Ho-sun Chan. The movie won wide acclaim in China and had amazing box office earnings of about 500 million Chinese yuan during its first month of release alone (Worldscreen, n.d.). What is noteworthy is the Chinese government's appraisal of *American Dreams in China*. The movie received the highest movie award in mainland China in the same year, including the Golden Rooster Award for Best Picture, the Golden Rooster Award for Best Actor, the Golden Rooster Award for Best Director, as well as the Hundred Flowers Award for Best Actor and the Flowers Award for Best Supporting Actor. It is recognized and praised for successfully portraying the life and struggle of entrepreneurs in the context of economic transformation and social change in China during the past three decades.

The movie also received the Best Works Award (五个一工程奖) in 2014, an award initiated by the Central Committee of the Communist Party of China aimed at promoting excellent work in the areas of drama, movie, television, broadcasting, songs and books that help spread the mainstream political and moral values among the general public, showcase the theme of the Chinese dream and narrate how ordinary Chinese people achieve success through their hard work. The award committee praised the movie as an inspirational biographic film that demonstrates the spirits of the Chinese Dream (Guancha, 2014).

The highly acclaimed English language learning industry in China therefore shows the internalization of the English hegemony and more importantly, the valorization of entrepreneurship in neoliberalizing China. In this process of commodifying English, there is the retreat of state from English education through decentralization which in turn gives more autonomy to local enterprises in the provision of English educational resources. This leads to the unequal distribution of, and access to, English among Chinese nationals. Nevertheless, given the gatekeeping role of English in both education and work, learning English constitutes an integral and important part of the cultivation of human capital. In other words, the national craze toward English triggers the formation of an English education industry. Also, as private enterprises become legitimate entities, the social-political condition for the commodification of English is also satisfied. In this context, individual entrepreneurship flourishes and the commodification of English results in the emergence of English language education as a big industry.

The Marketization of Mandarin Worldwide

Whereas the case of English shows effects of roll-back neoliberalism, the commodification of Mandarin is occurring during a time when China is attempting its peaceful rise as a global power (Zhou, 2015: 68–69). The promotion and marketization of Mandarin worldwide are believed to constitute one important strategy toward China's self-projection as a global power (Zhou, 2015; Zhu & Li, 2014), though how exactly such a link is contemplated by the Chinese government cannot yet be known because relevant official files are still classified (Zhou, 2015: 69). In what follows, I rely mainly on publicly available news reports to examine how the global promotion of Mandarin demonstrates roll-out neoliberalism as well as the consolidation of nationalism.

The teaching of Chinese as a foreign language has a long history. It had been taught and learned mainly for diplomatic purposes until the early 2000s when the Chinese government started to invest more efforts in promoting Chinese language and culture worldwide. Nevertheless, a market for Mandarin cannot simply be formed on its own; it needs a proper institutional framework to foster its formation and functioning. When such a market does not exist, as Harvey (2005) notes, the state usually intervenes to create one. This is exactly the case in regard to the formation of a linguistic market for Mandarin. Actually, since the establishment of the first Confucius Institute in 2004 in Seoul (Zhu & Li, 2014: 327), the involvement of the Chinese government has been taken as evidence of the politically charged nature of the promotion of Chinese language and culture (Gao, 2011; Gil, 2015; Paradise, 2009; Zhou, 2015). What has been less noticed, however, is that such initiative, though driven by political interest, is in reality also a market-based economic practice. In other words, power relations formerly framed in political terms are now recast as economic ones to re-legitimize them under the neoliberal economy (Heller, 2010: 103). As I will show below, it is clearly understood from the outset by the Chinese government that the promotion of Mandarin can never be purely about its teaching and learning. Such promotion can only achieve success and prosper based on the logic of economic transaction. Also, the promotion of Mandarin is very much caught up in the changing global geopolitics and increasing competition among nation states. In other words, the promotion of Mandarin constitutes one avenue through which neoliberal competition among nation states is lived out.

Neoliberal state and the creation of a linguistic market

Confucius Institutes are key establishments for promoting Chinese language and culture in general. The first Confucius Institute was established in 2004 and by the end of 2014 there were already 475 Confucius Institutes and 851 Confucius Classrooms in around 126 regions and countries (Chinanews, 2015). Confucius Institutes are mainly based in overseas universities targeting university/adult students, whereas Confucius Classroom was first proposed around 2007 to promote the teaching of Mandarin to school children. Confucius Classroom therefore emerges as a junior version of the institute, aiming in particular at secondary education. To further expand the impact of Mandarin learning, Confucius Institute Online was launched in 2008 to provide multimedia learning and teaching resources for its online users, and by 2014, it already had more than 3 million registered users.

The spearheading committee behind these establishments is the Office of Chinese Language Council International, also known as Hanban. According to the official website of Hanban, the Confucius Institutes:

> devote themselves to satisfying the demands of people, to strengthening educational and cultural exchange and cooperation between China and other countries, to deepening friendly relationships with other nations, to promoting the development of multi-culturalism, and to construct a harmonious world. (Hanban, 2016)

Hanban, therefore, is the executive body for the promotion of Mandarin. Despite being officially designated as a non-governmental and non-profit organization, Hanban is in reality affiliated to the Ministry of Education of China and led by high officials in the Communist Party of China (CPC), with its committee consisting of high officials from 'the State Council, the Ministry of Education, the Ministry of Foreign Affairs, and the Ministry of Culture' (Paradise, 2009: 651). Hanban provides funds to Confucius Institutes and similar establishments (Zhou, 2015: 75). As already mentioned, the political nature of such initiatives has been controversial (see e.g. Gil, 2015; Zhou, 2015), but if we look at the language ideologies and practices underlying the promotion of Mandarin worldwide, we can achieve a better understanding of the intertwining of politics and economy. This is concerned with the conceptualization of language, the provision of language textbooks, the implementation of language testing, all of which, as we shall see, are actually underpinned by the ideology of language as commodity.

'Language in itself is a product'

As the director of Hanban since 2005, Xu Lin is vocal in the media about promoting Mandarin worldwide. In an interview with one of the most authoritative news media in China, Xinhua News Agency, she explained that the way Confucius Institutes operate must be industrialized. The global promotion of Mandarin, she said, is never purely about education. This is because language in itself is a product, especially when being promoted to the world. It has to be a cultural product and its promotion must be industrialized according to the rules of the market. There is absolutely no way forward other than adopting a market perspective.[1] Noting some of the difficulties that Hanban has experienced so far in promoting Mandarin, including the issues of textbooks, teachers and the standard of Mandarin, Xu suggests that all can be solved through marketization and industrialization. In terms of textbooks, Xu states that

> Textbooks must withstand the test of the market, and teachers need to teach in a way that is acceptable to learners of Chinese as a foreign language, including their way of thinking, their customs, and their daily life. ... Chinese textbooks need to be localized, and our starting point should be 'what they want to learn', instead of 'what we ask them to learn'. ... Many of the textbooks we have now are very much based on Chinese as a mother tongue. But it is only when we have many foreigners involved in the design of the textbooks that its industrialization and promotion can be said to be successful. The UK has been promoting English worldwide long enough and knows this very well. A language can only become a prominent language when other countries are also actively involved in developing teaching materials for that language. (Xinhua News Agency, 2008)

The market, according to Xu, is the single most important way to test the feasibility and effectiveness of textbooks. In other words, the promotion of Mandarin is not to be based on a model of linguistic authority that lies solely within China and its relevant bodies of language promotion – the model of Chinese as a mother tongue is ineffective for the promotion of the language worldwide. Instead, textbooks need to be customized and adapted to the needs of target learners of Mandarin ('their way of thinking, their customs, and their daily life', 'what they want to learn'). This indicates that linguistic authority and authenticity are giving way to localization for the purpose of marketization. Indeed, as Zhu and Li (2014: 329) note, in Confucius Classrooms in the UK, the adopted Mandarin textbooks are locally produced. Thus, the state and its relevant bodies, while being actively involved in the promotion of Mandarin, do not assume sole authority in judging the legitimacy and effectiveness of language teaching materials. Instead, the role of state is to facilitate the formation of a favorable economic environment in which 'multiple sources of authority' coexist in the commodification of language (Heller, 2010: 106), so that they can compete in the market and then the fittest survive. Such a market perspective has also been put into practice, as Xu further explained:

> During the Expo languages in Paris in 2008, China, as the hosting country, brought over 10 publishers to the exhibition; the majority are private enterprises, others state-owned publishers. It turned out that the differences between the two are obvious. Whereas there were few visitors to state-owned publishers, private publishers were very popular; some of their products were even out of supply. … This shows the sharp difference between these two types of enterprises in developing and promoting textbooks. Private ones are more experienced with the market, and are therefore more responsive to the needs of the market, and can act faster. (Xinhua News Agency, 2008)

Xu further elaborated that one private company had published a textbook that used multimedia to illustrate the components of Chinese characters. It turned out to be very popular and the products were sold out on the very first day. Another private enterprise had brought over a textbook series very popular in the UK, which also attracted much interest. Xu concluded that these cases showed the importance of introducing private enterprises into the promotion of Mandarin so that their innovation and entrepreneurship can help foster a better linguistic market for Mandarin.

Related to the issue of textbooks is linguistic competence. Xu's elaboration below indicates a very flexible conception of language competence when she talks about learning and using Mandarin:

> Some people used to think of the teaching of Mandarin as part of elite education. The so-called elite path (精英道路) means that when teaching foreigners Chinese, we cannot tolerate any grammatical mistakes; we must make sure that they speak proper and beautiful Chinese. But the truth is that the elite path does not work. This is because… the number of elites we can produce then tend to be very small, which does

not match the image of China as a big country nor its urgent need to promote its soft power. So in promoting Mandarin, we should first of all popularize the language, so that people will want to learn, use, and understand it. We will not have Chinese speaking elites unless we could popularize it in the first place. (Xinhua News Agency, 2008)

Here, the learning of Chinese is linked to the learner's social identity. Speakers of Chinese as a foreign language do not need to be social elites, who speak proper and grammatical Chinese. Instead, we see here the loosening of linguistic standards in preference to its popularity. Such a flexible way of marketing Mandarin under the neoliberal economy indicates that linguistic authenticity and correctness are giving way to the popularity of the language, with no strict grammatical rules attached. In other words, it indicates a language ideology based on mass consumption wherein preference is given to securing a hopefully profitable mass market as opposed to having only a small elite market of education.

As Heller (2010: 106) notes, such flexibility under the neoliberal economy 'opens up the possibilities for staking claims for the value not only of a wide range of linguistic resources but also for the very possibility of being able to navigate them expertly'. So, when the standardness and correctness of language teaching and learning are loosened during the learning process, the evaluation of individual learners' language competence becomes more important. This is where the creation of adult Chinese language tests becomes relevant. According to Xu Lin, thanks to the establishment of a specific organization in charge of Mandarin tests for adult language learners (HSK), a market for HSK is now in place, which brings in revenue of about 10 million Chinese yuan each year (Xinhua News Agency, 2008).

At the same time, it is worth noting that Confucius Institutes not only serve to popularize the Chinese language and culture overseas according to the principle of market, but also help increase the competitiveness of Chinese universities in worldwide university rankings under the neoliberal economy (c.f. Piller & Cho, 2013). According to Sun et al. (2016), Confucius Institutes help increase the attractiveness of Chinese universities among international students – China has become the third most favored country for international students after the United States and the UK – which in turn helps raise Chinese universities' score in the criteria of internationalization in world university rankings (Sun et al., 2016: 10).

As we have seen, the promotion of Mandarin worldwide, while dubbed by many as politically charged, is actually embedded in the neoliberal economy in multiple ways. It involves a neoliberal state which seeks to create a market for Mandarin, which in turn helps produce and foster the global power of China under neoliberal globalization. Also, in this very process of commodification, the state does not impose linguistic standards or authority. Instead, the standardness, correctness and authenticity of Mandarin are recalibrated in relatively more flexible ways based on an ideology of mass consumption, so that the promotion of Mandarin becomes as much a neoliberal enterprise as a political propaganda.

Conclusion

In this chapter, I have taken a process-based historical approach to neoliberalism and analyzed how English and Mandarin, two main languages of great socio-political importance to China, are embedded in the neoliberal transformation of China during the past three decades. The commodification of the two language stakes parallel but different routes. The commodification of the English language has started to emerge and quickly expand since the early 1990s when China made the transition from planned to market economy. The commodification of English largely depends on the incorporation of English into the valorization of human capital under the neoliberal transformation in China. We see in this process what Peck and Tickell (2002) call roll-back neoliberalism. Whereas in the case of Mandarin, we see that it is not only very much a governmental initiative but it is also grounded in neoliberal globalization. While this may seem to be contradictory to the neoliberal template, it actually demonstrates the flexible and adaptable character of neoliberalism. On the one hand, as inter-spatial relationships themselves become neoliberalized, nation states actually find themselves in more competitive relationships with each other. Meantime, power relations are no longer simply understood in political terms, but also in economic terms, as the neoliberal state seeks to actively create a global market of language and culture amid increasing inter-state competition. On the other hand, we also see the ideology of mass consumption underlying the promotion of Mandarin, as the issues of standardness, correctness and authenticity are giving way to a more flexible way of defining and using language. The case of Mandarin therefore demonstrates roll-out neoliberalism (Peck & Tickell, 2002) in the later phase of neoliberal globalization.

The two cases also show that the commodification of language is not simply an inevitable process of neoliberal globalization. Instead, there are socio-historical, political and economic conditions that underpin the actual practice of commodifying and marketing language. As I have shown, the commodification of the two languages occurred around different phases of the neoliberalization process of China. Moreover, despite the apparent similarity of the commodification of language in the two cases, I have shown that the two languages are involved in neoliberal globalization in different ways and this has different implications for individuals, nation states and even the two languages discussed. This study therefore shows the importance of a socio-historical approach to the commodification of language. It is only by paying attention to such socio-historical situatedness that we can reveal the contradictories and contingencies of neoliberal enterprises and better critique how power relations are produced and reproduced under a neoliberal economy.

Note

(1) All extracts from the Chinese media are translated from Chinese by the author.

References

Bolton, K. (2003) *Chinese Englishes: A Sociolinguistic History.* Cambridge: Cambridge University Press.

Bolton, K. and Graddol, D. (2012) English in China today. *English Today* 28 (3), 3–9.

Brenner, N. and Theodore, N. (2002) Cities and the geographies of 'actually existing neoliberalism'. *Antipode* 34 (3), 349–379.

Chen, X. (2013) The 20 Years of New Oriental. See http://www.xdf.cn/xdftw/201311/9720006.html (accessed 1 February 2016).

Chinanews.com (2015) 475 Confucius Institutes have been established worldwide. See http://www.chinanews.com/cul/2015/06-22/7358791.shtml (accessed 1 February 2016).

'Yu Minghong has resigned' (2002) See http://www.china.com.cn/chinese/EDU-c/180264.htm (accessed 1 February 2016).

Gao, S. (2011) Facework and ideology in welcome speech. *Critical Approaches to Discourse Analysis across Disciplines* 5, 92–111.

Gao, S. (2012) Commodification of place, consumption of identity: The sociolinguistic construction of a 'global village' in rural China. *Journal of Sociolinguistics* 16 (3), 336–357.

Gao, S. (2016) Interactional straining and the neoliberal self: Learning English in the biggest 'English Corner' in China. *Language in Society* 45 (3), 397–421.

Gil, J. (2015) China's cultural projection: A discussion of the Confucius Institutes. *China: An International Journal* 13, 200–226.

Guancha (2014) *American Dreams in China* received the Best Works Award. See http://www.guancha.cn/indexnews/2014_09_16_267729.shtml (accessed 1 February 2016).

Hanban (2016) See http://english.hanban.edu.cn/hb/ (accessed 1 February 2016).

Harvey, D. (2005) *A Brief History of Neoliberalism.* Oxford/New York: Oxford University Press.

Heller, M. (2010) The commodification of language. *Annual Review of Anthropology* 39, 101–114.

Henry, E.S. (2010) Interpretations of 'Chinglish': Native speakers, language learners and the enregisterment of a stigmatized code. *Language in Society* 39, 669–688.

Hu, G. (2005) English language education in China: Policies, progress, and problems. *Language Policy* 4, 5–24.

Hu, G. and McKay, S.L. (2012) English language education in East Asia: Some recent developments. *Journal of Multilingual and Multicultural Development* 33 (4), 345–362.

Jin, L. and Cortazzi, M. (2002) English language teaching in China: A bridge to the future. *Asia Pacific Journal of Education* 22 (2), 53–64.

Kipnis, A. (2007) Neoliberalism reified: *Sushi* discourse and tropes of neoliberalism in the People's Republic of China. *Journal of the Royal Anthropological Institute* 13, 383–400.

Mok, K.H. and Lo, Y.W. (2007) The impacts of neo-liberalism on China's higher education. *Journal for Critical Educational Policy Studies* 5 (1), 316–348.

Nonini, D.M. (2008) Is China becoming neoliberal? *Critique of Anthropology* 28, 145–177.

Ong, A. (2006) *Neoliberalism as Exception: Mutations in Citizenship and Sovereignty*. Durham, NC: Duke University Press.

Ong, A. (2007) Neoliberalism as a mobile technology. *Transactions of the Institute of British Geographers* 32 (1), 3–8.

Pang, J., Zhou, X. and Fu, Z. (2002) English for international trade: China enters the WTO. *World Englishes* 21, 201–216.

Paradise, J. (2009) China and international harmony: The role of Confucius Institute in bolstering Beijing's soft power. *Asian Survey* 49 (4), 647–669.

Peck, J. and Tickell, A. (2002) Neoliberalizing space. *Antipode* 34 (3), 380–404.

Piller, I. and Cho, J. (2013) Neoliberalism as language policy. *Language in Society* 42 (1), 23–44.

Pride, J.B. and Liu, R. (1988) Some aspects of the spread of English in China since 1949. *International Journal of Sociology of Language* 74, 41–70.

Sun, J.J., Hu, P. and Ng, S.H. (2016) Impact of English on education reforms in China: With reference to the learn-English movement, the internationalization of universities and the English language requirement in college entrance examinations. *Journal of Multilingual and Multicultural Development* 1-14. http://dx.doi.org/10.1080/01434632.2015.1134551.

Wang, L. (2004) When English becomes big business. In T. Weiss and K-k. Tam (eds) *English and Globalization: Perspectives from Hong Kong and Mainland China* (pp.149–168). Hong Kong: Chinese University Press.

Worldscreen (n.d.) *American Dreams in China* boasts 2.5 billion Chinese yuan box office during its first 27 days of release. See http://www.worldscreen.com.tw/goods. php?goods_id=3123 (accessed 1 February 2016).

Xinhua News Agency (2008) In dialogue with Hanban director Xu Lin: The soft promotion of Chinese language and culture. See http://lw.xinhuanet.com/htm/content_3156.htm (accessed 15 September 2015).

Zhang, W. (2000) *Transforming China: Economic Reform and its Political Implications*. Houndmills/New York: Palgrave.

Zhou, M. (2015) Nation-state building in a rising China: PRC discourses on the Chinese language since the turn of the 21st century. In L. Tsung and W. Wang (eds)

Contemporary Chinese Discourse and Social Practice in China (pp. 59–80). Amsterdam: John Benjamins.

Zhu, H. and Li, W. (2014) Geopolitics and the changing hierarchies of the Chinese language: Implications for policy and practice of Chinese language teaching in Britain. *The Modern Language Journal* 98, 326–339.

3 'A Treasure' and 'A Legacy': Individual and Communal (Re)valuing of Isthmus Zapotec in Multilingual Mexico

Haley De Korne

Introduction

Before the sun rises the public market in *Juchitán de Zaragoza* is already full of activity. In this city in the center of the Isthmus of Tehuantepec, along the Pacific coastal plain of Oaxaca in the south of Mexico, the temperatures are high year-round and some people are happy to buy and sell before the intense sun is fully in the sky. The market remains active all day and into the night as well; when the early-morning fish vendors are gone (selling the catch from the nearby gulf of Tehuantepec) they are replaced by vendors of fruit, vegetables, hand-made tortillas, clothing, kitchenware, and many other things besides. When dusk falls, new vendors arrive to sell bread, locally-made cheeses, tamales, and *bupu* (a corn-cacao-cane sugar-plumeria flower drink). Both locally grown or prepared products and products brought in from elsewhere in Mexico and the world can be purchased in the market. In the noisy, lively atmosphere most vendors will happily sell their wares in Diidxazá, the local language, or in Spanish – although some vendors come from outside of the region and speak only Spanish, or Spanish and another Indigenous language. While transactions among adults and elders commonly occur in Diidxazá, most people speak only Spanish to children or adolescents who come to shop for their families or to stand outside the building and sell their mothers' *gueta suqui* (oven-made tortillas) out of baskets carried over their arms. Many youth are able to understand the Diidxazá use around them, but interact mainly or only in Spanish. When a *huada* (foreign woman), such as myself, addresses the adult vendors in Diidxazá to make a purchase, some simply carry out the transaction as normal with no visible reaction, while others break out into a grin or a look of surprise, commenting to their neighbors that this foreigner speaks Diidxazá. They often go on to provide compliments and encouragement, saying that it's good to speak Diidxazá, it's a beautiful language.[1]

Language practices in the marketplace, as in other social spaces of the Isthmus of Tehuantepec, are influenced by numerous social and historical factors. In this chapter, I explore changes in the use and valuation of Diidxazá (an Indigenous language of Mesoamerica also called Isthmus Zapotec [IZ][2]) in education and other social spaces. Beginning with an historical analysis of the status of IZ across four different political and economic eras, I then focus on discourses and counter-discourses about the symbolic capital of IZ in education and society in the contemporary context. By tracing how the educational use of Isthmus Zapotec has been valued under different political and economic systems, from before the waves of European invasion, through the eras of colonization, nationalism and under current neoliberal, internationally oriented politics, I argue the need to recognize different discourses of value across time and among social groups. On the one hand, it is clear that changes in political and economic conditions have had a significant impact on discourses and practices relating to Diidxazá education and use. On the other hand, this case illustrates how the perceived value of Diidxazá is subject to ongoing negotiation; as in the public market of Juchitán described above, the linguistic marketplace where Diidxazá is evaluated and exchanged is characterized by many voices and local forms of organization, which remain impactful alongside the influences of neoliberal politico-economic structures.

The following section describes the methodology, context and conceptual framing of this chapter. I then turn to shifts in the value of Diidxazá across different eras and among different social actors, concluding with a discussion of the multiple forms of value present in the current linguistic market.

Language and Value in the Isthmus of Tehuantepec

My analysis of this context draws on a larger study which employed ethnographic monitoring (De Korne & Hornberger, 2017; Hornberger, 2013; Hymes, 1980; Van der Aa & Blommaert, 2011) to examine the use of Isthmus Zapotec in a variety of formal and non-formal education settings (De Korne, 2016). This study spanned from 2013 to 2015, during which time I resided in the Isthmus for 17 months and made several shorter follow-up visits to observe and participate in a sample of IZ education initiatives and to interview a range of education stakeholders. As a non-Mexican researcher of European–American origin, I approached this context as an outsider, but quickly developed connections and collaborations with a variety of local actors who, like me, have backgrounds and interests related to issues of language education, literacy and multilingualism. In this chapter, I draw on field notes, interviews, document collection and linguistic landscape documentation collected during this time, as well as secondary sources which situate this ethnographic data historically. I triangulate the above sources of data in order to analyze discourses and practices of valuing Diidxazá manifested by the comments and practices of a range of actors in formal education, including parents and caregivers, primary school teachers and administrators and higher education teachers and students. This sample is not representative of the practices and perspectives of all Diidxazá speakers, learners and educators; however, through a longitudinal, ethnographic perspective I hope to offer a contextualized understanding of the multiple, often over-lapping discourses at play.

The territory that is now Mexico has been inhabited by numerous sociolinguistic groups, who have come into contact and conflict over many centuries, making it an apt context within which to consider changes in language valuation, educational practice and social well-being. Of the five Indigenous languages present in the Isthmus of Tehuantepec, Isthmus Zapotec is by far the most numerically dominant today with an estimated 85,000 speakers.[3] As described in the opening vignette, Diidxazá is currently an integral part of communication practices in Juchitán and several other municipalities in the Isthmus, including domains from local commerce to social gatherings and the home. There is an active Diidxazá literary movement dating at least to the early 20th century, including poetry, narrative, traditional music and hip-hop. A 'popular alphabet' was established in 1956 (La Sociedad Pro-Planeación del Istmo, 1956) and is used in formal written production, but the majority of speakers have not learned it (De Korne, 2017).

The vast majority of residents of the Isthmus also speak Spanish, and an increasing number are monolingual or dominant in Spanish, especially among younger generations. The dominance of Spanish has been and continues to be promoted through the education system, as discussed further in historical perspective in the following sections. The majority of youth attend Spanish-only schools, while a minority attend nominally 'bilingual' schools where IZ is taught one hour per week at the primary level and not at all at higher levels. Spanish occupies the most prestigious social spaces outside of education as well, such as government offices and banks.

In the Isthmus, as elsewhere in the world, schooling and wider politico-economic conditions play crucial roles in establishing the value of certain language practices and devaluing others (Bourdieu, 1991; Bourdieu & Passeron, 1970; Levinson *et al.*, 1996). Bourdieu's (1977) *market of linguistic exchanges* provides a framework for understanding how the perceived value or *symbolic capital* associated with Diidxazá use in school and society translates into political hierarchies and material inequalities. Formal education holds a key position in the linguistic market as an 'instrument of the reproduction of linguistic capital' (Bourdieu, 1977: 651–652). Schools often serve to validate power hierarchies and reinforce the marginalization of certain speakers and forms of speaking through both discursive or symbolic and physical forms of exclusion (Bourdieu & Passeron, 1970; Fairclough, 1989; Illich, 1970). In Mexico, a high value is placed on Spanish (and increasingly on English) in schooling, while Isthmus Zapotec and other Indigenous languages have historically been considered to have little or no value in education, giving their speakers little or no social capital. The relations of symbolic power that influence communication practices and control the linguistic market are context-specific, as Bourdieu (1977) states:

> Linguistic competence (like any other cultural competence) functions as linguistic capital in relationship with a certain market. This is demonstrated by generalized linguistic devaluations, which may occur suddenly (as a result of political revolution), or gradually (as a result of a slow transformation of material and symbolic power relations, e.g. the steady devaluation of French on the world market relative to English). (Bourdieu, 1977: 651)

This context-specific understanding of linguistic capital is crucial to an analysis of the changes that have taken place – and are ongoing – in relation to the values associated with Diidxazá. The competencies that constitute capital in education and society today are inevitably different than those valued in the past. In order to understand the current workings of the linguistic market, it is necessary to consider the material and symbolic power relations within which language practices occur. The value of Indigenous languages and the social capital of their speakers declined suddenly in Mexico due to the material and symbolic power relations under European colonization and subsequent nation-building. The value of Indigenous languages within national structures has fluctuated to some degree in recent decades however, as further explored in the following sections.

One of the changing features of power relations in Mexico has been the trend toward the privatization of services and resources and increasing integration in international economic markets (Overmyer-Velázquez, 2010; Stavenhagen, 2015). Commonly referred to as the neoliberal or late liberal era, these political and economic trends have been accompanied by an increase in policies of cultural recognition and human rights in Mexico and elsewhere in Latin America (García, 2005; Hale, 2005; Muehlmann, 2009). The ways that these changes in material and symbolic power relations may influence the linguistic marketplace and education practices are a subject of ongoing concern. Various impacts have been noted in Mexico, from changes in how public education is designed and implemented (Levinson, 2005; Sayer, 2015), to the creation of new discourses about language use (Muehlmann, 2008; Yoshioka, 2010). Although there is currently an increased emphasis on the recognition of cultural and linguistic diversity, this recognition is typically tokenistic and does little or nothing to change material inequalities (Hale, 2005; Overmyer-Velázquez, 2010). In recognition of this, scholars have warned that neoliberal politics of respect for multiculturalism or multilingualism can function to control and assimilate cultural difference, rather than promote it (Comaroff & Comaroff, 2009; García, 2005; Speed, 2005). As discussed further below, neoliberal policies and discourses of recognition for Indigenous languages in Mexico and abroad are influencing the linguistic market in the Isthmus of Tehuantepec, such that Isthmus Zapotec is taking on new forms of value relative to its status in local, national and global markets.

The influence of a prevailing politico-economic system, whether colonial, neoliberal or other, is always partial and incomplete, however. While new ways of valuing Isthmus Zapotec are present in the current era, the influences of nationalist and colonial era logics which devalue Indigenous languages remain in strong evidence in everyday life. Additionally, local agents in the Isthmus of Tehuantepec have a long history of struggling for change amid systemic and structural power imbalances, with notable results. This constructivist perspective of social change and inequality has driven scholarship on *counterpublics*, or 'parallel discursive arenas where members of subordinated social groups invent and circulate counter-discourses to formulate oppositional interpretations of their identities, interests, and needs' (Fraser, 1992: 123). Povinelli (2011) examines such *spaces of otherwise* and their endurance amid the dominating ideological and material conditions of the late liberal era in which she writes, despite attempts to bracket or erase them. Such spaces and endurance have arguably been present in all historical eras and all formations of social inequality. Bourdieu (1977: 651) acknowledges the agency present within the linguistic market, stating that 'Discourse is a compromise formation, emerging from the negotiation between the expressive interest [of the speaker] and the censorship inherent in particular linguistic production relations [...] which is imposed on a speaker'. Therefore, not only imposed factors but also 'expressive interest' play a role in determining how transactions will play out in the linguistic marketplace.

In this chapter, I aim to attend to these forms of compromise and negotiation among local actors in conjunction with the wider structural factors and politico-economic processes which influence them. By focusing on local agents who may be overlooked by generalizing structural analyses, I examine neoliberal influences in Isthmus Zapotec education on the ground level. This case illustrates the incomplete or limited reach of neoliberal logics within a context where other social formations and logics continue to structure education systems, communication practices and daily life. I begin by considering changes in the linguistic market upon which Diidxazá has been valued at different times, and then turn to an analysis of the multiple, negotiated interpretations of symbolic capital associated with Diidxazá use by education actors in the Isthmus of Tehuantepec during my study.

Shame and Silence Through Schooling: The Price of Colonialism and Nationalism

This section traces how Diidxazá has been valued in social and educational domains during pre-colonial, colonial, nationalist and internationalist political and economic eras up to the present day. The Zapotecs built far-reaching economic and political networks in pre-colonial Mesoamerica, developing a hierarchical empire which included much of what is now Oaxaca from around 500 BCE to 900 CE and subsequently maintaining smaller centers of power in regional city states. They created pictographic and semi-phonemic writing systems which were taught to the social elite, as well as sophisticated vigesimal (base 20) mathematics, astronomy and architecture (de la Cruz, 2008; Romero Frizzi, 2003; Urcid, 2005). Zapotecs from the valley city state of Zaachila migrated down to the Isthmus around 1400 CE as the Aztec influence was creeping into the region. The Zapotecs who settled in the Isthmus displaced and occasionally clashed with other Indigenous groups over land (Miano Borruso, 2002). These struggles amid Mesoamerican powers took an unpredictable turn a century later with the beginning of the Spanish invasion in 1519.

Although records of everyday Zapotec life under colonial rule are not numerous, it was generally a time of hardship, including heavy tolls from new diseases, forced labor in *haciendas*[4] and struggles to pay the tributes required by the colonial government. In 1521, there were 24,000 Indigenous residents of the Isthmus recorded as paying tribute; in 1550, there were 6,000 and only 60 years after the invasion, in 1580, the population paying tribute had dropped over 80% to 4,000 (Acuña, 1984, as cited in Barabas & Bartolomé, 1999: 71), indicating that the population as a whole was also in sharp decline. There were rebellions against Spanish exploitation throughout the 16th and 17th centuries, with the most famous being the 1660 rebellion of Tehuantepec, where the Isthmus Zapotecs succeeded in governing the city of Tehuantepec for one year before the colonial government retook the city, gruesomely punishing the local leaders (Miano Borruso, 2002). Despite the Spanish confiscation of most material resources, such as arable land and the prized salt flats along the Pacific coast, an alternative 'commercial circuit' of economic exchanges was maintained among the Indigenous communities of the region during the colonial era (Acosta Márquez, 2007: 14).

In addition to severe material and physical exploitation, the symbolic devaluing of Indigenous peoples and languages was firmly established under Spanish colonial rule, enhanced by the introduction of formal education and alphabetic literacy (Maldonado Alvarado, 2002). The Zapotec writing systems, previously restricted to a minority, were not transmitted and subsequently lost; the Indigenous population was considered illiterate and their languages, termed *dialectos*, lesser forms of communication. Indigenous forms of linguistic and cultural expression were accorded no social value and Indigenous people were positioned at the bottom of the colonial social hierarchy. As Robles (1977: 17) comments, 'Una organización predominantemente feudal colocaba a la gran mayoría de aborígenes en posición explotada y marginada de los favores del gran desarrollo de los servicios educativos de entonces'.[5]

Following independence from Spain in 1821, a nation-building ideology prevailed in Mexico with political leaders no longer ignoring the Indigenous population, but instead attempting to include and assimilate them (Heath, 1972). The Mexican revolution in 1910–1920 resulted in a further centralist, assimilationist political environment which the national *Secretaría de Educación Pública*[6] supported, following its founding in 1921 (Martínez Vásquez, 2004). The first regional teacher training college in the Isthmus, the *Escuela Normal Regional de Juchitán*,[7] opened in 1926 and an increasing number of primary and secondary schools followed (Ruíz Martínez, 2013). It was as a result of this aggressive national campaign for school construction and Spanish-language literacy that use of Spanish began to become more common among the general population in Oaxaca in the 1940s (Hamel, 2008b; Sicoli, 2011).

In summary, the era of mandatory public schooling in Mexico – officially beginning with the 1867 *Ley de Instrucción Pública*,[8] although not becoming truly established until the founding and subsequent expansion of the *Secretaria de Educación Pública* in 1920 (Robles, 1977) – has perpetuated social inequalities and has largely been a space that excludes Indigenous languages and sociocultural practices. López Gopar (2007) discusses the dominance of a Eurocentric and autonomous model of literacy (Street, 1984) which excludes past and present Indigenous multimodal literacies in favor of an alphabet-centric view of language development. Rebolledo (2008: 104) describes the 'national monolingual educational model imposed on bilingual students' as characterized by 'a series of conventional teaching patterns and the curricular rigidity of basic education: school has been designed for a culturally homogenous population, within which Indian characteristics do not fit'.

Although use of Diidxazá continues among adult generations and in specific social domains, as described above, widespread educational norms and practices that devalue Isthmus Zapotec have resulted in the association of shame and prejudice with the language. There is an increasing practice of raising children primarily through Spanish, in particular in middle- and upper-class neighborhoods (Augsburger, 2004; Cata, 2003; McComsey, 2015). I was told time and again that Diidxazá is not being passed on because many people continue to think that it is a *dialecto* (qualitatively different than a language like Spanish or English) and that if children grow up speaking it they will not speak Spanish well, or will have a hard time learning Spanish. As one mother commented,

LV-4: Mis hijos, la niña de 12 años y el niño de 9, no hablan el zapoteco. Ya hace como 10 años que los niños que vienen naciendo, a partir de diez años atrás, ya no están hablando, ya no están aprendiendo el zapoteco, ya nosotros los papás como que les hablamos más en el español, para no confundirlos con el zapoteco. Porque a veces cuando nosotros, en mi caso no, que desde niña hablé el zapoteco, y aprender el español sí fue un poco complicado, [...] la mezcla del español y zapoteco, era muy difícil. Pues la gente que según esto ya sabía mucho, se le parecía como naco, pues hablar así, sí, sí daba un poco de vergüenza. (LV-4 131113)[9]

As in many parts of the world, schooling played a significant role in placing Diidxazá and other local languages at the bottom of the linguistic hierarchy in Mexico (Skutnabb-Kangas, 2009; Tollefson, 1991). A nominally bilingual (Indigenous language-Spanish) education system has existed under different titles and formats since the 1960s, but has generally functioned to transition students to use of Spanish without developing bilingual or biliterate capacities (Coronado Suzán, 1992; Hamel, 2008a, 2008b; Rebolledo, 2010) and without significantly raising the symbolic capital of the language. While many people with whom I spoke felt that there was more prejudice toward use of Diidxazá in the past, others noted that it carries on in the present. A young woman in her early twenties was one of many people who discussed the legacy of school-based discrimination, describing her small town primary school in an interview:

H: ¿Cuándo estuviste en la escuela en [un pueblo pequeño] no había nada de zapoteco en la escuela?

LV-2:   Nada. Ahí tenía varios compañeros que sí hablaban el zapoteco y para eso deben estar callados toda la clase porque no se les permitía hablar el zapoteco. Entonces se quedaban sin recreo si hablaban, una palabra y se quedaban; entonces ahí fue donde ya se fue perdiendo poco a poco y dice mi mamá que desde que ella estaba, cuando ella empezó ir a la primaria le hicieron lo mismo que ya prohibían desde ese entonces que aprendieran que hablaran el zapoteco dentro del salón, dentro de la escuela más bien. Desde ahí ya como que ya se fue perdiendo. (LV-2 131107)[10]

Silence and the exclusion of Diidxazá have thus been part of the common educational experience of several generations of children in the Isthmus, contributing to the internalized prejudices that are widespread today. The devaluing of the symbolic capital of Diidxazá and other Indigenous languages during the colonial era, followed by the attribution of capital primarily to Spanish (and in particular to Spanish monolingualism) during the nation-building era, has had a clear and lasting effect on the linguistic market in the Isthmus, as elsewhere in Mexico and the post-colonial world.

Rights and Recognition: Negotiating the Neoliberal Multicultural Market

Mexico has shifted to an official policy of *pluriculturalism* with the recognition of the presence of Indigenous peoples in Mexico's constitution in 1992 (article 2), the San Andrés Accords in 1996 and the Law on the Linguistic

Rights of Indigenous Peoples in 2003 (*Ley general de derechos lingüísticos de los pueblos indígenas*, 2003; López Gopar, 2007; Overmyer-Velázquez, 2010). Numerous scholars have critiqued the 'politics of recognition' that appear increasingly popular in post-colonial, liberal states, noting that they objectify and ultimately control the social difference represented by Indigenous languages and cultures without substantially altering material disadvantages experienced by minority communities (Brown, 2006; Comaroff & Comaroff, 2009; Coulthard, 2007; Povinelli, 2011), resulting in 'folkloric poverty' (Overmyer-Velázquez, 2010). Hale (2005: 13) argues that a focus on cultural rights and recognition is a hallmark of current trends of neoliberal political and economic reforms, describing how 'neoliberal multiculturalism' in Latin America has involved 'restructur[ing] the arena of political contention, driving a wedge between cultural rights and the assertion of the control over resources necessary for those rights to be realized'.

The advancement of privatization and internationalization policies in Mexico[11] is a prime example; the same year that Mexico changed the constitution to recognize Indigenous languages (2003), they also changed the constitution to privatize land that had been communally held, a policy which has had dire consequences for subsistence farmers, among which Indigenous people are highly represented (Appendini, 2012). The 1994 North Atlantic Free Trade Agreement, including the restructuring of agriculture and resource management toward export crops and extraction, is another manifestation of neoliberal policy which has had a negative material impact on Indigenous Mexican communities (López Bárecenas, 2009), causing migration and demographic shifts which weaken cultural and linguistic ties (Pérez Báez, 2013; Yoshioka, 2010). As a result, apparent gains in struggles for social equality often remain at the rhetorical level; meanwhile 'The nightmare settles in as indigenous organizations win important battles of cultural rights only to find themselves mired in the painstaking, technical, administrative, and highly inequitable negotiations for resources and political power that follow' (Hale, 2005: 13).

While forms of colonial and national assimilatory governance still continue to be reflected in language education discourses in Mexico as discussed in the previous section, neoliberal and multicultural recognition politics also have an emerging influence. On the national level, recent efforts to make *interculturalism* part of public schooling are an example of superficial neoliberal multiculturalism, characterized by celebrating cultural difference without considering the hierarchies and power dynamics among groups (Velasco Cruz, 2010; Walsh, 2010). On the regional level, many teachers and school directors in the Isthmus have adopted a rhetorical alignment with Indigenous language promotion, even if their practices (and perhaps more significantly the centralized curricula and exams that police their practices) have not changed significantly. For example, the current director of the small town primary school attended by the young woman quoted above, who had worked there since before the time when she was a student, expressed regret that students in the school are now largely unable to speak Diidxazá:

E-4: Quién sabe cuál es la idea de que... este... que le diga a los niños: mira, no hables el zapoteco. Porque muchas veces... o... así pasa, ¿no? Te prohíben decirlo porque supuestamente es un dialecto que no está reconocido. En cambio, fuera el inglés, el francés, el alemán, bueno, ya es otra cosa. Pero el zapoteco como que lo prohíbe la gente aquí. Quién sabe por qué, ¿no? (E-4 140318)[12]

These comments made in a semi-structured interview with me, a foreign researcher known to be interested in Isthmus Zapotec, exemplify what I observed to be a common stance in favor of the equality of local languages. The director notes that people forbid their children from speaking Isthmus Zapotec due to the misconception that it is an unrecognized dialect – implying that if they were aware of its official recognition, perhaps they would view it in the same light as English, French or German, where it technically belongs. His egalitarian stance does not translate into active practices, however, as the school remains a space largely dedicated to Spanish monolingualism. Comments such as this and many others are indicative of a changing ideological climate surrounding language education in the Isthmus, in which the symbolic capital of Diidxazá has risen in value. The fact that not everyone has taken up this discourse of revaluing limits the degree to which schools put the discourse into practice; the opposition of parents to the use of Diidxazá is noted by several school directors as a key factor in their choices (Interviews E-3 140114; E-8 140513).

A positive valuation of local culture, and to a lesser extent language, is also evident among education actors that do not regularly interact with Diidxazá-speaking families, as these school directors do. One example comes from an advertisement for the *Centro Escolar Bilingüe Pestalozzi* (see Figure 3.1), a private school located in an urban part of the Isthmus where there is very little Diidxazá use and whose 'bilingual' title refers to English and Spanish. The advertisement shows a woman on a beach in a dress and headpiece worn for regional festivals and ceremonies (*traje istmeño*) and invites the public in Spanish to 'be part of our customs and traditions' through attending an exposition of student work, followed

Figure 3.1 Photograph of flyer advertising a school event, posted in Tehuantepec, 21 March 2015

by a slogan in English 'Isthmus, where culture florishes' (sic).[13] While in the past 'bilingual' schools were associated with under-funded public schools for Indigenous children, there are an increasing number of private Spanish–English bilingual schools, some affiliating with European names and pedagogies (such as Montessori, or Pestalozzi as in the case of this school). Interestingly, this school aligns with Isthmus 'culture' through visible indexes like clothing (*traje istmeño*) and geography (beach), but through the use of an English slogan they do not explicitly affiliate with local language.

Many people in the Isthmus are interested in learning English and especially in having their children learn it, seeing it as an important skill for success in schooling and employment in the future (e.g. Field notes 140801; Interviews IP 140915; LV-3 131113). Nonetheless, most children in the Isthmus would not be able to attend an English bilingual school like this due to the tuition fees. Josefa, a grandmother who cares for two bilingual (Diidxazá–Spanish) grandchildren explained in an interview how she (like many female caregivers in the region) makes just enough to sustain her family through the painstaking embroidery of the kind of garments shown in the private school's flyer. She is uncritically grateful for the public education provided to her grandchildren in their urban monolingual primary school and has impressed upon them the importance of studying hard in order to succeed. She also joked that I should take them with me in my suitcase so they can learn English (Interview J-4 141112).

The commodification of culture and language through neoliberal multicultural discourses would appear to be of little benefit to people like Josefa and her grandchildren who continue to lack basic material resources at the bottom of the economic hierarchy, despite being rich in the kinds of symbolic capital celebrated by the politics of recognition. At the same time, internationally oriented institutions capitalize from the positive association with local culture, making their affiliation with local culture visible and mobile through publicity such as the school's flyer. It is clear that the benefits of recognizing local culture and language as symbolic capital in recent decades have not been universally distributed by the linguistic market in Mexico.

The national-level politics of multiculturalism in Mexico may be superficial and mask ongoing inequities in many ways, yet it is misleading to view them as a unilateral product of neoliberal trends. Mobilizations of Indigenous communities at local, regional and national levels have played an important role in shifting policies and most importantly in negotiating what results they have locally. Beyond the high-profile work of the Zapatistas in Chiapas, responsible for the 1996 San Andrés Accords and to a large extent the 2003 Law of Linguistic Rights (López Bárecenas, 2009; Rebolledo, 2010), there are numerous local self-defining political and cultural initiatives in Indigenous communities across Mexico. In the Isthmus, the municipality of Juchitán is known for the election of the independent, left-wing COCEI (*Coalición Obrero-Campesino-Estundiantil del Istmo*)[14] party in 1981 at a time when the rest of the country was run by the PRI (*Partido Revolucionario Institucional*), a political movement which incorporated Diidxazá poetry and artwork as an important part of its public displays (Campbell, 1989, 1994; Rubin, 1994) and which continues to the present.

Through even the briefest contextualization of the struggles over language and culture recognition in Mexico, it becomes clear that there are multiple agents negotiating symbolic power. For example, the urban public school attended by Josefa's bilingual grandchildren, although officially a monolingual school, has facilitated several projects related to Diidxazá as part of a larger effort to improve the social cohesion of students and the participation of parents in the school. They hope that by validating local cultural and linguistic practices, they will help to counteract the effects of domestic violence, poverty and drugs that have increasingly appeared in the school (Interviews E-9 141717; E-10 140917). They were supported in this initiative by a branch of the state-level teachers union which is promoting participatory education and the revaluing of local knowledge through a proposed state-level reform, the *Plan para la transformación de la educación de Oaxaca*[15] (IEEPO, SNTE & CNTE, 2013). As a result of these state-level and school-level actors, Josefa's bilingual grandchildren performed at the top of their respective classes during Diidxazá activities, visibly proud of the capital that their ability to speak Isthmus Zapotec suddenly represented and eagerly taking up the challenge to write it (Field notes 140602, 140715).

In this example, the revaluing of Diidxazá goes beyond the tokenistic level (such as displaying traditional clothing in an advertisement) to influence communicative practices in the classroom through teaching IZ literacy. While these practices are not as highly visible or mobile as the private school's expo and flyer, they improved the educational experience and confidence of students who might otherwise feel marginalized by formal schooling. Additionally, the teachers' aim was not to promote language or culture in an objectified way but rather to improve the well-being of the school community, and revaluing local language was one of the strategies that they identified. While the national politics of multicultural recognition may be helping to create a discursive environment in which projects like this are more readily accepted by educational authorities, it is clear that they are not responsible for generating or determining such educational initiatives. Povinelli (2011: 72) argues that the influences of dominant political discourses are always partial, noting: 'It is vital [...] that although it can police the potential eruptions of political events, the politics of cultural recognition in late liberalism cannot saturate social worlds in such a way that no potentiality remains within the actual world'. In other words, the story of language and education practices in the Isthmus did not begin – nor does it end – within the tidy framework provided by the politics of neoliberal multiculturalism.

Revaluing Diidxazá: Negotiating Symbolic Capital on Multiple Markets

The public market of Juchitán offers a range of products from local to global points of origin; images of the *Virgen de Guadalupe* that were made in China, apples from the cooler state of Chiapas, duck eggs and nopal cactus from the *Ikoots* (Huave) zone near the coast and many local products, from tomatoes the size of small marbles to white-skinned cucumbers, leather sandals and the distinctive embroidered *traje*. Similarly, the linguistic market trades in discourses and forms of symbolic capital that can be sourced to different places and political economic conditions, resulting in the overlap of discourses which devalue Diidxazá as a *dialecto* alongside those which grant symbolic value to Indigenous language and culture, and those which incorporate Diidxazá use as part of wider social goals.

There are multiple voices currently raising the value of Diidxazá in some respect, from school directors who recognize the official status of Indigenous languages, to teachers and students who actively engage in Diidxazá practices. Actors who engage in Isthmus Zapotec education today are producing and negotiating discourses which value the language as capital for mobile individuals as well as capital for communal, place-specific ways of being. While the former is an interesting trend which can easily be linked to neoliberal multiculturalism, it is important not to ignore the counter-discourses that are not oriented to personal accumulation, but rather to social coexistence, or *convivencia*. Below, I briefly outline how these discourses of value are manifest by participants in formal education.

Diidxazá as symbolic capital on local markets

Diidxazá has value in the social life of the Isthmus and is seen by many as an important part of an *Istmeño* ontology or a place-based, descent-based way of living in the Isthmus. People who adopt this social or group orientation do not describe Isthmus Zapotec as a resource which can be exported or superficially acquired. When discussing why they value Isthmus Zapotec or are engaged in teaching or using it in some way, the most common response is related to family, social ties and place. A young teacher-in-training, when asked to define Zapotec, said:

> **X-1:** Yo siempre defino la palabra zapoteco como ese palabra sicarú que significa hermoso, bonito, porque al fin y al cabo es hermoso hablar zapoteco, convivir con otras personas. (X-1 131115)[16]

Being able to *convivir* – live with, interact and communicate – with people of all generations in the Isthmus, as monolingual Spanish speakers are not able to do, is valuable for him. Other people of younger generations commented that they use Diidxazá most when speaking with grandparents and that they enjoy this interaction (LV-3 131113; UT-4 150705).

Social interactions are also at the heart of the motivations of several of the young adults who participate in weekend Isthmus Zapotec classes at a university, as expressed by Reyna, a student:

> **U-6:** Ahorita lo que me interesa es poder hablarlo, no importa cómo pero hablarlo, y poderme comunicar con la gente, ir al mercado y poder hablar solo el zapoteco. Por el momento no me interesa ser muy científica y saber todas las reglas y todo eso, lo que me interesa ahorita es poder comunicarme. (U-6 131022)[17]

Although she turned to a formal education institution to learn more Isthmus Zapotec, her motivation is not to use it in a formal setting but to communicate in the markets and everyday social spaces. She went on to comment,

> **U-6:** Bueno pues el zapoteco así en palabras coloquiales pues es la lengua de mi abuelita, la lengua de mi madre y con el hecho de ser la lengua de las personas que me dieron la vida, por las que yo estoy aquí, se vuelve un legado y una herencia muy importante. (U-6 131022)[18]

Reyna's valuation of Diidxazá and her desire to develop beyond her passive bilingual abilities is rooted in her sense of family and place, and contrasts with the ideology that caused her parents to discourage her from learning Diidxazá as a child. It is also distinct from neoliberal discourses, through which the value of Diidxazá is determined on an international market.

Another student, Rosalinda, who grew up outside of the Diidxazá-speaking zone described how she was initially motivated to study it because of the social atmosphere of her university campus:

> **U-10:** [...]cuando empecé a estudiar acá en la facultad pues ya empecé a interactuar con personas que hablaban zapoteco, y pues me empezó a [gustar]---
>
> **H:** [Personas] de tu edad.
>
> **U-10:** Sí, de mi edad. Entonces--- y que me hablaban fluido. Era su primera lengua el zapoteco. Entonces... me interesó mucho y los escuchaba hablar, y quería yo entender lo que decían. [...] Entonces sí quería aprenderlo. Me gustó mucho, sí. Y ya cuando me empecé a meter en esos cursos, a integrarme a esos cursos, convivir más con personas que hablan el zapoteco, todo lo demás, este... empecé a platicar con mi familia, con mi papá. Entonces me dijo mi papá que sí, mis ancestros, eh mis familiares míos, abuelitas, mis abuelitas y todos ellos, ellas sí eran de acá del Istmo de Tehuantepec. Entonces ellos sí hablaban zapoteco. Mi bisabuelita hablaba zapoteco... y mi tatarabuelita era de Tehuantepec. Entonces quizá por eso también me emociona aprender zapoteco. (U-10 140513)[19]

Both using Diidxazá and some of the motivations for teaching or learning it are thus closely tied to the daily life of people in the Isthmus. These discourses of value orient toward the importance of communication and cohesion in today's social environments, as well as the awareness of language as a capital that is related to descent. Orienting toward the 'genealogical society' (Povinelli, 2011) can be seen as a form of resistance or a counter-discourse in an era when individual mobility (or in Povinelli's words, the 'autological subject') is promoted by neoliberal politico-economic systems.

Diidxazá as mobile capital and opportunities

In contrast to the speakers and learners who orient toward local ties when discussing Diidxazá, some people orient toward Diidxazá as a source of capital in relation to domains outside of the Isthmus. While not mutually exclusive of the local or community discourse described above, this discourse often takes on a more individualist tone, identifying opportunities for scholarships or other positions specific to speakers of Indigenous languages and the interest of outsiders (such as myself) in Isthmus Zapotec as motivations for valuing the language or learning to speak it.

The director of a semi-urban primary school where Isthmus Zapotec is taught one hour per week and occasionally promoted through other activities, commented,

E-8:   ...la lengua diidxazá es un tesoro, es un valor importante para nosotros. [Así-]
H: [Sí.]
E-8:   Así lo veo, Haley, yo así lo veo. Pero si niego mi tierra, niego...mi lengua por ejemplo, o dijera idiomas cualesquiera... ¡No! no, para nada. Nuestro zapoteco ha caminado muchos lugares. De veras, ha caminado mucho, ha alcanzado lugares, espacio más allá en otros, en otros países donde ha llegado. Sus costumbres han ido a Alemania igual, ¿no? Este pues... sus bailes, ¿no? Y esa es una ventaja del zapoteco porque pues... está creciendo. Y nosotros los que estamos acá, no le estamos dando importancia. (E-8 140513)[20]

This director links the value of Isthmus Zapotec to its presence in international spaces, evaluating the disinterest of people in the region in comparison with the interest of people from outside the region. Additionally, he commodifies the language itself as a 'treasure' which has great value. These comments stand out in contrast to his acknowledgement at other moments during the interview that it is not of great interest to all of his teaching staff nor to many of the parents of his students, and contrasts as well with my observations of the minimal use of Diidxazá within the school (Field notes 131218; 140714).

This discourse of valuing Diidxazá on linguistic markets controlled from the outside appears especially common among younger, educated or socially mobile people. A university student told me that although her parents had not wanted her to learn Diidxazá, she paid attention and learned it and now she argues that they need to teach her younger brother because of the scholarships and jobs available to speakers of Indigenous languages. Her greatest motivation is to travel and get out of her town, and she sees Isthmus Zapotec as a possible resource to achieve that goal (Interview UT-1 140717). Another university student who was not able to speak Diidxazá and had not (yet) traveled outside the Isthmus, began to attend classes, commenting to me that speaking a *lengua materna* (mother tongue) could be useful for him outside of the region (Field notes 130415). Both mobile and would-be mobile young adults are thus seeing Isthmus Zapotec as possible capital in spaces outside the region where it is actually spoken.

The message that Indigenous languages are assets that the outside world is interested in has been taken up by a significant number of educational actors in the Isthmus. However, this discourse does not negate other forms (or lack) of capital associated with the language. As previously discussed, most school directors acknowledge the equality of Isthmus Zapotec but do not give it equal educational time. Likewise, people who recognize the communal value of Diidxazá locally may also negotiate it as capital on external markets. For example, Rosalinda, the student who was motivated to study Diidxazá after hearing her fellow students speak it and learning her own heritage, also explained to me that her interest in IZ was one of the things she included in an application for a coveted scholarship to study in the US for one year which she felt may have helped its success:

U-10: Al momento de estar rellenando la solicitud de la universidad [...] te piden ciertas cosas [...]. Y una de esas era la forma en que tú ibas a, a enseñar el español. Inclusive también te... te piden tus intereses, que describas lo que a ti te gusta. Lo que te interesa, cursos... cosas que has hecho. Entonces, ahí me eché unas cosas de zapoteco. Y en el español pues también. Pues dije que lo voy a enseñar de una manera que pueda sacarlos más o menos. Eh... cosas que se puedan apegar al contexto real. Y también retomando un poco lo que es la cultura istmeña y obviamente zapoteca... (U-10 140513)[21]

Whether as a form of symbolic capital that increases access to scholarships or a skill for obtaining work in the new climate of official language recognition, there are numerous people who participate in individualist and external-oriented ways of valuing Diidxazá. They have found use for, or affiliation with, Diidxazá to be a resource for them that may increase their material well-being inside and outside of the Isthmus.

Conclusion

Over time, Mexican educational politics have institutionalized norms which largely devalue Diidxazá use and ultimately contribute to the material inequalities experienced by Diidxazá speakers, despite a shift toward policies of pluricultural recognition. The values associated with Isthmus Zapotec remain subject to negotiation however, as local actors continue to revalue IZ use within place-based systems of interaction and exchange, and to find ways to benefit from the shifting linguistic market in which they find themselves. Although there is potential for 'a commodification of language in service of transnational corporations' and a homogenizing neoliberal agenda (Flores, 2013: 515) to be pursued through some of the ways that IZ is valued by education actors today, this is only part of the story. The histories and ongoing movements of Indigenous communities demand a less generalized interpretation, one which recognizes local social and symbolic capital and the ongoing struggles through which Indigenous communities have gained increased rights and recognition within structures of inequality and exploitation.

Local discourses and negotiations of symbolic capital are by nature less mobile and less visible than those produced by actors holding more prominent positions in politico-economic structures, yet these alternative markets through which languages like Diidxazá maintain symbolic capital on their own terms represent significant counter-discourses. From a theoretical standpoint, it is important to attend to the *multiple modernities* (Taylor, 2004) being imagined and negotiated, and multiple spaces of otherwise which endure and develop despite the inequalities of the neoliberal era (Povinelli, 2011). While tracing the emerging influences of neoliberal logics in Isthmus Zapotec education, it is crucial not to overlook the other logics which continue to shape daily life for Diidxazá speakers and learners. The discourse of language as a *legacy* – a form of capital to be sure, but one that comes from somewhere and is bound up in histories and in the mouths of ancestors who spoke it – stands out starkly against the discourse of language as a commodity, a treasure whose worth is determined by exchange value on international markets and which can be cut free of a place and time. The ability to participate within genealogical and place-based networks retains significant value among education actors, while opportunities for individual mobility and the increased material well-being that this can bring are also valued.

While an orientation toward group and place-based ties is often analyzed as the influence of nationalist logics, I argue that the genealogical orientation expressed by Diidxazá learners and teachers should not be framed through the trope of essentialist nationalism any more than diverse cultural practices should be devalued by Western academic tropes of deconstructed authenticity (Briggs, 1996; Sahlins, 1993). In light of the enduring socio-economic realities of the Isthmus, where family ties and local exchange have remained crucial to survival during wave after wave of political domination and exploitation across the centuries, remembering this history is a form of resistance and a counter-discourse of ground-up recognition. From an educational standpoint, it is heartening to observe how people engaging in communally oriented forms of Diidxazá education are benefiting from the affirmation of their social ties and family histories, both of which are in danger of being erased through ongoing politico-economic inequalities. As such, the valuing of Isthmus Zapotec in education remains a key site of symbolic struggle, open to multiple discourses and compromises.

Notes

(1) This vignette summarizes numerous field notes collected during my 17-month ethnographic study, as discussed further in the introduction; e.g. field notes 130408, 131224, 141122. (Field note and interview notation lists the code of the interviewee and the year, month, day. All names of people are pseudonyms.)

(2) I use Diidxazá, Isthmus Zapotec and the abbreviation IZ interchangeably.

(3) Isthmus Zapotec is 1 of approximately 62 varieties that make up the Zapotec branch of the Oto-manguean language family (Pérez Báez, 2011). After Nahuatl and Yucatan Maya, Zapotec is considered the Indigenous language with most speakers in Mexico (441,769 according to the Ethnologue [Lewis *et al.*, 2015]), although these figures overlook the internal diversity and lack of intelligibility among varieties of Zapotec.

(4) Lands ceded to Spanish owners, including the Indigenous people who lived on them, and used for cattle and agricultural production.

(5) A predominantly feudal organization placed the vast majority of indigenous people in an exploited position, marginalized from the favors of the great development of educational services of the time. (All translations mine.)

(6) Secretary of Public Education.

(7) Regional Normal School of Juchitán.

(8) Law of Public Instruction.

(9) **LV-4:** My children, the 12-year-old girl and 9-year-old boy, don't speak Zapotec. Now for about 10 years the children who are being born, since 10 years ago, now they're not speaking, now they're not learning Zapotec, now we, the parents, it's like we speak to them more in Spanish, so as not to

confuse them with Zapotec. Because sometimes when we, in my case, that since childhood I spoke Zapotec and learning Spanish was a bit complicated, [...] the mix of Spanish and Zapotec, it was really difficult. Well the people who apparently already knew a lot, it appeared to them like naco [[uncouth, low class]], to speak like that, yes, yes it gave some shame.

(10) **H:**   When you were in the [primary] school in [a town] there was no Zapotec in the school?

    LV-2:   None. There I had several classmates that spoke Zapotec and because of that they have to be silent for the whole class because they weren't permitted to speak in Zapotec. So they stayed without recess if they spoke, one word and they stayed; so that was where it went being lost bit by bit and my mom says that since when she was there, when she began to go to primary school they did the same to her, that they already forbid back then that people would learn, would speak Zapotec inside the classroom, inside the school rather. From there already, like that's how it's been getting lost.

(11) A topic well beyond the scope of this chapter. See Appendini (2012), Guillén Romo (2005), Overmyer-Velázquez (2010), among others.

(12) **E-4:**   Who knows what the idea is that...um...that they say to the children: Look, don't speak Zapotec. Because many times...or... that happens, right? You're forbidden to speak it because supposedly it's a dialect that's not recognized. In contrast, if it were English, French, German, well, then it's another thing. But Zapotec, like people here forbid it. Who knows why, right?

(13) The full text reads: Bilingual School Center, Pestalozzi, Expo-Cultural-Presentation: We invite you to be part of our customs and traditions through expositions of work made by the students, on the 19th and 20th of March starting at 5:00 PM in the municipal plaza, don't miss it!! Isthmus, where culture florishes.

(14) Laborer-peasant-student coalition of the Isthmus.

(15) Plan for the transformation of education in Oaxaca.

(16) **X-1:**   I always define the word Zapotec like that word *sicaru* that means beautiful, pretty, because ultimately it's beautiful to speak Zapotec, interact/ socialize with other people.

(17) **U-6:**   Right now what I'm interested in is to be able to speak it, it doesn't matter how [well], but to speak it, and to be able to communicate with people, go to the market and be able to speak only Zapotec. For the moment I'm not interested in being really scientific and knowing all the rules and all that, what interests me right now is being able to communicate.

(18) Well Zapotec in everyday words well it's the language of my granny, the language of my mother and with the fact of being the language of the people who gave me life, because of who I am here, it becomes a very important legacy and an inheritance.

(19) **U-10:**   [...]when I started to study here in the university well then I started to interact with people who spoke Zapotec. And well I started to like [it]--

    H: [People] your age.

    U-10:   Yes, my age. So – and that spoke to me fluently. Zapotec was their first language. So... I was really interested and I listened to them speak and I wanted to learn it. I liked it a lot, yes. And then when I started going to those classes, integrating myself [participating] in those classes, socializing more with people who speak Zapotec, everything else, um... I started to talk with my family, with my Dad. So he told me that yes, my ancestors, uh my relations, grannies, my grannies and all of them, they were from here from the Isthmus of Tehuantepec. So they did speak Zapotec. My great-grandmother spoke Zapotec... and my great-great grandmother was from Tehuantepec. So maybe for that also I am excited to learn Zapotec ...

(20) **E-8:** ...the Diidxazá language is a treasure, it's an important value for us. [So –]

H: [Yes]

E-8: That's how I see it Haley, I see it like that. But if I deny my homeland, I deny... my language for example, or say whatever languages... No! No, definitely not. Our Zapotec has walked many places. Truly, it has walked a lot, it has reached places, space beyond in other, in other countries where it has arrived. Its customs have gone to Germany too, right? Um so ... its dances, right? And that is an advantage of Zapotec because well... it's growing. And those of us who are here, we're not giving it importance.

(21) **U-10:** When you are filling out the application for the university [...] they ask you for certain things [...]. And one of those was the form in which you would teach Spanish. Also they ask for your interests, that you describe what you like. What interests you, classes... things that you have done. So there I threw in a few things about Zapotec. And in Spanish well also. Well I said that I will teach in a way that could get them out [ahead] more or less. Um... things that they could attach to the real context. And also taking up again a bit of what is the Istmeño culture, and obviously Zapotec [culture]...

References

Acosta Márquez, E. (2007) *Zapotecos del Istmo de Tehuantepec*. Mexico, D.F.: Comisión Nacional para el Desarrollo de los Pueblos Indígenas (CDI).

Appendini, K. (2012) Interpreting property rights from below: The land certification program (PROCEDE) in Mexico. In V. Andersson and S. Christensen (eds) *Latin American Responses to Neoliberalism: Strategies and Struggles* (pp. 121–140). Aalborg: Aalborg University Press.

Augsburger, D. (2004) Language socialization and shift in an Isthmus Zapotec community of Mexico. PhD dissertation, University of Pennsylvania.

Bourdieu, P. (1977) The economics of linguistic exchanges. *Social Science Information* 16 (6), 645–668.

Bourdieu, P. (1991) *Language and Symbolic Power*. Cambridge, MA: Harvard University Press.

Bourdieu, P. and Passeron, J.-C. (1970) *La Reproduction:Éléments d'une Théorie du Système d'enseignement*. Paris: Minuit.

Briggs, C. (1996) The politics of discursive authority in research on the 'Invention of Tradition'. *Cultural Anthropology* 11 (4), 435–469.

Brown, W. (2006) *Regulating Aversion: Tolerance in the Age of Identity and Empire*. Princeton, NJ: Princeton University Press.

Campbell, H. (1989) Juchitán: The politics of cultural revivalism in an Isthmus Zapotec community. *The Latin American Anthropology Review* 2 (2), 47–55.

Campbell, H. (1994) *Zapotec Renaissance: Ethnic Politics and Cultural Revivalism in Southern Mexico*. Albuquerque, NM: University of New Mexico.

Cata, V. (2003) Tehuantepec: Las últimas voces. *Guiña Ndaga (Baúl Rústico)* 1 (1), 1–22.

Comaroff, J. and Comaroff, J. (2009) *Ethnicity, Inc.* Chicago, IL: University of Chicago Press.

Coronado Suzán, G. (1992) Educación bilingüe en México: Propósitos y realidades. *International Journal of the Sociology of Language* 96, 53–70.

Coulthard, G. (2007) Subjects of empire: Indigenous peoples and the 'politics of recognition' in Canada. *Contemporary Political Theory* 6 (4), 437–461.

De Korne, H. (2016) Imagining convivial multilingualism: Practices, ideologies and strategies in Diidxazá/Isthmus Zapotec Indigenous language education. PhD dissertation, University of Pennsylvania.

De Korne, H. (2017) 'That's too much to learn': Writing, longevity, and urgency in the Isthmus Zapotec speech community. In P. Lane, J. Costa and H. De Korne (eds) *Standardizing Minority Languages: Competing Ideologies of Authority and Authenticity in the Global Periphery.* London: Routledge.

De Korne, H. and Hornberger, N.H. (2017) Countering unequal multilingualism through ethnographic monitoring. In M. Martin-Jones and D. Martin (eds) *Researching Multilingualism* (pp. 247–258). London: Routledge.

de la Cruz, V. (2008) *Mapas Genealógicos del Istmo Oaxaqueño.* Oaxaca: Culturas Populares, CONACULTA.

Fairclough, N. (1989) *Language and Power.* Harlow: Longman.

Flores, N. (2013) The unexamined relationship between neoliberalism and plurilingualism: A cautionary tale. *TESOL Quarterly* 47 (3), 500–520.

Fraser, N. (1992) Rethinking the public sphere: A contribution to the critique of actually existing democracy. In C. Calhoun (ed.) *Habermas and the Public Sphere* (pp. 109–142). Cambridge, MA: MIT Press.

Garcia, M.E. (2005) *Making Indigenous Citizens: Identities, Education, and Multicultural Development in Peru.* Stanford, CA: Stanford University Press.

Guillén Romo, H. (2005) *México Frente a la Mundialización Neoliberal.* Mexico, D.F.: Era.

Hale, C.R. (2005) Neoliberal multiculturalism: The remaking of cultural rights and racial dominance in Central America. *Political and Legal Anthropology Review* 28 (1), 10–28.

Hamel, R.E. (2008a) Bilingual education for indigenous communities in Mexico. In J. Cummins and N.H. Hornberger (eds) *Encyclopedia of Language and Education, Volume 5: Bilingual Education* (2nd edn, Vol. 5, pp. 311–322). New York: Springer.

Hamel, R.E. (2008b) Indigenous language policy and education in Mexico. In S. May and N.H. Hornberger (eds) *Encyclopedia of Language and Education, Volume 1: Language Policy and Political Issues in Education* (2nd edn, Vol. 1, pp. 301–313). New York: Springer.

Heath, S.B. (1972) *Telling Tongues: Language Policy in Mexico, Colony to Nation.* New York: Teachers College Press.

Hornberger, N.H. (2013) On not taking language inequality for granted: Hymesian traces in ethnographic monitoring of South Africa's multilingual language policy. *Working Papers in Educational Linguistics* 28 (1), 1–21.

Hymes, D. (1980) Ethnographic monitoring. In D. Hymes (ed.) *Language in Education: Ethnolinguistic Essays* (pp. 104–118). Washington, DC: Center for Applied Linguistics.

IEEPO, SNTE and CNTE (2013) *El Proceso de la Masificación del PTEO como Movimiento Generador de Conciencias Críticas.* See http://www.transformacion-educativa.com/attachments/article/94/CuadernilloPTEO.pdf (accessed 12 July 2017).

Illich, I. (1970) *Deschooling Society.* London: Marion Boyers Publishers.

La Sociedad Pro-Planeación del Istmo (1956) *Alfabeto Popular para la Escritura de Zapoteco del Istmo*. Mexico, D.F.: La Sociedad Pro-Planeación del Istmo. See http://www.sil.org/resources/archives/39117 (accessed 22 May 2017).

Levinson, B.A. (2005) Programs for democratic citizenship in Mexico's Ministry of Education: Local appropriations of global cultural flows. *Indiana Journal of Global Legal Studies* 12 (1), 251–284.

Levinson, B.A., Foley, D.E. and Holland, D.C. (1996) *The Cultural Production of the Educated Person: Critical Ethnographies of Schooling and Local Practice*. Albany, NY: State University of New York Press.

Lewis, M.P., Simons, G.F. and Fennig, C.D. (eds) (2015) Zapotec. In *Ethnologue: Languages of the World, Eighteenth Edition*. Dallas, TX: SIL International. See http://www.ethnologue.com/language/zap (accessed 1 August 2015).

Ley General de Derechos Lingüísticos de los Pueblos Indígenas (2003) Mexico. See http://www.diputados.gob.mx/LeyesBiblio/pdf/257.pdf (accessed 1 August 2015).

López Bárecenas, F. (2009) *Autonomías y Derechos Indígenas en México*. Mexico, D.F.: MC Editores.

López Gopar, M.E. (2007) El Alfabeto Marginante en la Educación Indígena: El Potencial de la Multilectoescrituras. *Lectura Y Vida* September, 48–57.

Maldonado Alvarado, B. (2002) *Los Indios en las Aulas: Dinamica de Dominación y Resistencia en Oaxaca*. Mexico, D.F.: Instituto Nacional de Antropologia y Historia.

Martínez Vásquez, V.R. (2004) *La Educación en Oaxaca*. Oaxaca de Juarez: IISUABJO.

McComsey, M. (2015) Bilingual spaces: Approaches to linguistic relativity in bilingual Mexico. PhD dissertation, University of California San Diego.

Miano Borruso, M. (2002) *Hombre, Mujer y Muxe' en el Istmo de Tehuantepec*. Mexico, D.F.: INAH.

Muehlmann, S. (2008) 'Spread your ass cheeks': And other things that should not be said in indigenous languages. *American Ethnologist* 35 (1), 34–48.

Muehlmann, S. (2009) How do real Indians fish? Neoliberal multiculturalism and contested indigeneities in the Colorado delta. *American Anthropologist* 111 (4), 468–479.

Overmyer-Velázquez, R. (2010) *Folkloric Poverty: Neoliberal Multiculturalism in Mexico*. University Park, PA: Pennsylvania State University Press.

Pérez Báez, G. (2011) Semantics of body part terms in Juchiteco locative descriptions. *Language Sciences* 33 (6), 943–960.

Pérez Báez, G. (2013) Family language policy, transnationalism, and the diaspora community of San Lucas Quiaviní of Oaxaca, Mexico. *Language Policy* 12 (1), 27–45.

Povinelli, E.A. (2011) *Economies of Abandonment: Social Belonging and Endurance in Late Liberalism*. Durham, NC: Duke University Press.

Rebolledo, N. (2008) Learning with differences: Strengthening Hñahño and bilingual teaching in an elementary school in Mexico city. In N. Hornberger (ed.) *Can Schools Save Indigenous Languages? Policy and Practice on Four Continents* (pp. 99–122). New York: Palgrave Macmillan.

Rebolledo, N. (2010) Indigenismo, bilingüismo y educación bilingüe en México: 1939–2009. In S. Velasco Cruz and A. Jablonska Zaborowska (eds) *Construcción de Políticas Educativas Interculturales en México: Debates, Tendencias, Problemas, Desafíos* (pp. 113–157). México, D.F.: Universidad Pedagógica Nacional.

Robles, M. (1977) *Educación y Sociedad en la Historia de México*. Mexico, D.F.: Siglo XXI Editores.

Romero Frizzi, M. de los A. (2003) *Escritura Zapoteca: 2500 Años de Historia*. Mexico, D.F.: INAH CONACULTA.

Rubin, J.W. (1994) COCEI in Juchitan: Grassroots radicalism and regional history. *Journal of Latin American Studies* 26 (1), 109–136.

Ruíz Martínez, D. (2013) *Faro Inextinguible de la Niñez: 75 Aniversario de la Escuela Primaria Matutina Centro Escolar Juchitán*. Oaxaca, Mexico: IEEPO.

Sahlins, M. (1993) Goodbye to tristes tropes: Ethnography in the context of modern world history. *The Journal of Modern History* 65 (1), 1–25.

Sayer, P. (2015) 'More & Earlier': Neoliberalism and primary English education in Mexican public schools. *L2 Journal* 7 (3), 40–56.

Sicoli, M.A. (2011) Agency and ideology in language shift and language maintenance. In T. Granadillo and H.A. Orcutt-Gachiri (eds) *Ethnographic Contributions to the Study of Endangered Languages* (pp. 161–176). Tucson, AZ: University of Arizona Press.

Skutnabb-Kangas, T. (2009) Multilingual education for global justice: Issues, approaches, opportunities. In T. Skutnabb-Kangas, R. Phillipson, A. Mohanty and M. Panda (eds) *Social Justice Through Multilingual Education* (pp. 32–62). Bristol: Multilingual Matters.

Speed, S. (2005) Dangerous discourses : Human rights and multiculturalism in neoliberal Mexico. *Political and Legal Anthropology Review* 28 (1), 29–51.

Stavenhagen, R. (2015) Ruta Mixteca: Indigenous rights and Mexico's plunge into globalization. *Latin American Perspectives* 42 (4), 92–102.

Street, B.V. (1984) *Literacy in Theory and Practice*. Cambridge: Cambridge University Press.

Taylor, C. (2004) *Modern Social Imaginaries*. Durham, NC: Duke University Press.

Tollefson, J. (1991) *Planning Language, Planning Inequality*. London: Longman.

Urcid, J. (2005) *Zapotec writing: Knowledge, Power and Memory in Ancient Oaxaca*. See http://www.famsi.org/zapotecwriting/zapotec_text.pdf (accessed 1 August 2015).

Van der Aa, J. and Blommaert, J. (2011) Ethnographic monitoring: Hymes's unfinished business in educational research. *Anthropology & Education Quarterly* 42 (4), 319–334.

Velasco Cruz, S. (2010) Políticas (y propuestas) de educación intercultural en contraste. In S. Velaso Cruz and A. Jablonska Zaborowska (eds) *Construcción de Políticas Educativas Interculturales en México: Debates, Tendencias, Problemas, Desafíos* (pp. 63–112). Mexico, D.F.: Universidad Pedagógica Nacional.

Walsh, C. (2010) Interculturalidad crítica y educación intercultural. In J. Viaña, L. Tapia and C. Walsh (eds) *Construyendo Interculturalidad Crítica* (pp. 75–96). La Paz: Instituto Internacional de Integración del Convenio Amdrés Bello.

Yoshioka, H. (2010) Indigenous language usage and maintenance patterns among indigenous people in the era of neoliberal multiculturalism in Mexico and Guatemala. *Latin American Research Review* 45 (3), 5–34.

4 From Language-as-Resource to Language-as-Struggle: Resisting the Coke-ification of Bilingual Education

Nelson Flores

Introduction

A few years ago, I was working with a large urban school district on transforming its bilingual education programs. My primary role was to provide professional development to the district's bilingual teachers as they prepared for a shift away from transitional bilingual education that temporarily used Spanish with the goal of transitioning the students to English by third grade toward dual language bilingual education that sought to use both languages throughout elementary schools with the goal of bilingualism and biliteracy for participating students. A primary focus of this professional development was to introduce teachers to the concept of translanguaging which challenges the idea that dual language bilingual programs should be designed to keep the languages strictly separated and instead argues that they should be designed so that the two languages can be strategically brought together in ways that maximize bilingual language development (García, 2009). The teachers responded positively to the workshops and began to interrogate how they could maximize translanguaging as a tool for supporting their students in the move toward a dual language bilingual model that had the explicit goal of developing both languages.

As part of this initiative, we also held parent meetings at all of the participating schools. One of the schools was in a gentrifying area of the district. A white mother came up to me after the meeting and wanted to consult with me about the possibility of having her children grow up trilingually. Her plan was for the children to get English from her,

Spanish from the new dual language bilingual program and Chinese from their nanny. Another school was in a low-income predominately Latinx[1] area of the district. Here, a Puerto Rican mother who came to the meeting reported that she had been a victim of domestic violence and that she and her daughter had been homeless for some time. She was worried that this had affected her daughter and though she did not know what a dual language bilingual program was, she was looking for any program that could provide her daughter with special support when she came to the school the following year. Both of these mothers were trying to navigate a large and complex urban school district in ways that would ensure their children received the best education possible. Of course, the vast differences in their life circumstances made their attempts at doing this look extremely different.

Being confronted with these stark inequalities, I began to realize that while I had been prepared in my doctoral work to provide professional development for teachers related to the latest thinking in bilingual education, I was completely ill-equipped to address the larger political and economic inequalities that prevent these programs from reaching their full potential. This realization has led me to begin to reflect on how it is that I can advocate for bilingual education in a context of such vast inequalities. Though on the surface this question may seem like a question about the here-and-now, as I have begun this process of reflection it has quickly become apparent that the only way to begin to answer this question is through an examination of the historical context that has led to these vast inequalities.

In this chapter, I examine this history. I do not seek to discuss the specifics of this particular urban school district. Instead, I seek to take a global perspective on these issues by situating the roots of contemporary inequalities within the rise of neoliberalism as a backlash to the global struggles for liberation that emerged post-World War II. Using the case of bilingual education for Latinxs in the United States, I will examine the ways that neoliberalism politically incorporated the demands of these social movements through the commodification of diversity in ways that left white supremacist and capitalist relations of power intact. In this context, bilingual education initiatives, like the one I am working to support, are positioned as anti-racist while in reality doing little to combat structural racism. My intention is not to critique such initiatives, especially since I continue to be an active participant in many of them. Instead, my goal is to attempt to envision an approach to language education policy that reconnects advocacy work for bilingual education to broader political struggles that seek to dismantle white supremacist and capitalist relations of power.

Neoliberalism, Race and Applied Linguistics

Neoliberalism is often described as the coalescing of institutional forces in support of the free flow of capitalism in ways that benefit transnational corporations and economic elites (Harvey, 2003; Klein, 2007). A major element of a movement toward corporatist governance is a process that Harvey (2003) refers to as accumulation by dispossession – namely the process of making a profit by extracting wealth from marginalized populations. Accumulation by dispossession has always been an integral part of the working of capitalism. Historically, this came in the form of colonization, where Europeans invaded and conquered territories in order to force colonized peoples to extract the raw materials from these lands to support the industrialization of Europe and eventually the United States. With the rise of neoliberalism in the 1970s, this accumulation by dispossession has taken on a new form through the privatization of public goods and the imposition of this privatization on much of the world's population through the efforts of both national governments and international organizations such as the International Monetary Fund (IMF) and the World Trade Organisation (WTO) (Harvey, 2003).

Critical applied linguists have used neoliberalism as a framework for analyzing the hegemony of English on the global market (Phillipson, 2009) as well as the role of transnational corporations in the development of English language curricula (Block et al., 2012). They have also used neoliberalism as a framework for theorizing the commodification of language itself. Heller (2003: 474) uses the case of francophone Canada as an illustrative study that documents 'a shift from understanding language as being primarily a marker of ethnonational identity, to understanding language as being a marketable commodity on its own, distinct from identity'. She connects the francophone Canadian context to larger global trends where there is a changing relationship between the nation state and transnational corporations that has simultaneously led to the decreased influence of national identities alongside an increased interest in commodifying these same identities as part of the global tourism trade.

An often overlooked aspect in studies of neoliberalism, both within and outside of critical applied linguistics, is the role of race in the production of and perpetuation of neoliberalism. In most cases, racial inequalities are considered a byproduct of neoliberalism. Yet, some scholars have challenged this unidirectional relationship and have, instead, argued that new racial formations are integral to the production of neoliberalism. In particular, Omi and Winant (2015) argue that neoliberalism is not simply a political and economic process but also a racial project that politically incorporates the demands of the US Civil Rights Movement and other global struggles against white supremacy that emerged in the post-World War II context in ways that 'insulated the racial state from revolutionary transformation and absorbed anti-racist movements in a reform-oriented transition' (Winant, 2004: 112).

Ferguson (2012) provides the example of the famous Coca-Cola hilltop commercial first released in 1971 as an example of this political incorporation. The commercial begins with a young white woman dressed in countercultural clothing of the era singing 'I'd like to buy the world a home and furnish it with love'. The camera then pans out to gradually reveal a multiracial group of young men and women on a hilltop who begin to sing the following in unison:

Grow apple trees and honey bees and snow white turtle doves.
I'd like to teach the world to sing in perfect harmony,
I'd like to buy the world a Coke and keep it company.
It's the real thing, what the world wants today.

At the end of the commercial, the following words appear on the screen:

On a hilltop in Italy, we assembled young people from all over the world to bring you this message from Coca-Cola bottlers all over the world. It's the real thing. Coke.

This Coca-Cola commercial can be understood as an illustration of the ways in which the rise of neoliberalism served to politically incorporate the political struggles of the era in ways that accommodated superficial celebrations of diversity while doing little to challenge racial inequality. As Ferguson (2012: 65–66) argues, 'in one fell swoop the commercial manages to represent the various feminist, peace, anti-racist, and anticolonial movements, bringing them together through the universalizing potential of a commodity'. Building on this argument, I refer to attempts to commodify diversity in ways that reinforce the racial status quo as the Coke-ification of diversity. The Coke-ification of diversity was not a byproduct of neoliberalism but rather an integral part of the production of neoliberalism with the creation of a utopic vision of superficial celebrations of diversity becoming the barometer for measuring the state of human progress toward racial justice. That is, the Coke-ification of diversity is part of the accumulation by dispossession that characterizes neoliberalism. By commodifying diversity it makes it into a product that can be taken from minoritized communities in ways that benefit majoritized communities.

In the next section, I analyze the ways in which this process of accumulation by dispossession played out in the context of bilingual education for US Latinxs. I situate the struggle for bilingual education for US Latinxs within changing orientations of language education policy that entered mainstream global discourses in the 1960s as language-minoritized communities worldwide began to demand linguistic rights. I will examine the ways in which the institutionalization of bilingual education in the US context separated bilingual education from larger political struggles in ways that undermined its potential to be part of a larger anti-racist struggle against white supremacy. I then examine the ways in which this institutionalization of bilingual education paved the way for the Coke-ification of bilingual education as part of the racial formation that lies at the core of neoliberalism.

Changing Orientations to Language Education Policy

Ruiz (1984) conceptualizes three orientations toward language education policy: (1) language-as-problem, which positions language diversity as a threat to national unity; (2) language-as-right, which argues that language-minoritized communities have a fundamental right to speak their heritage language; and (3) language-as-resource which argues that language diversity should be treated as a resource to be harnessed and developed. Though all three orientations often co-exist with one another, scholars have examined the shifting prominence of these orientations in mainstream political discourses. In the case of the United States, Crawford (2000) examines the ways that the xenophobia that emerged as a response to World War I led to the entrenchment of a language-as-problem orientation that would not be challenged until the US Civil Rights Movement which witnessed a shift toward a language-as-right orientation as Latinxs and other language-minoritized communities began to demand bilingual education. More recently, the growth in dual language bilingual education programs throughout the United States has been part of a shift toward a language-as-resource orientation with bilingualism reframed as a tool that all children need for the 21st century (Lindholm-Leary, 2000).

García (2009) connects this US-specific dynamic to larger global shifts that characterized the last century. García characterizes the global context pre-World War II as primarily characterized by a language-as-problem orientation with nation states working to eradicate multilingualism. She situates the US Civil Rights Movement within a larger post-World War II shift toward a language-as-right orientation with language-minoritized communities mobilizing for linguistic rights in conjunction with post-colonial struggles worldwide. Finally, she situates the recent small steps toward a language-as-resource orientation in the US context within the larger context of the post-Cold War era with language increasingly being seen as a resource in a context of increasing mobility. Below, I broaden this analysis to demonstrate that these shifting orientations are part of a larger process of politically incorporating the global racial struggles that emerged in the post-World War II era.

Though US Latinxs have always resisted the language-as-problem orientation, the rise of the US Civil Rights movement in the 1960s allowed for the emergence of a national movement in favor of language diversity. In this era, Latinx community activists rejected a language-as-problem orientation in favor of a language-as-right orientation that positioned bilingual education as a right to which all Latinx children were entitled. Importantly, these calls for bilingual education as a right for all Latinx students were positioned within broader demands to dismantle the racial hierarchies of US society. For example, Chican community activists in the American Southwest situated calls for bilingual education within the larger political project of rebuilding Aztlán – the lands that had been taken from Mexico as part of the Mexican-American War (Trujillo, 1996). Similarly, Puerto Rican community activists in New York City advocated for the right to bilingual education within a larger struggle for local community control of governance structures that sought to develop an anti-racist participatory democracy (Nieto, 2000).

An examination of the 10-point plan of the Brown Berets, a prominent Mexican-American activist group active during the US Civil Rights movement, helps to illustrate this connection of a language-as-right orientation with broader political struggles:

(1) Unity of all of our people, regardless of age, income or political philosophy.
(2) The right to bilingual education as guaranteed under the treaty of Guadalupe-Hidalgo.
(3) We demand a Civil Police Review Board, made up of people who live in our community, to screen all police officers, before they are assigned to our communities.

(4)   We demand that the true history of the Mexican-American be taught in schools in the five Southwestern states.

(5)   We demand that all officers in Mexican-American communities must live in the community and speak Spanish.

(6)   We demand an end to 'Urban Renewal Programs' that replace our barrios with high rent homes for middle-class people.

(7)   We demand a guaranteed annual income of $8000 for all Mexican-American families.

(8)   We demand that the right to vote be extended to all people regardless of the ability to speak the English language.

(9)   We demand that all Mexican-Americans be tried by juries consisting of only Mexican-Americans.

(10) We demand the right to keep and bear arms to defend our communities against racist police, as guaranteed under the Second Amendment of the United States Constitution.

As can be seen from this 10-point plan, calls for bilingual education as a right for Mexican-American children (mentioned explicitly in point 2) were embedded within larger demands to dismantle racial inequality through calls for self-determination that included community-controlled policing, racially equitable housing policies and a living wage. That is, language was one right among many that the Brown Berets identified as necessary in order to address the root causes of racial inequality.

Latinx community activists were successful in getting the federal government along with state governments to adopt bilingual education programs to serve Latinx students. Yet, the institutionalization of these programs divorced them from these community struggles against racial inequality within which their original demands were situated (Del Valle, 1998; Grinberg & Saaverda, 2000; Reyes, 2006). In particular, as bilingual education became institutionalized, it shifted from being an intrinsic right for all Latinx students that would provide them with tools to dismantle racial hierarchies toward a temporary right for 'limited English proficient' students to receive remedial programs that would then allow them to assimilate into the racial status quo. In 1978, this culminated in the federal government moving to provide federal funding only for transitional bilingual education programs that were designed exclusively for 'limited English proficient' students with the goal of mainstreaming them into English-Only classrooms as quickly as possible (Crawford, 2000). In short, it reframed the barriers faced by Latinx children in US schools as solely a linguistic issue that could be resolved through the temporary use of Spanish, erasing the many other political and economic issues that groups such as the Brown Berets sought to bring attention to (Reyes, 2006).

It was within this context of the institutionalization of bilingual education that prominent advocates for bilingual education began to shift away from a language-as-right orientation to a language-as-resource orientation in their advocacy work. Ruiz (1984) was the first scholar who explicitly made this argument. As a strong advocate for language-minoritized communities, Ruiz laments the deficit perspectives of the language-as-problem orientation that squanders the linguistic resources of these communities through the imposition of English-Only educational programs and transitional bilingual education programs. Yet, he also notes the limitations of a language-as-right orientation – in particular the problem of noncompliance of states and districts and the confrontational process that is necessary for pursuing legal options. The challenge of noncompliance leads Ruiz to reject a language-as-right orientation as the most effective approach to addressing language diversity. As an alternative, he offers the language-as-resource orientation, which he defines as starting 'with the assumption that language is a resource to be managed, developed, and conserved' (Ruiz, 1984: 28). He argues that adopting such an orientation would 'have a direct impact on enhancing the language status of subordinate languages [and] help to ease tensions between majority and minority communities' (Ruiz, 1984: 25).

At the time of its proposal, the language-as-resource orientation offered an important intervention that challenged deficit framings of Latinxs and other language-minoritized students. Yet, as was the case with the institutionalization of a language-as-right orientation, the institutionalization of a language-as-resource orientation has also entailed a process of political incorporation that has reinforced the racial status quo. This is because proponents of a language-as-resource orientation have overlooked the most important lesson to be learned from the barriers faced by a language-as-right orientation – namely, that institutionalizing an orientation in ways that divorces it from community struggles against racial inequality leads to its complicity in reproducing the racial status quo. In the case of the institutionalization of the language-as-rights orientation, it was through the creation of remedial programs that placed the onus on children and their families in combatting racial inequalities. In the case of the institutionalization of the language-as-resource orientation, it was through the Coke-ification of bilingual education as part of the racial formation that lies at the core of neoliberalism.

Coke-ifying Bilingual Education Through a Language-As-Resource Orientation

The Coke-ification of the language-as-resource orientation is already alluded to in Ruiz's original conceptualization where he discussed language as a possible resource for two areas: national security and competitiveness in the global economy. In both of these areas, the language resources of language-minoritized populations become a commodity that is harnessed in ways that reproduce the racial status quo. This commodification of language-minoritized populations can be seen in an example that Ruiz offers of how a language-as-resource orientation might be implemented. He provides an example of students of Japanese preparing for foreign service with the state department by working in a Japanese community center in San Francisco in order to take advantage of the linguistic resources of the Japanese community. In this example, the Japanese speakers become a tool to serve the linguistic needs of language-majoritized (presumably white) people seeking to learn Japanese to further their own career objectives. It is unclear what exactly the Japanese community gains from this implementation of a language-as-resource orientation.

To be clear, I am not suggesting that Ruiz was proposing this as the only model of what a language-as-resource orientation could look like nor am I suggesting that he was advocating the exploitation of language-minoritized communities. It is clear throughout the article that he was a strong advocate for language-minoritized communities and a strong proponent of bilingual education for these communities. Instead, I use this example to demonstrate the danger in institutionalizing a language-as-resource orientation outside of the context of community struggles against racial inequality. The danger is that the institutionalization of a language-as-resource orientation may become incorporated into the neoliberal racial project of accumulation by dispossession that exploits diversity by converting the linguistic resources of language-minoritized communities into commodities that can be exploited by language-majoritized communities in ways that reinforce the racial status quo. In short, the danger is that a language-as-resource orientation can be Coke-ified (Petrovic, 2005; Valdés, 1997).

This Coke-ification of a language-as-resource orientation can be illustrated in a more recent Coca-Cola commercial that was released in 2014. Similar to the hilltop commercial, this commercial consciously includes a cast of multiracial people. In contrast with the hilltop commercial, this commercial is not exclusively in English. Instead, images of multicultural

America appear alongside a multilingual rendition of 'America the Beautiful'. This celebration of linguistic diversity stands in sharp contrast to the discourses of community empowerment expressed by Latinx community activists fighting for bilingual education during the US Civil Rights movement. During the US Civil Rights movement, bilingual education was a community demand that was part of a larger effort to address the racial inequities of US society. In contrast, in the multilingual Coke commercial it was a way of superficially celebrating diversity in order to market a product to the increasingly linguistically diverse US consumer.

During its initial release as part of the 2014 Super Bowl it caused quite a firestorm. On one side of the debate were conservative critics who chastised Coca-Cola for undermining American unity through embracing multilingualism in place of an English-Only ideology. In fact, conservative political commentator Glenn Beck explicitly referred to the hilltop commercial in his criticism of the new multilingual commercial when he argued 'remember when Coke used to do the thing on the top and they would all hold hands ... Now it's "have a coke and we'll divide you"' (Kaczynski, 2014). These conservative critics were not willing or able to accept the Coke-ification of multilingualism. For them, multilingualism continued to be an inherent threat to national unity that should never be commodified. This backlash provides evidence that the language-as-problem orientation is still prevalent throughout many sectors of US society.

On the other side of the debate were (neo)liberal supporters who applauded Coca-Cola for treating linguistic diversity as a resource rather than a problem. For them, the criticisms offered by conservative critics were a sign of racism linked to personal ignorance. For example, the public shaming tumblr defended the commercial, arguing:

> If you're a human being you might say to yourself 'that was a decent commercial, what's the big deal?' But if you're a vile monster void of emotion and compassion you might have realized that America the Beautiful was sung in MULTIPLE LANGUAGES. DEAR GOD, NO. Some people were pissed it was not sung in ENGLISH. (Public Shaming, 2014, n.p.)

Tumblr goes on to share tweets posted by conservative critics of the commercial alongside commentary that seeks to illustrate the ignorance of the tweeter. For example, in response to one tweet by a person named Olivia that lamented the fact that the commercial included the national anthem in multiple languages, tumblr notes:

Olivia has no fucking clue that it was 'America the Beautiful' in the Coke commercial, not God Bless America. But who cares? REAL AMERICANS don't need to know the difference between the songs as long as they're sung in ENGLISH!! ... And, she's not the only one. Apparently, the Star-Spangled Banner is no longer the United States' national anthem ... (Public Shaming, 2014, n.p.)

In these comments, racism is understood to be a problem of individual ignorance with no attention to the ways in which structural racism continues to permeate US society. Indeed, considering the fact that the celebration of linguistic diversity demonstrated in the commercial stands in sharp contrast to the long track record of Coca-Cola's accumulation by dispossession through efforts such as attacks on labor unions (Gill, 2005), campaigns to privatize water (Aiyer, 2007) and aggressive efforts to shape school curricula to maximize their corporate profits (Saltman, 2004), the only way to applaud Coca-Cola's efforts are precisely to ignore structural racism.

In summary, the multilingual Coca-Cola commercial and those who defended it from conservative critics celebrate linguistic diversity outside of any community struggle against racial inequality. Therefore, as with the hilltop commercial, the multilingual commercial manages to convert civil rights struggles into a commodity that the company can sell. In this case, Coca-Cola has turned struggles for language rights into an apolitical celebration of diversity that paints Coca-Cola as an advocate for progressive values while allowing the company to tap into the quickly growing multilingual American consumer – including Latinxs, who are the fastest growing segment of the US population (Filipovic, 2014). In this neoliberal framing of multilingualism, Latinxs and other bilingual communities become a market that Coca-Cola can tap into to serve its own interests while simultaneously prompting policies worldwide that exploit these same populations. It is this Coke-ification of bilingualism that has transpired in the institutionalization of a language-as-resource orientation to bilingual education. That is, while civil rights activists framed calls for bilingual education within a critique of the racial inequalities caused by global capitalism, this institutionalized version of a language-as-resource orientation positions bilingual education as an integral tool for the perpetuation of global capitalism.

This framing of bilingual education has become pervasive among bilingual education advocates. It can be found in official policy positions proposed by contemporary advocates of bilingual education. For example, the 'English Plus Resolution' that has been introduced into Congress several times explicitly frames the importance of bilingualism within a language-as-resource orientation. This orientation is articulated within a commodification of bilingualism:

> Whereas multilingualism, or the ability to speak languages in addition to English, is a tremendous resource to the United States because such ability enhances American competitiveness in global markets by permitting improved communication and cross-cultural understanding between producers and suppliers, vendors and clients, and retailers and consumers. (English Plus Resolution, 2009, n.p.)

This framing of bilingualism can also be found in the discourse of many professional organizations that have been ardent supporters of bilingual education in the United States. For example, the New York State Teachers of English to Speakers of Other Languages (NYTESOL) position statement opposing English-only legislation explicitly connects the value of bilingualism with free trade agreements developed as part of neoliberalism:

> While many of the proponents of English-only policies cite the economic advantages of learning English, restricting the use of other languages in the social, cultural, and educational life of US citizens and residents would ultimately result in unintended and unfortunate consequences for the US economy. It makes little sense to promote monolingualism at a time when multilingualism is becoming an economic imperative. Trade agreements such as NAFTA and GATT formalize the growing trend toward export-driven economies, and the ability to communicate in the global marketplace is a skill US business can ill afford to neglect. Speakers of languages other than English represent a valuable economic resource that would be wasted or even destroyed by policies promoting English only. (NYTESOL, 1995, n.p.)

More recently, when I attended the 2012 National Association for Bilingual Education (NABE) conference, several of the speakers utilized a language-as-resource orientation in justifying bilingual education. One speaker argued that the only way to ensure that the United States beats China in the race for dominance in the new global economy is to ensure that bilingual education is made available to all students. In this framing of the issue, bilingual education is only valued when profitable for corporations and to maintain US hegemony. Though this framing of the issue was likely not the speaker's intent, by uncritically accepting this commodified view of a language-as-resource orientation, this speaker along with many other advocates for bilingual education may be contributing to a shift in bilingual education that will marginalize language-minoritized students in new ways.

This bilingual education for all mantra has coalesced around almost unanimous support among bilingual education advocates for 'dual language' (also known as 'two-way immersion') bilingual programs which seek to place language-majoritized and language-minoritized students together to develop bilingualism in both English and the home language of the language-minoritized students. Justification for these programs is often framed within the language-as-resource orientation. Lindholm-Leary (2000), in a report written for the US Department of Education, provides an example of this framing of dual language programs:

> Dual language education is a program that has the potential to promote the multilingual and multicultural competencies necessary for the new global business job market while eradicating the significant achievement gap between language minority and language majority students. The appeal of dual language programs is that they combine successful education models in an integrated classroom composed of both language majority and language minority students with the goals of full bilingualism and biliteracy, academic excellence for both groups, and multicultural competencies. (Lindholm-Leary, 2000: 5)

In the same report, descriptions of the success of these 'dual language' bilingual programs are also oftentimes framed within this same orientation:

> Results demonstrate that the dual language education model can be successful. Students learn the communication skills and multicultural competencies to work on multicultural teams. Further, research reveals that students develop the types of competencies required by the global economy job market:
>
> - Bilingual proficiency;
> - Biliteracy;
> - Achievement in content areas; and
> - Multicultural competencies. (Lindholm-Leary, 2000: 35)

Through positioning language as a resource that all should have, this support for dual language bilingual education commodifies language in ways that connect the development of bilingualism with the new global economy.

Though there has been fairly unanimous support for these programs among supporters of bilingual education, some scholars have raised some concerns about an uncritical acceptance of these programs. As Petrovic (2005) argues:

> Bilingual proponents have begun to campaign for two-way programs with little consideration of issues of power, and a seeming collusion in the mooting of discussion and organization around other types of traditional bilingual education programs predominantly serving language minority students. (Petrovic, 2005: 407)

Valdés (1997) positions her concerns about these programs directly within the language-as-resource orientation that lies at their core:

> While it is tempting to bill dual-language immersion programs as examples of implementations in which language is a resource rather than a problem it is important to note the arguments ... within the critical language awareness perspective, which contend that educators need to carefully examine who the main beneficiaries of these language 'resources' will be. (Valdés, 1997: 419)

In a society with racial hierarchies between language-majoritized and language-minoritized communities, language as a resource for all is likely to benefit the language-majoritized community more than the language-minoritized community. Valdés elaborates on her point, thinking explicitly in terms of the economic justifications oftentimes used to defend these programs:

> Being bilingual has given members of the Mexican American community, for example, access to certain jobs for which language skills were important. Taken to its logical conclusion, if dual-language immersion programs are successful, when there are large numbers of majority persons who are also bilingual, this special advantage will be lost ... At this moment in time, given strong anti-immigrant sentiments, it is not difficult to imagine that an Anglo, middle-class owner of a neighborhood Taco Bell might choose to hire people like himself who can also talk effectively to the hired help instead of hiring members of the minority bilingual population. (Valdes, 1997: 419–420)

Thinking about this in terms of education, one of the reasons Latinxs were first able to enter the teaching workforce was because of the need for bilingual teachers (Reyes, 2006). As more white children are educated within these dual language bilingual programs and develop bilingual linguistic resources, they will now be in competition with Latinxs for bilingual positions, and in a racially stratified society will likely take many of these positions. In this way, the bilingualism of their Latinx peers in the program will be accumulated by these white children in ways that ensure the continued dispossession of the Latinx community.

Yet, this is not even the worst case scenario. Another concern is that as more language-majoritized white families enter these programs to prepare their children to be competitive in the global economy, they risk being transformed into programs exclusively for the privileged. For example, the city of Holyoke currently has a dual language bilingual program that is reserved for 'gifted and talented' students with the English language learning (ELL) director of the district noting that 'it's a certain type of student who can come in and embrace the many ways that it will be challenging. The curriculum is pretty fast paced' (Williams, 2014: n.p.). This 'certain type of student' seems to be disproportionally English dominant with the first kindergarten class serving 7 students reported to be Spanish dominant and 16 students reported to have had little to no exposure to Spanish before attending the program. How soon is it before the commodification of bilingualism leads to all dual language bilingual programs becoming 'gifted and talented' programs for language-majoritized white students with Latinxs and other language-minoritized students pushed out of these programs into less desirable English-Only classrooms? The irony is that this accumulation by dispossession can now be done under the guise of a celebration of diversity through the offering of a bilingual education option to white students.

To be clear, I am not questioning the motives of proponents of this commodified version of bilingual education nor am I suggesting that they would be supportive of this worst case scenario. As Petrovic (2005) notes, many proponents of framing bilingual education through this language-as-resource orientation see it as a pragmatic way of advocating for language-minoritized students since it makes bilingual education easier to swallow by emphasizing the instrumental nature of these programs and soliciting support from the language-majoritized white community. Yet, he argues that despite these intentions this commodification of bilingualism 'can serve only to perpetuate the inequitable linguistic status quo driven by capitalism in the first place' (Petrovic, 2005: 404–405). Therefore, while the language-as-resource framework was devised with the intention of empowering language-minoritized populations, it has become institutionalized in ways that adopt a very limited view of bilingualism that does little to challenge linguistic hierarchies that are the product of larger racial inequalities. Instead, it perpetuates the neoliberal racial project of accumulation by dispossession through commodifying diversity in ways that reify white supremacy under the guise of a celebration of multiculturalism.

It is this realization that has led me to reconsider the work that I am doing to promote bilingual education in the community where I work and live. Being confronted with the stark inequalities of contemporary neoliberalism, I have begun to realize that my good intentions are not enough and that I can no longer divorce my advocacy for bilingual education from struggles to dismantle the accumulation by dispossession that maintains white supremacy. Yet, I do not feel demoralized. Instead, I feel inspired by the models of the past that we have to build on. I seek to continue in this tradition by situating the struggle for bilingual education within a language-as-struggle orientation that centers the perspectives of the language-minoritized communities who have the most to gain from these programs and the most to lose should they become Coke-ified. It is to this language-as-struggle orientation that I now turn.

From Language-As-Resource to Language-As-Struggle

Below, I lay out four principles that could become part of a language-as-struggle orientation. These principles are not meant to be an exhaustive list of all things that should be considered when adopting a language-as-struggle orientation nor are they meant to be a recipe book that can be easily applied in any context. Instead, they are meant to provide a schematic of what the major components of a language-as-struggle orientation might be. I am also not suggesting that any of these ideas are new. What is new is the attempt at bringing all of them together in the hopes of developing a coherent orientation that can be offered as an alternative to the language-as-resource orientation.

Embed notions of language proficiency in the context of the racial inequalities exacerbated by neoliberalism. A lack of an explicit focus on the racial formation that lies at the core of neoliberalism has made a language-as-resource orientation vulnerable to Coke-ification. A language-as-struggle orientation would resist this political incorporation by making the racial project of neoliberalism an explicit focus of critical analysis. It would begin from the premise that in a society shaped by racial inequities and exacerbated by the accumulation by dispossession at the core of neoliberalism, white students who become bilingual are often seen as exceptional students while language-minoritized students who become bilingual are at best seen as 'English proficient' with no acknowledgment of these bilingual skills and at worse seen as 'semilingual' with no proficiency in either language. A language-as-struggle orientation would both seek to examine the structural processes that produce these different social positionings as well as seek to develop counter-narratives that resist the deficit framings of language-minoritized students and expose the racializing ideologies that lie at the core of these framings (for an example of an attempt at such a counter-narrative see Flores *et al.*, 2015).

Situate calls for bilingual education within calls for larger social transformation. Developing a more robust analysis of neoliberalism and the ways in which neoliberalism contributes to the continuing racialization of the language practices of language-minoritized students offers the opportunity to begin to develop a comprehensive approach to bilingual education that situates it within larger political struggles that seek to combat the racial inequities of our current political and economic context. This might mean situating calls for bilingual education programs in low-income neighborhoods within larger efforts to enact comprehensive revitalization in these neighborhoods. Similarly, this might mean situating calls for bilingual education programs in affluent and gentrifying neighborhoods within larger effort to create mixed-income neighborhoods through the development of affordable housing within the catchment areas of these programs (see Warren [2005] for an attempt at applying this principle to educational policy more broadly).

Connect with community organizations that are working to address larger racial inequalities. A language-as-struggle orientation would also entail moving beyond an engagement with organizations that focus explicitly on issues related to language diversity toward a more comprehensive approach that engages with community organizations focused on other issues that have been identified as integral to combatting the racial inequalities of US society as they are manifested in the current neoliberal context. This might include an engagement with social service agencies, advocacy groups that are working to address issues in education not directly related to bilingual education as well as advocacy groups focused on issues not directly related to education at all such as income inequality, housing segregation and immigration policy. The goal is to work to push bilingual education into the conversation in all of these areas of advocacy work while bringing insights from these other areas of advocacy work to shape the agenda of bilingual education advocacy (see Anyon [2014] for an attempt at applying this principle to educational policy more broadly).

Bring language struggle into the classroom. By this point, I hope it is clear that the burden on combatting racial inequalities cannot be placed on bilingual programs and the teachers who work in them. Much of this work has to be done through advocacy work outside of the classroom. Yet, bilingual programs and teachers can play a role in this social transformation by bringing a language-as-struggle orientation into the classroom. Though there is certainly no recipe for what this would entail, the general principle would be to treat language use as ideological and embedded in relations of power as well as to provide space for students to develop strategies for negotiating these power relations. This might include critically analyzing linguistic diversity in US society, examining the rhetorical strategies used by bilingual authors and offering students opportunities to blend the languages in ways that seek to express their bilingual identities (see García & Li [2014] for an example of what this approach might look like).

In summary, a language-as-struggle orientation would avoid uncritically celebrating bilingual education. Instead, it would make the concerns of language-minoritized students and communities central to any advocacy for these programs. It would raise questions about the unequal racial distribution of political and economic resources that lies at the core of neoliberalism. It would challenge the racialized discourses that position the bilingualism of white students as more valuable than the bilingualism of language-minoritized communities. At its core would be the belief that social transformation can only develop through political struggle – not through the feel-good commodification of difference. That is the real thing that Coke does not want us to see.

Note

(1)   I use 'Latinx' or 'Latinxs' as gender neutral terms for people of Latin American descent.

References

Aiyer, A. (2007) The allure of the transnational: Notes on some aspects of the political economy of water in India. *Cultural Anthropology* 22 (4), 640–658.

Anyon, J. (2014) *Radical Possibilities: Public Policy, Urban Education, and a New Social Movement.* New York: Routledge.

Crawford, J. (2000) *At War with Diversity: US Language Policy in an Age of Anxiety.* Clevedon: Multilingual Matters.

Del Valle, S. (1998) Bilingual education for Puerto Ricans in New York City: From hope to compromise. *Harvard Educational Review* 68 (2), 193–217.

English Plus Resolution (2009) H. Con. Res 3, 111th Cong., 1st Sess.

Ferguson, R. (2012) *The Reorder of Things: The University and Its Pedagogy of Minority Difference.* Minneapolis, MN: University of Minnesota Press.

Filipovic, J. (2014) Coca-Cola's America is beautiful ad: Why liberals should be upset. *The Guardian.* See http://www.theguardian.com/commentisfree/2014/feb/03/coca-cola-america-is-beautiful-ad (accessed 24 January 2016).

Flores, N., Kleyn, T. and Menken, K. (2015) Looking holistically in a climate of partiality: Identities of students labeled 'long-term English language learners'. *Journal of Language, Identity, and Education* 14 (2), 113–132.

García, O. (2009) *Bilingual Education in the 21st Century: A Global Perspective*. Malden, MA: Wiley-Blackwell.

García, O. and Li, W. (2014) *Translanguaging: Language, Bilingualism and Education*. New York: Palgrave Macmillan.

Gill, L. (2005) 'Right there with you': Coca-Cola, labor restructuring and political violence in Colombia. *Critique of Anthropology* 27 (3), 235–260.

Grinberg, J. and Saavedra, R. (2000) The constitution of bilingual/ESL education as a disciplinary practice: Genealogical explorations. *Review of Educational Research* 70 (4), 419–441.

Harvey, D. (2003) *The New Imperialism*. New York: Oxford University Press.

Heller, M. (2003) Globalization, the new economy, and the commodification of language and identity. *Journal of Sociolinguistics* 7 (4), 473–492.

Kaczynski, A. (2014) Glenn Beck: Multilingual Coke ad meant to 'divide us politically'. *Buzz Feed*. See http://www.buzzfeed.com/andrewkaczynski/glenn-beck-bilingual-coke-ad-meant-to-divide-us-politically#.abgp2LGmg7 (accessed 24 January 2016).

Klein, N. (2007) *The Shock Doctrine: The Rise of Disaster Capitalism*. New York: Picador.

Lindholm-Leary, K. (2000) *Biliteracy for a Global Society: An Idea Book on Dual Language Education*. Washington, DC: George Washington University.

New York State Teachers of English to Speakers of Other Languages (NYTESOL) (1995) *Position Statement Against Official English Legislation and Policy*. See http://www.nystesol.org/pdf/ppapers/posipaper09.pdf (accessed 24 January 2016).

Nieto, S. (2000) Puerto Rican students in US schools: A brief history. In S. Nieto (ed.) *Puerto Rican Students in US Schools* (pp. 5–38). Mahwah, NJ: Lawrence Erlbaum Associates.

Omi, M. and Winant, H. (2015) *Racial Formation in the United States*. New York: Routledge.

Petrovic, J. (2005) The conservative restoration and neoliberal defenses of bilingual education. *Language Policy* 4 (4), 395–416.

Phillipson, R. (2009) *Linguistic Imperialism Continued*. New York: Routledge.

Public Shaming (2014) Speak English!: Racist revolt as Coca-Cola airs multilingual 'America the Beautiful' SuperBowl ad. 14 February. See http://publicshaming.tumblr.com/post/75447787843/speak-english-racist-revolt-as-coca-cola-airs (accessed 24 January 2016).

Reyes, L. (2006) The ASPIRA consent decree: A thirtieth anniversary retrospective of bilingual education in New York City. *Harvard Educational Review* 76 (3), 369–400.

Ruiz, R. (1984) Orientations in language planning. *NABE Journal* 8 (2), 15–34.

Saltman, K. (2004) Coca-Cola's global lessons: From education for corporate globalization to education for global justice. *Teacher Education Quarterly* 31 (1), 155–172.

San Miguel, G. (2004) *Contested Policy: The Rise and Fall of Federal Bilingual Education in the United States, 1960–2001*. Denton, TX: University of North Texas Press.

Trujillo, A. (1996) In search of Aztlán: Movimiento ideology and the creation of a Chicano worldview through schooling. In B. Levinson, D. Foley and D. Holland (eds) *The Cultural Production of the Educated Person: Critical Ethnographies of Schooling* (pp. 119–152). Albany, NY: State University of New York Press.

Valdés, G. (1997) Dual language immersion programs: A cautionary note concerning the education of language-minority students. *Harvard Educational Review* 67 (3), 391–429.

Warren, M. (2005) Communities and schools: A new view of urban education reform. *Harvard Educational Review* 75 (2), 133–173.

Williams, M. (2014) Como se dice? Kindergarten students at Metcalf in Holyoke learn lessons in English and Spanish. *Mass Live*. See http://www.masslive.com/living/index.ssf/2014/12/dual_language_metcalf_holyoke.html (accessed 24 January 2016).

Winant, H. (2004) *The New Politics of Race: Globalism, Difference, Justice*. Minneapolis, MN: University of Minnesota Press.

5 English as the Medium of Instruction in Korean Higher Education: Language and Subjectivity as Critical Perspective on Neoliberalism

Joseph Sung-Yul Park

Introduction

The current conditions of neoliberalism press us to focus on the political economic basis of the relationship between language and education. The processes through which educational institutions and values are rapidly being reconfigured to more explicitly respond to the demands of capital foreground the material and economic basis of education that is often overlooked in paradigms which view learning and teaching in purely cognitive or cultural terms (Hill & Kumar, 2009; Hyslop-Margison & Sears, 2006). In particular, the way in which language increasingly takes up a central position within education as a skill that correlates with an individual's marketability highlights the intersection of language and education as a contested site where class-based interests are at stake (Macedo *et al.*, 2003; Urciuoli, 2011).

At the same time, neoliberal reframing of language and education is a prominent site where we can see how such political economic conditions are deeply interconnected with problems of subjectivity. Recent work on governmentality and biopolitics has shown how neoliberalism operates through guiding the conduct of individuals and inculcating self-modulation (Foucault, 1991; Lemke, 2001, 2011). That is, neoliberalism is closely invested in the formation of selves which becomes a mechanism for molding ideal neoliberal subjects. This partly explains the significance of language and education as a site for neoliberal transformation. Modern education has historically served as the institutional basis for the constitution of ideal citizens of the newly formed nation state, and in this context, ideologies of standard language promoted by educational institutions helped perpetuate a shared subjective orientation to different ways of speaking and images of speakerhood (Agha, 2007; Bourdieu, 1991). Changing the material conditions of the neoliberal economy, then, may be seen as recalibrating the image of the ideal subject that is to be reproduced through educational institutions and their language ideologies; they valorize the entrepreneurial branding of the individual self that is consonant with the increasingly flexible mode of production and reconceptualize language as a commodifiable skill that supports such flexible image of the self (Urciuoli, 2008).

Contesting neoliberal transformations of education and their resignification of language in market-based terms, then, requires us to attend to how dimensions of political economy and subjectivity intersect. A critical reflection on this nexus will help us problematize the way in which the ideology of neoliberalism gets rationalized and naturalized, opening up a space for challenging the dominant order of capitalism that subsumes all aspects of social life and reclaims language and education as a site for collective and alternative imagination (Bourdieu, 1988). In this chapter, I elaborate on this issue through a discussion of how English has been promoted as a medium of instruction (MOI) in South Korean higher education. I first identify subjectivity as an important key for understanding the place of English in South Korea, discussing how a deep sense of anxiety about English characterizes Koreans' relationship with the language. Then, I review how the policy of English MOI in Korean higher education is driven by the broader neoliberal transformation of Korean society, pointing out that the growing presence of English in Korean universities not only reflects specific political economic conditions of neoliberalism but is also mediated in important ways by the subjective positioning of Koreans as illegitimate speakers of English. Based on this discussion, I consider how a focus on the dimension of subjectivity can be a key point for contesting the neoliberal policy of English MOI in Korean universities.

Subjectivities of English in South Korea

Through the use of the term *subjectivity*, I orient to the affective yet politically grounded dimensions of our social experience that shape us as particular kinds of selves (Kramsch, 2009; Ortner, 2005). The notion of subjectivity implies that we are constantly molded and positioned as subjects, as we interact with historical and material conditions of our lives to derive meaning, both consciously and unconsciously, about who we are. Language is a prominent element in this process – the sense of anxiety, desire, pride, fear and uneasiness, etc., that we feel when speaking a language always works to condition us as a specific type of speaker occupying a particular position in the world. In this sense, our subjectivity as speakers and the language ideologies through which it is mediated serve as an important site for reproducing and negotiating relations of power.

The English language in South Korea (hereafter Korea) is a helpful example of this. The way in which Koreans relate to English can be characterized in terms of a deep sense of anxiety. This anxiety is manifest in a wide range of practices, such as the way Koreans recurrently apologize for how bad their English is; the jokes they tell about running away from a foreigner asking for directions due to fear of speaking English; the exorbitant investments parents make in the English language learning of their children, in hope that they will not grow up to be incompetent speakers of English like their parents are; and widespread complaints that Koreans' inability to communicate effectively in English is holding the country back on the economic global stage (for a more detailed account, see Park, 2009). We may note that these anxieties are not mere learner insecurities that can be understood purely in terms of inner psychological feelings which a language learner may feel in the process of learning the language but eventually overcomes upon reaching a certain level of fluency. Indeed, Koreans who have acquired reasonable competence in English often still engage in and orient to such practices. Rather, such anxieties should be seen as a socially shared way of positioning oneself as a particular subject, inculcated in Koreans through a common social and historical experience (Park, 2011).

Since Korea's first encounter with English at the end of the 19th century, the language frequently and consistently functioned as an emblem of the modern, representing a more advanced and cultured civilization that exists outside the borders of Korea (Park, 2012, 2015). This was particularly the case after the end of Japanese colonial rule when the United States started to exert a significant influence on Korean society. The United States presented itself as a wonderful benefactor, aiding Korea with its economic power and protecting it from communist invasion through its military prowess. US-educated elites took up important positions of power, including the first president Syngman Rhee, strengthening Korea's dependence on the United States. But at the same time, the United States was also seen as an unreachable other, representing the truly advanced world which the backward Korea would constantly dream of becoming but never quite reach. In this context, English, as the language of the United States, represented the modern ideals that Koreans were constantly supposed to strive for but would never be able to attain. Also contributing to this was the native speakerism (Holliday, 2005) that permeates the English language teaching industry in Korea, where the white native speaker of English is seen as the enduring source of linguistic authority that the non-native Korean learner of English could perhaps approximate but would be unable to replicate.

For this reason, these anxieties about English are not purely a matter of individual psychology but an embodied manifestation of a socially dominant language ideology (Kroskrity, 2000; Schieffelin *et al.*, 1998) – in this case, the belief that Koreans are illegitimate speakers of English who lack any practical competence in the language despite the huge investments they make in English language learning – which I called the ideology of *self-deprecation* elsewhere (Park, 2009). Language ideologies are powerfully connected to the formation of subjectivities because they are not abstract statements about language but deeply grounded in figures of personhood or socially recognizable images of speaker types and characteristics (Agha, 2007). In the Korean context, the Korean speaker of English is imagined as a helplessly incompetent speaker of the language, with particular behavioral and affective characteristics, such as being nervous about speaking English, avoiding situations in which English should be spoken and so on (Park, 2009). Such figures of personhood, widely circulated through Korean discourses about English, are powerful ways through which subjectivities of English are forged in Korean society. These figures offer a specific and tangible model according to which Koreans may modulate their behavior, thoughts, feelings and beliefs, effectively shaping them as subjects who internalize and rationalize their illegitimacy as speakers of English. And the affect and feelings that Koreans learn to display and enact become a highly effective basis for reifying them as subjects, for such anxieties and insecurities about English, as embodied responses, work to naturalize the powerless position they occupy in relation to English and the political conditions that serve as its basis.

In this sense, material conditions of power that accrue to the hegemony of English in Korea are inseparable from the subjectivities of English that shape Koreans' imagination of their relationship to English. The power of English in Korea is not merely a static reflection of global-level relations in which the country is positioned but is mediated in an important way through the lived experiences and subjectivities of Koreans that are reified in dominant figures of personhood circulated throughout society. For this reason, tracing the subjectivities of English can provide us with a useful window for understanding how the logic of neoliberalism comes to insinuate itself into Korean higher education. It reminds us that such processes are not put into place by material conditions alone but are also mediated by language ideological processes that have deep implications for how Koreans understand themselves as feeling and thinking subjects. In the following sections, I illustrate this through a discussion of how the trend of increasing use of English as MOI within the context of the neoliberalization of Korean higher education is both mediated by and contributes to the reproduction of subjectivities of English.

English as a Medium of Instruction in Korean Universities

Since the early 21st century, Korean universities have invested significant efforts in expanding the use of English as an MOI. As Korea is a country with a relatively strong degree of monolingualism, virtually all campus activities in Korean universities had been expected to take place in the Korean language. But from the early 2000s, many Korean universities started to aggressively introduce English into their classrooms, as part of their drive for globalization and pursuit of competitiveness (J. Cho, 2012).

An early example of this was Korea University, one of the oldest and most prestigious private institutions of higher education in Korea. During the early 2000s, the university went through an aggressive drive of reform, attempting to rewrite its nationalistic and traditional image into a modern and global one. Led by the management-minded president Euh Yoon-dae, the university actively raised a huge university development fund, expanded campus facilities and brought in a large number of foreign exchange students, aiming to reinvent itself as a global institution. One of the most prominently discussed aspects of this reform was boosting the number of courses offered in English. During Euh's presidency (2003–2006), the percentage of lectures taught in English rose from 4% to 34%, rapidly expanding the presence of English on campus (Yi, 2006). Due to such aggressive promotion of English, Korea University at the time was considered one of the most prominent examples of the increasing importance of English in Korean society.

Another salient example of universities pursuing English as an MOI was the Korea Advanced Institute of Science and Technology (KAIST). This top public research institution for science and engineering had also been actively engaged in a drive to boost its standing as a global institution. Suh Nam-Pyo, elected as president in 2006, pushed for a series of reforms that enhanced competition on campus, including more stringent reviews for promotion and tenure of faculty members and punitive tuition for students whose academic performance did not meet a certain standard. Suh's reform also included instituting English as the sole MOI for all classes. This promotion of English was again a subject of great media attention, particularly in the aftermath of a series of student suicides in 2011 that were widely attributed to the stress and anxiety caused by the intense climate of competition (Piller & Cho, 2013). Such criticism led to the resignation of Suh by 2013, as well as a loosening of the 100% English MOI policy, but with all of its major courses being taught in English, KAIST is still at the vanguard of English language instruction in Korean universities.

The most active university in promoting English as an MOI, however, might be the Ulsan National Institute of Science and Technology (UNIST). A new university founded in 2007 in the industrial city of Ulsan, UNIST was established with the ambitious goal 'to be ranked within the top 10 science and technology university by 2030' (sic), displayed prominently on the university's webpage.[1] The same page also explains that one of the four strategies for achieving this is 'globalization', which is most saliently represented by the fact that 'all courses at UNIST are conducted in 100% English'. While the English-only instruction policy of the newly founded UNIST was not subject to negative public reaction that bigger and more prominent institutions like KAIST had to deal with (Yi, 2012), it may nonetheless be one of the clearest examples of how Korean universities understand the role of English in the future of higher education; UNIST's explicit orientation to English as a key for reaching global academic excellence starkly illustrates how Korean universities have come to accept English MOI as a necessary condition for preserving their relevance in the rapidly changing global economy.

A variation on this theme can be found in Underwood International College (UIC), a liberal arts college established in 2006 within the prestigious Yonsei University. As part of Yonsei University's internationalization efforts, UIC was explicitly built as a highly international educational environment, focusing its faculty hiring on non-Korean scholars and actively recruiting international students, and it was also declared an English-speaking institution. To prospective students from Korea, UIC presents itself as an environment that will facilitate their growth as global leaders, 'touting its Western faculty members and English language medium as incentives to enroll that capitalize on Korean students' anxieties that the accumulation of global capital is essential for professional advancement' (Kim, 2016: 122–123).

The above examples are only some of the most notable ones that represent Korean universities' race to expand their offering of classes in English. English MOI lectures are now recognized as an unavoidable part of university education; while institutions that aim to offer all of their courses in English in the way KAIST and UNIST do are rare, most of the top universities in the Seoul metropolitan region currently tend to provide around 30% of their courses in English, though regional universities fall behind at around 10%. To meet such numbers, new staff members are often required to lecture in English at least for a certain number of years or are offered financial incentives for teaching classes in English (Choi, 2010). As a consequence, the ability to teach in English also becomes an important criterion for the hiring of new faculty members (Kim, 2013). The policy of English MOI has been highly controversial, with many issues raised ranging from the potential danger of academic dependence on the English-speaking West, to inequalities that can be caused by privileging those with better access to English language learning, to the undemocratic process through which such policies are often introduced (J. Cho, 2012).

So, what drove Korean universities to so actively pursue English as MOI? The expansion of English as MOI was ultimately motivated by the belief that English is a key indicator of competitiveness in the market. The growth of the policy of English MOI was part of the drastic neoliberalization of Korean higher education, in which universities, once seen as bastions of academic authority, are now under pressure to adhere to the logic of the market and strategize their goals to more actively meet the demands of capital. Such pressure was linked with greater promotion of English in two different but closely related ways.

First, the state induced greater competition among universities as a way of pushing them to develop as global research universities that could contribute to the country's advancement in the global economy. Arguing that the shift toward an information-based economy required universities to play a more active role as producers of knowledge, the government pressured universities toward greater integration in the US-centered order of academic research. For instance, through national projects like Brain Korea 21, a huge research funding program introduced in 1999 with the goal of developing world-class research universities, the Korean government consolidated research funds that used to be distributed among universities and channeled them to a smaller number of institutions, selected through stringent evaluation according to market principles.

Such pressure toward 'internationalization' led to the growing presence of English on Korean university campuses. For instance, there was greater pressure to publish in international indexed journals, most of which are in English (Lee & Lee, 2013), and to recruit greater numbers of foreign staff and students which implied wider use of English for communication both in and out of the classroom. English as MOI came to serve as an important indicator of a university's internationalization and was taken up by universities as an important strategy for competition. The culture of university ranking that was perpetuated by the powerful conservative media intensified such competition. *JoongAng Ilbo* and *Chosun Ilbo*, two of the largest newspaper companies with strong ties to the dominant status quo of Korean society, started to publish an annual ranking of Korean universities from 1994 to 2009, respectively, modeled upon global rankings such as that of *Times Higher Education* or Quacquarelli Symonds (QS). As highly influential institutions of power that closely represent the interest of capital, the conservative media promoted through these rankings the idea that Korean universities must follow a market logic and compete for recognition of their authority in order to stay relevant to the global economy. As those rankings considered the percentage of lectures offered in English as an important criterion for evaluating an institution's degree of internationalization, they also had a significant effect on establishing English as a crucial indicator for a university's competitiveness (Piller & Cho, 2013).

Second, the changing condition of the job market led to a reconceptualization of the ideal worker. Increasing competition in the market and the resulting volatility and unpredictability meant a more flexible and precarious workplace and corporations presented the ideal worker as someone who does not rely on past achievements but happily engages in projects of self-development to constantly develop new skills and adapt to the changing demands of the workplace. In this context, English came to be seen as an index for this ideal neoliberal subject. The significance attributed to English as the language of global competition led competence in the language to be seen as evidence of one's effort of self-development as well as global orientation. More importantly, because for Koreans, as non-native speakers, learning English was an endless task, it was perceived as a particularly apt index of the ideal neoliberal subject's continuous investment in self-improvement (Park, 2010). English MOI, then, was seen as an important way through which universities were preparing their graduates as neoliberal subjects. Forcibly immersing the students into an English-speaking classroom context was expected to break their inability to communicate in English and to push them into playing a more active role in their own English language learning.

In short, the discussion above shows how the promotion of English as MOI was deeply rooted in the neoliberalization of Korean higher education. This is an effect of neoliberalism (and not simply globalization, capitalism or liberalization) in the sense that it was grounded in the retreat of state support for educational institutions, a domain that was previously conceived as representing the public good, exposing those institutions to the logic of the market defined by increasing competition and audit culture. At the same time, it is neoliberal also because the policy of English MOI was framed as providing a basis for the students' self-development, where development of communicative competence in English was seen as an ideal way of cultivating the value of one's human capital in a job market which is characterized by endlessly intensifying competition.

Our discussion also shows how the ideology of self-deprecation, as a dominant ideology of English in Korean society, shapes the policy of English MOI and the discourses that support it. Universities' investment in English as a means of internationalization presumes the *lack* of English in Korean universities which is seen as evidence of their backwardness; English serves as an index of continuous self-development precisely because Koreans' presumed incompetence in English calls for constant and never-ending investment in English language learning; and underlying all this is a firm belief that any competence in English that Koreans have acquired so far must be insufficient for competition in the global economy. Moreover, for our purposes, it is also important to note how the dimension of subjectivity is involved in the way the ideology of self-deprecation is manifest. As noted above, the policy of English MOI was not simply an issue of status planning, assigning English to the domain of higher education; it was about how to transform Koreans into competent speakers of English, competent enough to compete globally in the field of knowledge production and academic research. As such, logic presumed the figure of the Korean as an incompetent speaker of English; it had the effect of reifying and circulating that image further, thereby reinforcing the anxieties and insecurities of English that constitute the subjective grounding of self-deprecation. In this way, the English MOI policy in Korean higher education was constructed as a site of anxiety which in turn worked to further rationalize the material conditions of neoliberalism that gave rise to the policy. Indeed, it is difficult to fully account for the intensity with which Korean universities pursued English as MOI without taking into consideration the dimension of subjectivity. While a range of political economic conditions, including structures of competition reflecting the interest of capital and the changing conditions of the workplace, served as the material basis for the policy, the sense of inferiority and anxiety about

Koreans' own competence in English made such policy, which blatantly adheres to the interests of the English-speaking West and global capital, to appear compelling and worth pursuing. This can be demonstrated through a more detailed analysis of metalinguistic discourse surrounding the policy of English MOI which we now turn to.

Metalinguistic Discourse on the English-Medium Classroom

The media coverage of Korean universities' pursuit of English frequently invokes the figure of the incompetent Korean speaker of English, foregrounding the anxieties of English that are associated with that figure of personhood. Examples of this can be found from the titles of many articles that report on the state of the policy, some of which are shown below.

공포의 영어강의 캠퍼스 'The fearsome campus of English-lectures' (*Hankook Ilbo*, 13 March 2006)

'정보전달 안돼, 울며 겨자먹기식'...영어 강의 문제점 '"No information conveyed, reluctant implementation"... problems of English language lectures' (*GyeonghyangSinmun*, 11 April 2011)

대학교 영어 강의는 '개그쇼'?...교수도, 학생도 '영어 공포증' 'University English language lectures as "comedy"? ... Professors and students suffering from "English phobia"' (*Pressian*, 19 March 2010)

'교수는 겉만 훑고 수강생은 말문 닫고' 대학 영어강의 논란 '"Professors skim the surface, students close their mouths": Controversy over English language lectures' (*Sindonga*, September 2014)[2]

These titles problematize the current state of English-medium lectures in Korean universities by invoking the image of Koreans as incompetent speakers of English. The inability of Korean professors and students to achieve meaningful communication in the classroom is presumed in descriptions such as 'no information conveyed' and 'professors skim the surface (of instructional content), students close their mouths (due to their discomfort in speaking in English)'. More crucially, these titles do not simply describe the English MOI classroom but imbue it with affective meaning; the characterization of the English-speaking campus as 'fearsome' and the professors and students as overwhelmed with 'English phobia' construct the Korean members of the university as not only lacking good competence in English but also highly nervous about the fact that they need to communicate in the language. In this way, the reader is expected to link the English MOI classroom with the widespread figure of the incompetent Korean speaker of English and to anticipate the problems that would occur in such classrooms.

The content of many articles also draws upon specific anecdotes in which the figure of the incompetent speaker of English takes center stage. The following excerpt from an article in *Chosun Ilbo*, one of the major conservative papers, is an example of this.

> 서울 유명 사립대 사회과학계열 4학년 박모씨는 지난해 영어로 진행하는 전공 강의를 들을 때 도저히 알아들을 수 없었다. 교수의 영어에 지방 사투리 억양이 잔뜩 녹아들어가 있었기 때문이다. 강의방식도 교수가 학생들을 자연스럽게 바라보며 하는 것이 아니라 거의 미리 작성한 파워포인트 자료를 읽는 형태였다.
>
> 같이 수업을 듣던 10여명의 외국인 교환학생들은 수업 도중 교수에게 내용을 이해할 수 없다며 7~8차례 질문을 던졌지만 교수는 무슨 뜻인지 모를 영어로 더듬더듬 대답을 했다. 박씨는 '비슷한 강의가 몇 달째 계속되자 외국인 학생들도 나중에는 포기한 듯 교과서만 들여다봤다' 고 말했다.
>
> Mr. Park, a senior at the social sciences faculty of a major private university in Seoul, could not understand at all the English lecture at the class he took for his major last year. It was because the professor's English was fully blended with a regional accent. In terms of delivery as well, the professor did not speak naturally facing the students but merely read through the powerpoint slides that were prepared earlier.
>
> The 10 or so foreign exchange students who were attending the class asked questions to the professor 7–8 times during the lecture, saying that they could not understand the content but the professor answered haltingly in indecipherable English. Mr. Park said, 'after the lectures unfolded in a similar manner for a few months, the foreign students seemed to give up and just focused on the textbook'. (*Chosun Ilbo*, 23 February 2011)

Here, through the voice of one student, the horrible quality of the professor's lecture is reported, constructing the professor as an incompetent speaker of English. The professor's English is characterized as 'fully blended with a regional accent (of Korean)', apparently encouraging the reader to draw upon the social stigma associated with regional dialects to imagine the incomprehensibility of the professor's language. The report further highlights the problematic delivery of the lecture and by depicting the professor as just 'reading through the powerpoint slides prepared earlier', an inference is again invited that the professor lacks proper competence to speak 'naturally' in English. Further representation of the professor as answering the foreign students' questions 'haltingly in an indecipherable English' reinforces the constructed incompetence of the professor, as the text invokes intertextual connections with the common image of Koreans struggling with anxiety when having to converse with foreigners in English. The reaction of the foreign students, reported through the voice of the Korean student, finally characterizes the situation as utterly helpless, as they 'give up and just focus on the textbook'.

The same article goes on to present a similar picture of the students as well. Later in the article, we find the following:

> 교수들은 교수들대로 학생들 영어 이해력의 부족함을 지적하고 있다. 연세대 인문계열 한 교수는 '수업시간에 의사 소통이 잘 안 돼 강의가 제대로 진행이 안 된다. 수업이 끝나고 찾아와 "아까 말씀하신 게 이런 뜻이에요?"라고 묻는 학생도 있고, 심지어 시험 날짜가 언제냐고 묻는 학생들도 있다'고 말했다.

> The professors, for their part, point out how students lack the ability to comprehend English. A professor at the humanities faculty of Yonsei University said: 'I cannot teach properly because it is difficult to communicate during class. Some students come to me after class and ask, "what was it that you said during the lecture?" and some even ask when the exam is'. (*Chosun Ilbo*, 23 February 2011)

In this case, the fact that the students come to the professor after class with questions about the class content and 'even ask when the exam is' is not presented as evidence of the professor's bad English but of the students' 'lack of the ability to comprehend English'. Their active inquiries outside the English-medium lecture hall (in Korean) serve as a foil for their lack of communication in class, again invoking the image of the Korean who becomes silent when it is necessary to speak in English. This is therefore another manifestation of self-deprecation, in which both professors and students, as Koreans, are equally represented as incompetent speakers of English. The contrast with 'foreign exchange students', who supposedly represent 'global' subjects who have no problem communicating in English or asking questions in class, further highlights the illegitimate status of Koreans as speakers of English and their concomitant sense of insecurity; it is the foreign students' reactions – i.e. their giving up on the professor and their choice to simply self-study through the textbook – rather than the Korean student's account that is ultimately presented as authoritative evidence of the failure of the English MOI classroom.

The ideology of self-deprecation is not only found in media discourse, however. The large body of academic research that has investigated lecturers' and students' perception of the effectiveness of the use of English as MOI in Korean universities based on questionnaire and interview data (Byun *et al.*, 2011, 2012; D. Cho, 2012; Cho & Hwang, 2013; E. Kim, 2014; K. Kim, 2011; Kym & Kym, 2014; among others) confirm that Korean students and instructors in the English MOI classroom share a view similar to that reflected in the media. For instance, Korea University students quoted in Byun *et al.* (2011) complain about how the professors' incompetence in English renders the English MOI lectures ineffective:

> Non-native [i.e., Korean] professors explained things briefly and simply. It's hard to understand them when there aren't enough explanations. When asked to clarify, they merely repeated themselves.
>
> The class does not move smoothly, and things stall from time to time. And it gets boring when there's a break in the flow. (Byun *et al.*, 2011: 442)

Similarly, the professors acknowledged the problems caused by the students' limited English language competence as well as their own incompetence in English:

> when preparing for class, I try to organize subject content in several formulated phrases, taking into consideration the low level of the students' capabilities. During class, I simply paraphrase and repeat them. This kind of instruction method is the best I could come up with at this moment. Still, every class I become overwhelmed when trying to deliver more than I had outlined, immediately feeling the limits of my English ability. (Byun *et al.*, 2011: 442)

It is important to keep in mind that what we see in the examples above is not so much an 'objective' observation of Koreans' communicative ability but an instance of metalinguistic discourse through which Koreans are constructed as incompetent speakers of English. Recent linguistic anthropological work highlights how linguistic competence must be seen as an ideological construct (Park, 2010). First of all, contrary to popular belief, a person's competence in a language is not observable or measurable in objective terms; while language assessment allows us to identify how much an individual is able to fluently and consistently use a particular linguistic form, the ordinary notion of 'how well one speaks a language' cannot be reduced to such tests (Lowenberg, 2000). More fundamentally, our evaluation of a speaker's competence is not independent from our evaluation of the speaker (Bourdieu, 1991) and in the Korean case, speaker characteristics such as race, ethnicity and nationality work to categorize a person as a 'native speaker' with absolute authority to determine what counts as 'good' or 'correct' English. For this reason, the broader discourse surrounding the policy of English MOI, in which Koreans are depicted as incompetent speakers of English, should be seen as an ideological construct, molding Koreans into particular subjects and guiding them to take up a particular subject position in relation to the structural forces that push for the English MOI policy on university campuses.

The ideological nature of such metalinguistic discourse about English MOI lectures can be seen from some studies which show that students' self-evaluation of their own comprehension of the English MOI lectures is not as bad as such discourse might suggest. For example, Byun et al. (2011) indicate that, in their data, average student response to the question of whether their knowledge of English had hindered their understanding of course content was 3.09 on a scale of 1–5, with 5 indicating greatest difficulty. They interpret this as showing that 'students' English proficiency levels did not play a major role in their understanding of subject knowledge in EMI [English medium instruction] courses' (Byun et al., 2011: 440). This shows that the students' and professors' negative evaluations of their own and each other's competence in English, while reflecting some practical realities of the communicative context of the English MOI classroom, nonetheless involves a considerable degree of erasure (Irvine & Gal, 2000), downplaying the extent to which Koreans are actually able to communicate successfully through the medium of English. For this reason, the negative depiction of Koreans' competence in metapragmatic discourse about the policy of English MOI in Korean universities should not be taken at face value but should be interpreted as an important way through which anxieties about English are reproduced, leading to a deeper internalization of the unequal social and political relations that gave rise to the policy of English MOI in the first place.

Subjectivity and Contestation of the Neoliberal Order

Our discussion above shows how the dimension of subjectivity serves as an important mediating link between neoliberalism and the policy of English MOI on Korean university campuses. On the one hand, the ideology of self-deprecation allows the logic of neoliberal competition permeating

Korean universities to be translated into the language policy of English MOI lectures, due to the anxiety it induces about Koreans lacking the competence in English to stay ahead in global competition. On the other hand, the metalinguistic discourse on English MOI lectures enhances and naturalizes the figure of the illegitimate speaker of English, providing further ground for constructing English as an index of an ideal neoliberal subject that all Koreans should pursue. This means that problematizing and challenging the neoliberal order that is being imposed upon Korean universities require a serious analysis and critique of the ideological processes by which such subjectivities are reproduced.

This is an important point because much research on English as MOI in Korean higher education has focused on the Korean students' and professors' perceived lack of competence as a key for critiquing this policy. For instance, one strand of research tries to critically evaluate the effectiveness of English-medium lectures, arguing that the policy of English MOI has been blindly pursued without sufficient evidence of pedagogical efficacy and usefulness. These studies then highlight the self-reported lack of comprehension and ineffectiveness of learning and teaching through the medium of English as evidence that the policy was introduced without adequate support for students and instructors to help them cope with the use of English as MOI. On this basis, they call for greater intervention and systematic support that can ensure more effective communication in the English MOI classroom (Cho & Hwang, 2013; E. Kim, 2014; K. Kim, 2011; Kym & Kym, 2014; among others). Many of them further critique the undemocratic process that pushed for a language policy that members of the campus community are clearly not prepared for in terms of linguistic competence (Byun et al., 2012; D. Cho, 2012). While such studies are valuable, it is important that we take a more critical perspective on such self-reported incompetence in English. As we noted above, Koreans' anxieties about English are not simply a transparent reflection of their lack of proficiency in English but a historically and materially grounded construction that is rooted in the formation of subjectivities. Therefore, our analysis of what goes on in the English MOI classroom should also question the nature of such anxieties and consider alternative ways in which the subjectivities of the Korean students and professors may be imagined.

For instance, Choi et al.'s (2014) study of interaction in an English MOI classroom analyzes how a dialogic teaching method (which employs authentic, contextualized questions to help students connect their previous knowledge with new knowledge) managed to elicit active participation from the Korean students, unlike what would stereotypically be expected of Korean speakers of English. In explaining their findings, the authors refer to Blommaert's (2010) concept of truncated repertoire which problematizes the assumption that a competent speaker of a language will have mastery of the full range of possible repertoires of a given language and suggests that it is unreasonable to expect Korean students to have perfect control of all repertoires in the English language for them to meaningfully engage in the English MOI classroom. Thus, they argue: 'if having perfect competence in English is not a prerequisite for learning a new subject in [English-medium instruction], EFL students may be able to use their limited competence in classroom settings' (Choi *et al.*, 2014: 371). In the sense that they highlight the situated nature of what constitutes successful communication, then, the authors manage to avoid taking the figure of the incompetent Korean speaker of English for granted and allow for an alternative positioning of the students as legitimate users of English.

The above study is one example of an approach that does not presume Koreans' illegitimacy as speakers of English. While most Korean professors and students clearly do not have a competence equal to traditionally conceived 'native speakers' of English, this by no means precludes the possibility of them making meaningful communication through English (or through a mixture of English, Korean and whatever linguistic resources they have at their disposal). This, in turn, can be a useful basis for contesting the neoliberal order of the university in which competence in English, imagined in terms of globally valued standard varieties, is seen as one of the ultimate index of the ideal subject. Denying the purported 'otherness' of English and acknowledging that English is already a part of the linguistic repertoire of the members of the Korean university may help Korean students and professors imagine themselves as different kinds of subjects – as speakers of English who are endowed with the legitimacy to negotiate meaning through the language, despite not having the same kind of access to the resources of the English language as a native speaker does. This perspective will help us question the assumption that improving the students' proficiency in English, defined in terms of native-speaker norms, should be a major concern for Korean higher education.

Such reconceptualization of competence, however, also requires challenging the ideology of language as a bounded entity (Park & Wee, 2012). The classroom that Choi, Tartar and Kim studied was one in which English was presented as the sole medium, disallowing for the use of linguistic resources from Korean or other languages. But if we do take seriously Blommaert's (2010) notion of truncated repertoire, we would have to acknowledge that a perspective of competence as a social construct should remain sensitive to communicability that takes place within modes of communication in which mixing of resources from different languages are commonplace. This is indeed a highly relevant question for the policy of English as MOI because mixing of Korean into an English-medium lecture is frequently subject to criticism. Such practices, which are commonly found in English MOI lectures across universities in Korea (Hong & Yi, 2013), are often disparaged in media discourse, pejoratively referred to as 'English medium lecture in appearance only' (무늬만 영어강의: Chae, 2014). Notably, they are usually treated as embarrassing evidence of the instructor's and students' inability to sustain an interaction in English, thus again serving as a site for reproducing the anxieties and insecurities about English. A broader conceptualization of competence and repertoire would allow us to see such instances not as shameful failure to adhere to the principle of English as MOI but as a translingual practice (Canagarajah, 2013) that demonstrates how English, even in ostensibly monolingual Korea, has always already been local (Pennycook, 2010).

The Korean case that we have explored in this chapter, then, points to the importance of looking at dimensions of subjectivity as a strategy for problematizing the way neoliberal transformation of education resignifies language according to the logic of the market. Contesting such neoliberal transformations requires systematic resistance and political action but it also calls for close attention to how such transformations build upon our sense of insecurity and anxiety by naturalizing unequal relations of power underlying regimes of standardness, competence and legitimacy. Such regimes are not merely about language but through the mediation of language ideologies, also about subjectivities, about the ideal neoliberal subject and about what constitutes valued identities in the global world. Thus, an important contribution that the study of language and language education can make toward a critique of neoliberalism is to uncover such processes and to subvert the highly naturalized views of language, competence and speakerhood, so that an alternative can be imagined.

Notes

(1) http://www.unist.ac.kr/about-unist/overview/vision. Accessed 20 October 2015. Original in English.
(2) All translations from Korean are my own.

References

Agha, A. (2007) *Language and Social Relations*. Cambridge: Cambridge University Press.
Blommaert, J. (2010) *The Sociolinguistics of Globalization*. Cambridge: Cambridge University Press.

Bourdieu, P. (1991) *Language and Symbolic Power.* Cambridge: Harvard University Press.

Bourdieu, P. (1998) The essence of neoliberalism. *Le Monde diplomatique (English edition).* See http://mondediplo.com/1998/12/08bourdieu (accessed 2 November 2015).

Byun, K., Chu, H., Kim, M., Park, I., Kim, S. and Jung, J. (2011) English-medium teaching in Korean higher education: Policy debates and reality. *Higher Education* 62 (4), 431–449.

Byun, K., Jeon, J., Jo, Y., Kim, N., Kim, H. and Mun, H. (2012) 대학 유형 및 특성에 따른 국제화 추진 전략 연구 (II): 대학 영어강의 정책의 효과적 추진전략 탐색. Research Report RR 2012–03. Seoul: Higher Education Policy Research Institute.

Canagarajah, S. (2013) *Translingual Practice: Global Englishes and Cosmopolitan Relations.* New York: Routledge.

Chae, J. (2014) 한국 고전문학을 영어로? '무늬만 영강' 판치는 대학가. *Hankook Ilbo.* 25 September. See http://www.hankookilbo.com/v/b651918fc30946d193dc3c8 d4da609ca (accessed 2 November 2015).

Cho, D. (2012) English-medium instruction in the university context of Korea: Tradeoff between teaching outcomes and media-initiated university ranking. *Journal of Asia TEFL* 9 (4), 135–163.

Cho, J. (2012) Campus in English or campus in shock? *English Today* 28 (2), 18–25.

Cho, S. and Hwang, S. (2013) 대학교 전공과목 영어강의 현황 파악 및 미래 방향 탐색: 영어능력차이에 따른 인식 및 만족도 조사를 중심으로. *Hyeondaemunbeobyeongu* 71, 175–194.

Choi, J., Tartar, B. and Kim, J. (2014) Can EFL speakers communicate in English-mediated classes?: A case of a liberal arts class for engineering students in Korea. *Journal of Intercultural Communication Research* 43 (4), 369–385.

Choi, S. (2010) 업적평가 학과평가로 확대 … 교육효과 의문에도 일단 'GO'. *GyosuSinmun,* 15 March. See http://www.kyosu.net/news/quickViewArticleView.html?idno=19949 (accessed 20 October 2015).

Foucault, M. (1991) Governmentality. In G. Burchell, C. Gordon and P. Miller (eds) *The Foucault Effect: Studies in Governmentality* (pp. 87–104). London: Harvester Wheatsheaf.

Hill, D. and Kumar, R. (eds) (2009) *Global Neoliberalism and Education and Its Consequences.* New York: Routledge.

Holliday, A. (2005) *The Struggle to Teach English as an International Language.* Oxford: Oxford University Press.

Hong, J. and Yi, G. (2013) 대학 영어전용강의 실태와 학습효과성 연구. In *Proceedings of the 7th KELS (Korean Education Longitudinal Study) Conference* (pp. 455–479). Seoul: Korean Educational Development Institute.

Hyslop-Margison, E.J. and Sears, A.M. (2006) *Neo-Liberalism, Globalization and Human Capital Learning: Reclaiming Education for Democratic Citizenship.* Dordrecht: Springer.

Irvine, J.T. and Gal, S. (2000) Language ideology and linguistic differentiation. In P.V. Kroskrity (ed.) *Regimes of Language: Ideologies, Polities, and Identities* (pp. 35–83). Santa Fe, NM: School of American Research Press.

Kim, B. (2013) 영어 잘 해야 교수 된다? 신규임용 영어평가 어떻게 하나. *GyosuSinmun,* 4 November. See http://www.kyosu.net/news/articleView.html?idxno=27931 (accessed 2 November 2015).

Kim, E. (2014) Korean engineering professors' views on English language education in relation to English-medium instruction. *The Journal of Asia TEFL* 11(2), 1–33.

Kim, K. (2011) Korean professor and student perception of the efficacy of English-medium instruction. *Linguistic Research* 28 (3), 711–741.

Kim, S.K. (2016) English is for dummies: Linguistic contradictions at an international college in South Korea. *Compare: A Journal of Comparative and International Education* 41 (1), 116–135.

Kramsch, C. (2009) *The Multilingual Subject*. Oxford: Oxford University Press.

Kym, I. and Kym, M. (2014) Students' perceptions of EMI in higher education in Korea. *The Journal of Asia TEFL* 11 (2), 35–61.

Lee, H. and Lee, K. (2013) Publish (in international indexed journals) or perish: Neoliberal ideology in a Korean university. *Language Policy* 12 (3), 215–230.

Lemke, T. (2001) 'The birth of bio-politics': Michel Foucault's lecture at the Collège de France on neo-liberal governmentality. *Economy and Society* 30 (2), 190–207.

Lemke, T. (2011) *Biopolitics: An Advanced Introduction*. New York: New York University Press.

Lowenberg, P.H. (2000) Non-native varieties and the sociopolitics of English proficiency assessment. In J.K. Hall and W.G. Eggington (eds) *The Sociopolitics of English Language Teaching* (pp. 67–85). Clevedon: Multilingual Matters.

Macedo, D., Dendrinos, B. and Gounari, P. (2003) *The Hegemony of English*. Boulder, CO: Paradigm Publishers.

Ortner, S. (2005) Subjectivity and cultural critique. *Anthropological Theory* 5 (1), 31–52.

Park, J.S. (2009) *The Local Construction of a Global Language: Ideologies of English in South Korea*. Berlin: Mouton de Gruyter.

Park, J.S. (2010) Naturalization of competence and the neoliberal subject: Success stories of English language learning in the Korean conservative press. *Journal of Linguistic Anthropology* 20 (1), 22–38.

Park, J.S. (2011) Framing, stance, and affect in Korean metalinguistic discourse. *Pragmatics* 21 (2), 265–282.

Park, J.S. (2012) English as border-crossing: Longing and belonging in the South Korean experience. In V. Rapatahana and P. Bunce (eds) *English Language as Hydra: Its Impacts on Non-English Language Cultures* (pp. 208–220). Bristol: Multilingual Matters.

Park, J.S. (2015) Structures of feeling in unequal Englishes. In R. Tupas (ed.) *Unequal Englishes: The Politics of Englishes Today* (pp. 59–73). New York: Palgrave Macmillan.

Park, J.S. and Wee, L. (2012) *Markets of English: Linguistic Capital and Language Policy in a Globalizing World*. New York: Routledge.

Pennycook, A. (2010) *Language as a Local Practice*. New York: Routledge.

Piller, I. and Cho, J. (2013) Neoliberalism as language policy. *Language in Society* 42 (1), 23–44.

Urciuoli, B. (2008) Skills and selves in the new workplace. *American Ethnologist* 35 (2), 211–228.

Urciuoli, B. (2011) Neoliberal education: Preparing the student for the new workplace. In C.J. Greenhouse (ed.) *Ethnographies of Neoliberalism* (pp. 162–176). Philadelphia, PA: University of Pennsylvania Press.

Yi, J. (2012) UNIST 세계무대 떠오르는 강자. *Gwahak Donga*. September. See http://science.dongascience.com/supplementviews/group-view?acIdx=11872 (accessed 20 October 2015).

Yi, W. (2006) 4년간 고려대 개혁 이끈 어윤대 총장. *Joongang Ilbo*. 26 November. See http://news.joins.com/article/2518923 (accessed 20 October 2015).

6 Internationalization and English Language Learning in Higher Education in Canada: A Case Study of Brazilian STEM Scholarship Students

Jonathan Luke

Introduction

In recent years, student mobility has emerged as one of the central components of the internationalization of higher education. In Canada and other English-dominant host nations such as the US, the UK and Australia, expanding enrollment of international students is identified as an important strategy for successful internationalization across all levels of educational governance (e.g. Altbach & Knight, 2007; Association of Universities and Colleges Canada [renamed Universities Canada, April 2015], 2011; Chakma et al., 2012). Similarly, over the last decade, countries such as Saudi Arabia and Brazil have launched ambitious mobility programs, sending greater numbers of students abroad with the aim of increasing competitiveness and entrepreneurship both in the labor market at home as well as on the global stage (Ciência sem Fronteiras, n.d.b; Saudi Arabia Ministry of Education, 2015).

With expanding global flows of students from nations where English is not a dominant language to English-medium educational contexts comes a greater need for understanding the status and role of English and English language learning (ELL) within particular internationalization initiatives (Kubota, 2009) and for documenting student subject positions in relation to ELL policies which often emerge from complex transnational assemblages of governmental strategies, tactics and mechanisms (Johnson, 2013b;

McCarty, 2011; Shohamy, 2006). Recent higher education research across fields including anthropology, applied linguistics and education (e.g. Holborow, 2013; Olssen & Peters, 2005; Urciuoli, 2008) has mapped the ways in which perspectives on language and language learning emerge from and interact with neoliberal discourses and the rationalities they instantiate. Extending on this work, this chapter draws on a larger ethnographic investigation of the ELL experiences and language policy engagement of Brazilian students over the duration of their study abroad sojourns in Canada as recipients of *Ciência sem Fronteiras* (Science without Borders [SwB]) scholarships. Considering empirical materials including university ELL classroom observations, scheduled and impromptu interviews and government documents and media reports, this case study employs Foucault's (1988, 1997, 2007) notions of governmentality and technologies or practices of the self to document ways in which this particular policy assemblage emerged and evolved for these students and to highlight the key neoliberal discourses which run through it. I demonstrate that while these students appear to be largely adherent and/or sympathetic to skills-based and labor market-oriented discourses of English and ELL, some reject an exclusively instrumentalist approach and also cultivate more personal or social and/or intercultural perspectives on the relevance of their language learning and flourishing bilingualism.

Science Without Borders: A Brief Overview

SwB was a national study abroad mobility program for Science, Technology, Engineering and Mathematics (STEM) students that was launched in 2011 and was funded primarily by the Brazilian federal government. Its chief stated aim was 'to promote the consolidation and expansion of science, technology and innovation in Brazil by means of international exchange and mobility' (Ciência sem Fronteiras, n.d.a). As a strategic plan, it was thus markedly different in design from more traditional models of study abroad that focus on foreign language learning and the development of cultural awareness. Of the 100,000 scholarships of the first phase of the program, approximately 80% were given to undergraduate students and over 60% of the total number of students travelled to English-speaking destinations (Ciência sem Fronteiras, n.d.c; Piovezan, 2015). A new phase was announced in mid-2014 with plans for another 100,000 scholarships scheduled for completion by 2018; however, in September 2015, the program was suspended for an indefinite period of time due to federal budgetary constraints (Cruz & Foreque, 2015).

For undergraduates, the program was piloted as one year in length, including eight months of academic study followed by a four-month internship either as a research placement on the campus of the host institution or as an industry placement with a nearby business. These internships were the key selling feature of the program to both the student participants and the general public, with the stated intention of increasing the interaction between academics and the private sector while also providing students with experiential learning in workplaces relevant to their chosen fields of study (Ciência sem Fronteiras, n.d.b). However, these parameters were adjusted a number of times over the first few cohorts. One problem that arose immediately was that there were not enough students in Brazil with adequate language proficiency to gain entry to institutions abroad and study in a foreign language. As a result, Portugal became a popular choice with over 30,000 students selecting it as their first choice (British Council, 2015).

In early 2013, it was decided that Portugal would be closed as an option, and in order to continue to meet target numbers, CAPES (*Coordenação de Aperfeiçoamento de Pessoal de Nível Superior* or Coordination for the Improvement of Higher Education Personnel), one of the Brazilian higher education agencies linked to the Ministry of Education responsible for managing the program, permitted a large number of students who had initially selected Portugal to choose another destination. This group became known informally as the *Reoptantes do Portugal* – the second 'choicers' of Portugal, or the Portugal cohort. Two features stand out in distinguishing this cohort from those that preceded it: first, many of these students travelled abroad (the majority of them to English-speaking countries) with very little or no knowledge of the medium of instruction of their host country; second, and relatedly, these students were not all pre-accepted into academic programs, as was the case with previous cohorts, but were placed in intensive (non-credit) English language programming with promotion to academics contingent on performance. In the case of Canada, the Canadian Bureau of International Education (CBIE), which managed the majority of SwB scholarships on behalf of the Canadian government, was then responsible for assisting this cohort of students in gaining acceptance to academic programs.

At this time the Brazilian Minister of Education explained to the media that the government would not consider scholarships to Portugal in order to encourage students to develop proficiency in other languages and that the English language was now one of the priorities of the program (G1, 2013). The duration of the sojourn for this group of students was extended to a maximum of 16 months, including in some cases up to 12 months of language study. The internship component was also cancelled partway through their sojourn abroad. In order to address the language proficiency of subsequent cohorts as well as for other mobility programs, the Brazilian government launched a supplementary program featuring both distance and classroom language learning within Brazil called *Inglês sem Fronteiras* (English without Borders) in December 2012, followed by the more inclusively named *Idiomas sem Fronteiras* (Languages without Borders) in November 2014 which, at the time of this writing (July 2015), also offered French as an additional language option.

The case study presented in this chapter draws on the experiences of 11 undergraduate student members of the Portugal cohort, first while studying English and later while enrolled in general academic programming (in all but two cases) at four different Canadian universities. By examining this particular group of students who are members of a decidedly exceptional cohort, I am less interested in mapping the experiences abroad of SwB scholarship students generally, but rather aim to highlight the expected and unexpected results of a fragile and dynamic policy process at a particular moment in time. And, by focusing in on this moment, it is not my intention to vilify or evaluate the decisions made and the implementation or the intentions of policymakers and stakeholders across all scale levels or even the students themselves in terms of how they engaged with the policy assemblage in the midst of which they found themselves. As one senior coordinator of SwB described it, the program was made with a sledgehammer, involving a wide range of domestic and international agencies in a number of countries learning how to work together and make rapid changes *in medias res* (Piovezan, 2015). My interest lies instead in identifying the key discourses that informed stakeholder decisions which affected this particular cohort of students, as well as the responses to and subject positions these students took up within the ELL policy assemblage that emerged from these decisions. In the following sections, I present a more detailed explanation of what Foucault's concepts of governmentality and practices or technologies of the self contribute to this analysis and also how they inform the notions of both language policy and neoliberalism I draw on here.

Governmentality, Language Policy and Technologies of the Self

Foucault's (2007: 108) neologism governmentality links together the idea of government which has the broad purpose of arranging populations and things toward particular ends, with that of 'mentality', i.e. a political disposition or rationality which is made manifest in the complex 'ensemble formed by institutions, procedures, analyses and reflections, calculations, and tactics'. Central to the concept is the idea that government is accomplished through 'the conduct of conduct', with this phrase invoking several senses of the word conduct, including (a) comportment or directing of oneself or another and (b) a particular set of behaviors or actions, typically under normative or evaluative scrutiny (Dean, 2010: 17–18). As governmentality applies Foucault's conception of power as progressive or productive rather than simply repressive, a number of key insights are possible. First, unlike repressive or disciplinary power, governmentality depends on the agency of individuals to act freely but within limits that are set out for them. It does not stem from the total control of repressive power relations. What follows from this first point is that rather than emanating from 'a monolithic state operating as a single source of power', government is in fact the result of a heterogeneous and often fragile alliance of a range of practices proposed by a range of agents spanning from the level of state institutions down to more local organizations and even to micro-level social group norms (Li, 2007: 276).

Within the field of language policy, a number of scholars have taken up the concept of governmentality as a means of moving beyond a state-centered or top-down view of policy to a model that accounts for a greater plurality of ways in which language-related practices are managed or governed (e.g. Flores, 2014; Johnson, 2013a; Pennycook, 2002, 2006). Doing so has required going beyond the analysis of legislation and other official policy texts produced by states to consider a more 'expanded view of language policy as overt and covert, top-down and bottom-up, *de jure* and *de facto*' (McCarty, 2011: 2). Scholars working with this expanded view have often turned to ethnography as an approach which provides the means for considering the range of agents, goals or objectives, processes and discourses at play as well as the complex social histories of particular contexts (Johnson, 2009; McCarty, 2011). Similarly, a number of researchers in public policy and anthropology have advocated for ethnographic approaches as providing the ability to access 'the multiplicity of power relations and practices within the present, as well as the actual processes through which subjectivities are formed' (Brady, 2014: 13; Li, 2007). Of particular interest for the current study is that this turn also enables the researcher to focus 'greater attention on how individuals interpret and engage with language policies, and how they position themselves relative to those policies and to the language politics more generally across a wide range of contexts' (King & De Fina, 2010: 652).

In contrast to the flourishing interest in governmentality in language policy research and public policy research more broadly, less attention has been given to Foucault's (1988, 1997) later concept of the technologies of the self which refers especially to the conduct of the self, rather than the conduct of others. In most cases, these practices of the self on the self have been considered as simply alternate modes of coercive government by the state or some larger administrative body. While the production and transformation of subjectivities via particular technologies of the self are indeed sanctioned and encouraged by governmental agents, Foucault (1997, 2007) also recognized and elaborated another approach to this idea of technologies or practices of the self taken only as governmental domination of the subject by other means. The philosopher Arnold I. Davidson (2011: 26) identifies the notion of counter-conduct from Foucault's lecture series from 1977 to 1978 as a 'conceptual hinge' that links his political reflections which focus on state power to his later focus on the self. Thinking of certain practices of the self as a form of counter-conduct allows for the possibility to imagine active 'struggle against the processes implemented for conducting others' and how they affect the self (Foucault, 2007: 201). These practices can thus be understood also as agentive struggles that have transformative power in terms of enabling the possibility for different subjectivities. It is important to stress, however, that counter-conduct is not exterior to conduct and there are limits to these possibilities. Nevertheless, practices or techniques of the self as Foucault presents them contain the potential for two opposing qualities: first, as systems of rules or norms for behavior established by the dominant governmental rationalities, yet also, as a form of action which opens up spaces for agency through subversion, resistance or adherence to alternative rationalities.

Neoliberalism and Applied Linguistics

Foucauldian treatments of governmentality as a rationality of rule also help to elaborate the notion of neoliberalism that informs this study. Neoliberalism has exploded as an analytic category in the social sciences generally over the last 15 years and is more recently emerging in applied linguistic research (e.g. Block et al., 2012; Chun, 2009; Kubota, 2011; Park, 2010). An often cited definition proposed by David Harvey (2005: 2) describes it as 'a theory of political economic practices that proposes that human well-being can best be advanced by liberating individual entrepreneurial freedoms and skills within an institutional framework characterized by strong private property rights, free markets and free trade'. However, increased use of the term has also led to a proliferation of typological classifications of the term. These include, but are not limited to, considering neoliberalism as: an ideology, a policy package, an Anglo-American form of capitalism, a governmentality or mode of governance or as a more general all-purpose denunciation (Brady, 2014: 16). Although these conceptions of neoliberalism are not necessarily mutually exclusive, and instead reflect particular ways of making sense of phenomena in particular places and times, in this chapter I take an ethnographic approach to neoliberalism as a form of governmentality (Brady, 2014) for several reasons. First, taking neoliberalism exclusively as an ideology suggests the mono-causality or singular will of a particular dominant group of agents and makes it difficult to account for the multiplicity of heterogeneous processes and fragile alliances which contribute to the policy process (Dardot & Laval, 2013; Li, 2007). Second, and relatedly, taking neoliberalism primarily as a policy package implies a uniformity that may or may not be present in actual practice. This approach focuses on the (often top-down) intentions of a small group of agents and is less suited to understanding not only the complexities that arise when these policies are taken up by their target populations but also the ways in which these policies interact with other policies and rationalities which are not so easily characterized as neoliberal. As Brady (2014: 13) notes, it is important for researchers 'to acknowledge the presence of non-liberal rationalities and to incorporate these rationalities into their theoretical frameworks'. Lastly, taking a governmentality approach highlights the productivity of neoliberal rationalities which are not simply destructive of rules and rights by means of, for example, the push towards privatization and individual responsibility, but also constitute new kinds of social relations and subjectivities (Dardot & Laval, 2013).

Within the field of applied linguistics a number of neoliberal discourses on language and language learning have been mapped out which are germane to the current study. Wee (2008: 32) proposed the notion of linguistic instrumentalism to describe an emphasis on the economic value of language 'in terms of its usefulness in achieving specific utilitarian goals such as access to economic development or social mobility'. Building on this work, in a study on language learning and testing in Japan, Kubota (2011: 248) further qualifies instrumentalism as taking a view of English proficiency as an essential skill in the global new economy which both 'strengthens a nation's economic competitiveness and increases individual economic returns'. She cautions that although instrumentalism as a neoliberal discourse assumes an unproblematic link between language proficiency and individual prosperity, in actual practice the connection is more complex. Focusing on another aspect of this promise of individual benefit through

English in the Korean context, Park (2010) identifies a discourse circulating in the press that attributes successful language learning to individual tenacity and responsibility, erasing any structural differences that may affect different outcomes in different learners. In the analysis that follows, these discourses of instrumentalism and responsibility play an important role in situating the language learning of these students within the larger neoliberal approach to knowledge transfer in higher education that the SwB program appeared to subscribe to.

Method

The empirical materials discussed in the analysis that follows are drawn from a larger ethnographic study of internationalization and student mobility in higher education in Canada. Taking an ethnographic approach to language policy research (Johnson, 2009), I conducted fieldwork following 11 student members of the Portugal cohort described above for a period of 12 months (February 2014–January 2015). This group included five males and six females between the ages of 21 and 27. Background information on each of the participants is provided in Table 6.1; however, in order to preserve participant anonymity this information is necessarily limited.

Fieldwork was divided into two phases. For the first four months of my fieldwork the students completed intensive non-credit English language study at one university language institute in a major Canadian metropolitan area. During this phase, I regularly observed their classes and frequently socialized with the students between classes and in the cafeteria. I interviewed each of these students (with one exception) at least three times scheduled in advance with these semi-structured interviews lasting between 45 and 90 minutes each. In addition to scheduled interviews, I also conducted impromptu interviews and conversations with the students and their peers between classes several times each week.

Participants were initially selected via email promotional materials circulated by the head teacher at the language institute with subsequent snowball recruiting as they suggested their friends and classmates. During the second phase of the study, nine of the students were accepted to continue their studies at four universities in two different Canadian provinces. Two returned to Brazil at the end of the semester as they were not accepted into any Canadian universities (more on this below). Of the remaining students, two completed a subsequent single semester of academic programming but chose to quit the program and return to Brazil prior to the end of the scholarship period. The remainder stayed in

Table 6.1 Participants

Name	Gender	Age	Field of study	Home university	Home region in Brazil	Duration of sojourn in Canada (months)
Beatriz	F	22	Engineering	Private	Southeast	12
Bruna	F	26	Information Systems	Private	Southeast	8
Clara	F	23	Health Sciences	Public	Northeast	12
Carlos	M	27	Physics	Public	South	12
Daiane	F	27	Engineering	Private	Southeast	16
Daniel	M	21	Information Systems	Public	Northeast	16
Fernanda	F	23	Health Sciences	Public	South	16
Lucas	M	24	Health Sciences	Private	South	16
Paulo	M	21	Engineering	Public	Southeast	8
Thiago	M	22	Computer Science	Private	Southeast	16
Vanessa	F	23	Engineering	Public	Southeast	16

Canada for the full 16-month program duration. During this second phase, regular interviews were conducted in person with the participants who remained within commuting distance of the researcher; interviews with participants farther afield in Canada and back in Brazil were conducted via Skype. Interviews were also conducted with teachers of the English language institute and administrators of the program from both the university where the ELL for these students took place and CBIE.

Alongside media reports and policy documents from each country, data from the semi-structured interviews constitute the focus of the discussion below. In total, these interviews resulted in approximately 50 hours of audio recordings. Interview transcripts and policy documents went through multiple processes of coding and as is the case with all ethnographic research, the analysis is interpretive. Interviews were conducted primarily in English, as most of the participants took part in the study as a means to access further speaking practice. However, Portuguese was also used when the participants preferred it, as well as for occasional clarification purposes. All excerpts included were originally in English unless otherwise indicated. In this study, I have employed a broad approach to transcription, omitting detailed conversational features as I was predominantly 'interested in the content of the talk rather than how it was actually conducted' (Stroud & Wee, 2012: 84).

Science Without Borders: Official Plans and Agendas

With generous monthly stipends allotted to each student and the large number of applicants accepted to the program, it may on the surface appear odd to consider SwB through the lens of neoliberalism given the prominence of efforts to dismantle the welfare state in contemporary neoliberal practice. This is especially the case when the program is viewed alongside domestic social programs implemented in higher education by recent left-wing PT (*Partido dos Trabalhadores* – the Worker's Party) governments in Brazil such as PROUNI (*Programa Universidade para Todos* – the University for All Program) and more recent quota laws for Afro-Brazilian, Indigenous and low-income students in public universities (Lloyd, 2014). Nevertheless, bearing in mind Brady's (2014) caution that multiple and at times competing rationalities may exist alongside and intersect with one another, governmental statements about SwB clearly foreground a particular set of neoliberal discourses. The official aims of SwB as a mobility program include: (a) 'exposing students to an environment of high competitiveness and entrepreneurship' (Ciência sem Fronteiras, n.d.a); (b) providing them with access to state-of-the-art technological innovation and practice in the best and most relevant universities around the world; (c) enhancing 'the interaction between academic and both the business sector and civil society'; and (d) promoting 'international collaborations in scientific publications' (Science without Borders, n.d.d). This list is drawn from pages on the front of the official program website bearing subheadings such as 'Motivation' and 'Goals' and based on this positioning, a number of observations can be made about these aims. First, while this list is obviously not exhaustive in terms of outcomes desired by the program's administrators, several outcomes of the program are conspicuous in their absence. Most glaringly absent is language learning itself and the development of social and cultural awareness and intercultural sensibilities that are typical of more traditional perspectives on the international student mobility experience. Yet, for the members of this cohort, language learning has been central to the experience. The exclusion of the social sciences and humanities from the program also highlights these absences.

Second, the discourses of competition and entrepreneurship presented above apply at both the level of the individual and that of the state's economy as bolstered by the private sector (Dardot & Laval, 2013). In an enthusiastic account of the program as a public-private partnership, the former US Ambassador to Brazil, Thomas Shannon Jr. (2012: 47), explained 'the vast majority of the students who participate in Science without Borders will not return to government jobs, but are instead likely to work in private companies – thus expanding Brazil's already-growing entrepreneurial class'. As the Ambassador articulates it, this exposure to competitive entrepreneurship can be seen as beneficial both to the students as individuals, as they invest their time and effort in mobility in hopes of gains in their future workforce trajectories and also for the state and its economic development through the growth of a class of like-minded citizens.

The desire to send students to the so-called best universities of the world reflects a growing reliance on global rankings of universities such as the Times Higher Education World Universities Rankings. These rankings serve as key arbiters of the quantified value of particular institutions, also fostering greater competition both between institutions and at the level of the state. In the case of the 11 students in this study, rankings played an important role in their aspirations. As their acceptance to academic programming happened after their arrival in Canada, they were allowed to propose a short list of choices. In almost all cases, the students chose the most prestigious (and difficult to gain access to) universities in the country. When I pressed them for why they had made these choices (i.e.

if they had knowledge of a particular program or department), they told me they had relied on rankings found on the internet. Several lived to regret selecting these schools. As a student called Bruna (all names used are pseudonyms) told me: 'I'm laughing [at myself] because "why did you choose this?" because the required score is so high' (February 21, 2014). In actual fact, the schools attended by the students who were successfully placed in academic programs in Canada were lower-ranking schools based on Canadian sources such as the Maclean's University Rankings.

Related to these notions of entrepreneurship and private-public partnerships and spanning across the host and sending nations is a focus on commercialism and monetization. The Inaugural Action Plan of a related body, the Canada–Brazil Joint Committee for Cooperation on Science, Technology and Innovation (2012, sec. 2a), which counted SwB as one of its key modes of exchange, advocates strongly for a focus on research in specific STEM areas and the 'the development of products and/or services that can be successfully commercialized by the industry partners in Brazil and Canada'. This narrowing of focus to research in particular fields, products and services that can be then monetized reveals a prioritization of market logic at work in the decision-making process.

Government literature from Canada reveals similar desired outcomes for the program to those described above but also includes a number of domestic benefits, such as the contribution to local economies. In 2012, international students spent an estimated 8.4 billion dollars in Canada, providing substantial financial opportunity to Canadian universities facing diminishing endowments, while also addressing skilled labor shortages and looming demographic challenges to the labor force more generally by encouraging immigration (Foreign Affairs, Trade and Development Canada, 2014: 7). A Senate report on intensifying strategic partnerships with 'The New Brazil' highlights language education as an opportunity: 'Canada can build on its strong foundation as the largest venue for English-language training for Brazilian students' (Canada Senate Committee on Foreign Affairs and International Trade, 2012: 27). Other reasons are also given for why it is opportune for Canada to be developing partnerships with Brazil at this particular point in time. For example, in his announcement of Canada's participation in the SwB program, Governor General of Canada David Johnston (2012) declared, 'Brazil is on an impressive trajectory and has truly arrived as a significant player on the international stage', while the above-mentioned Canada Senate Committee on Foreign Affairs and International Trade (2012: vii) calls for action on Canada's part based on 'Brazil's emergence as an economic and political force in our own hemisphere and internationally'.

Looking at the institutional level, the university language institute where these students were enrolled moved quickly to accept them. As one of the instructors describes it, 'We stepped in and said we'll take the contract thank you very much. It was a great move on [the program director's] part [...the institute] is just expanding like crazy which is good if you want to make money' (January 13, 2015). In order to further accommodate these students, the institute piloted an adapted curriculum, compressing a 64-week program (beginning at the lowest level) into 32 weeks through the addition of supplemental programming. In the following section, I describe the student experiences with this language learning program and in the cases of those who passed through to the next phase, their subsequent experiences in academic courses of study.

Student Perspectives: Expectations and Adjustments

Upon arriving in Canada, all the students in this study had high hopes for their sojourns and imagined they would be progressing through their language learning courses rapidly, despite the fact that most of them were initially enrolled in the lowest possible levels. Thiago described what they assumed would happen:

> We got a letter to explain. So it says oh, you are doing four months of English course from September to December and then you are going to be tested. And if you need more English you are going to do more English from January to April and then from May to September you are going to do an internship [...] in December we weren't tested. We didn't have any test, so in January we started to receive emails that we were going to do the test. (October 10, 2014)

At this point, it was clear that they would be completing at least eight months of English instruction. Clara elaborated on her expectations:

> When I came here I thought I would just take four months of English but now I see it's not enough for a person who didn't talk before [...] my plans were to take the TOEFL in December and start university in January but everything changed. (February 6, 2014)

Over the winter months, the students wrote The Test of English as a Foreign Language (TOEFL) on a staggered timetable set by CAPES that was far from transparent. As one instructor described: 'in February, the students at the lowest levels of our program received letters that they had to write the TOEFL exam with 48 hours notice […] they had no chance and none of them got the TOEFL scores they were hoping to' (June 4, 2014). Students who were enrolled in higher levels were asked to take the test later in the semester. By April, many of the cohort had been accepted into Canadian universities but a considerable number were informed that they had not been accepted into academic programming in Canada and they would be returning home after completing eight months of English instruction. Of the students participating in this study, two fell into this group and they struggled to make sense of the decision-making process, given the fact that a number of their colleagues would be permitted to keep studying English in Canada at their new host institutions. University and scholarship administrators in Canada I spoke with assured me that language proficiency was not the only criteria for acceptance which was corroborated by the fact that of the students who had been accepted to Canadian universities, many had test scores far lower than are typically accepted by their respective host departments. However, at this time, a number of articles in the Brazilian press emphasized low levels of English as the primary factor for the recall (e.g. Globo, 2014). Students studying in Canada organized a protest against the decision to send them home which was met with little response and a tacit endorsement of the role of language in the decision-making process from the president of CAPES, who argued that the number of unsuccessful students was statistically insignificant and that the government had never expected 100% of the students to have sufficient proficiency in English to progress to academics (Globo, 2014). The question of fairness in terms of the test scheduling and preparedness was not addressed.

As the summer began, the students were disappointed that the internship had been cancelled for their entire cohort and also with the additional language training (bringing the total duration of time up to 12 months) that some of them were required to complete. As Fernanda related, 'I expected to do the internship here, and like, the articles, in my major, with professors, doctors' (April 9, 2014). Two of the students attempted to circumvent the formal cancellation of the internship portion of the sojourn by going out and searching for other opportunities on their own. Clara told me, 'I'm just trying to find out everything about [my field] in Canada on the Internet. I just spread some emails – a lot of emails and I got some replies and I didn't get some […] I was just trying to find someone who would like to help me' (March 21, 2014). Lucas cold-called all of the professors in related departments at his university and was eventually given an opportunity to work as a research assistant (September 22, 2014).

At the end of the summer semester, two of the participants in this study who had progressed to academics in Canada decided to quit the program early. In a letter written to CAPES at the time, Beatriz explained her decision:

> Os meus principais objetivos ao me inscrever no programa Ciência sem Fronteiras era aprimorar o meu conhecimento na língua inglês, já que e algo muito importante atualmente para o mercado de trabalho, e realizar um estágio ou pesquisa no exterior para ter outro visão do mercado da engenharia em um pais de primeiro mundo [My main goals when I signed up for SwB were to improve my knowledge of the English language, as it is very important now for the labor market and to carry out an internship or participate in research abroad in order to gain perspective on the engineering market in a first world country].

In a Skype conversation shortly after her return to Brazil, she repeatedly stressed that given the adjustments to the features of the program, she had completed everything of value that she had hoped to do in Canada and had no choice but to return home. A number of other students in the cohort not participating in this study also chose to end their sojourns early, with an additional factor being the ability to match up dates with the beginning of the school term in Brazil.

Student Perspectives: Outcomes and Reflections

As their sojourns in Canada progressed, the students' perspectives on the outcomes of the program went through a number of changes. At least in part, these perspectives were influenced by the fact that what they had thought would happen had failed to take place. Whereas in earlier conversations and interviews they had spoken often of internships and the possibility of participating in research and publication, they now spoke more frequently of English in increasingly pragmatic and instrumental terms. As Vanessa told me in our final conversation: 'I think the first thing is English for sure [...] to bring this to Brazil and like for my resume' (February 3, 2015). Daiane concurred, looking forward to her return home to Brazil:

> I need to finish here and my life will be there so I think that I can't stop everything just to stay studying English because I think my English, it's enough now to have a good job in Brazil [...] to be different from the rest of the people, because that's the idea. (April 10, 2014)

What had begun as the pursuit of academic knowledge in her field is reduced here to making the best of her acquisition of English not as a form of knowledge in its own right, but rather as a form of distinction directly related to competition in the labor marketplace after her graduation.

Beatriz and Clara chose to leave the program after eight months of ELL and four months of academic study, opting out of four more months of academic study. Back at home, Clara reflected on her return via Skype:

> Everybody was like oh, what did you learn in Canada and I was like – I didn't learn a lot of things about [my field] and I don't have a lot of things to share with you. My professors are like oh, what did you learn? Tell us the new things that you know? And I said oh, I have to study more again the old things because I didn't – I wasn't in touch with the things related to my field and to my profession. And I told them I was a little frustrated, disappointed about that. They were like oh, what did you do there? And I told them I learned English. It was great. I was in a new country, a new people, a new culture. (September 12, 2014)

This emphasis on the social and intercultural benefits was mentioned by others as well. Lucas praised his language program for the international connections he had made, describing '... the new different cultures. For example, I have never seen Saudi people in my life [...] and people from Turkey, Russia, let me see more different from me. And Chinese and Japanese also' (September 22, 2014). Similarly, just prior to her return, Beatriz praised what she referred to as the interpersonal aspects of her sojourn which she connected to her time learning and using English:

> Here was totally different because I needed to solve everything for myself and I never stayed a long time alone and it was very good to get to know myself better. [...] Talking to my friends in Brazil I saw that they have a different point of view in some situations than I have now and I was like my friends in the past but I think I am more mature now. I don't know [laughs]. A broad experience opened our minds and it's very nice to live with different people and cultures and we see and learn different things. I think it's one of the most important things I learned on this program. (July 16, 2014)

Discussion

As can be seen from the early plans and agendas for the SwB program on the part of a range of stakeholders including two national governments as well as host country educational institutions, what I have described here as a language policy assemblage constitutes only one part of the larger education policy assemblage that it is embedded within. Additionally, importance ascribed to, or attention given to this subcomponent of the larger policy can be seen to vary considerably based on explicit statements, plans and actions taken (or not) by the various stakeholders. In fact, in this case, language policies appear to be composed in large part of reactive measures intended to address unforeseen difficulties in the rolling out of the larger plan. However, by considering these statements and measures, as well as attending to the ways in which individual students interpreted, engaged and positioned themselves relative to these policies, it becomes possible to tease out some of the dominant discourses and the rationalities they instantiate in terms of how they inform consecutive stages of the policy process both at the broad level of the SwB program generally and in terms of language specifically.

Looking at the larger scholarship program, neoliberal discourses of competition and entrepreneurship informed plans to enhance the country's global position and collective benefit. This was to be operationalized by sending individual students to the best universities in the world and exposing them to the higher levels of competition and entrepreneurship assumed to exist in these universities. But when second language learning emerged as an unforeseen requirement, these same notions of competition and entrepreneurship were applied to the individual students and their performance in language learning programming abroad. And from the perspective of the state scholarship administrators in Brazil as well as the administration of the particular language institute these students attended, rapid language learning was presented as a necessary preamble or skilling required to access STEM knowledge capital rather than representing valuable knowledge and experience in its own right. Framing language learning as a challenge, or competition, in this way fashioned it as a form of gatekeeping, performed in large part by TOEFL tests, where those who did not achieve success took individual responsibility for their failure. What was missing from the conversation around language learning and testing were questions of the viability and fairness of this planning and the way that it was implemented, predicated on the possibility of learning a language, in some cases from scratch in eight months and in the cases of the students in the lower levels who wrote the test at an earlier date than the higher levels, an even shorter period of time. One of the students sent home remarked that he wrote his first essay in English while writing the TOEFL test.

When the students who were successful in moving through to academics in Canada realized that they were not going to be accessing what they had anticipated, they in turn began to reflect on what it was that they were acquiring on the sojourn. As they came to understand that English was to be the chief outcome of their time in Canada, they revised their aims from internships and the possibility of contributing to academic publications, to thinking of English as a form of distinction that they could use to their advantage in the job market after graduating. In this way, the loftier ideas of working to make the Brazilian collective more competitive in the global marketplace appear to have been reduced instead to thoughts of individual competition between peers for personal gain. For students like Daiane, this investment needed to match the outcome; for her, time spent achieving a higher level of English than was necessary to compete in the local job market could be considered as time wasted. In her case, not only was her idea of English largely reduced down to the level of an instrument but also further qualified on her departure from Canada as 'good enough' for the purposes she intended it for.

However, this neoliberal-inflected and economically oriented instrumentalist perspective on English and ELL was not shared by all, as the excerpts from Beatriz, Lucas and Clara demonstrate. These three students found the experience to also be a time of great personal growth and were proud of the intercultural awareness and social benefits that learning a second language afforded them. In this way, somewhat ironically, what they ended up taking from the program most resembles the more traditional aims of study abroad sojourns, in contrast to the more ambitious outcome of scientific and economic development through exposure to international competitiveness and entrepreneurship initially proposed.

As a demonstration of the shifting and at times contested status and role of English and ELL for one cohort of SwB scholarship recipients, the case study presented above highlights the ways in which in recent times, even socially generous and/or altruistic internationalization initiatives draw on or are influenced by particular discourses of language and language use. These discourses in turn instantiate rationalities of neoliberal governmentality that are often manifested in the policy efforts of an ensemble of transnational stakeholders. However, as was shown in the case of several of these students, the neoliberal subject positions on offer were not entirely taken up or accepted by them, as they navigated their own ways through the shifting expectations and policy landscape of the program. It is important to note, however, that even though these students were able to forge their own paths and value the program on their own terms, this all took place within the scant wiggle room of the larger education policy assemblage and its gatekeeping measures.

References

Altbach, P. and Knight, J. (2007) The internationalization of higher education: Motivations and realities. *Journal of Studies in International Education* 11 (3/4), 290–305.

Association of Universities and Colleges of Canada (2011) Trends in higher education: Volume 1 – Enrollment. See http://www.aucc.ca/wp-content/uploads/2011/05/trends-2011-vol1-enrolment-e.pdf (accessed 3 July 2015).

Block, D., Gray, J. and Holborow, M. (2012) *Neoliberalism and Applied Linguistics*. New York: Routledge.

Brady, M. (2014) Ethnographies of neoliberal governmentalities: From the neoliberal apparatus to neoliberalism and governmental assemblages. *Foucault Studies* 18, 11–33.

British Council (2015) English in Brazil: An examination of policy, perceptions and influencing factors. See http://englishagenda.britishcouncil.org/books-resource-packs/english-latin-america-examination-policy-and-priorities-seven-countries (accessed 24 April 2017).

Canada Senate Committee on Foreign Affairs and International Trade (2012) *Intensifying Strategic Partnerships with the New Brazil* (5th Report. 41st Parliament, 1st session). See http://www.parl.gc.ca/content/sen/committee/411/aefa/rep/rep05may12-e.pdf (accessed 24 April 2017).

Ciência sem Frontieras (n.d.a) Goals. See http://www.cienciasemfronteiras.gov.br/web/csf-eng/goals (accessed 24 April 2017).

Ciência sem Fronteiras (n.d.b) O programa. See http://www.cienciasemfronteiras.gov.br/web/csf/o-programa (accessed 24 April 2017).

Ciência sem Fronteiras (n.d.c) Painel de controle do programa Ciência sem Fronteiras. See http://www.cienciasemfronteiras.gov.br/web/csf/painel-de-controle (accessed 24 April 2017).

Ciência sem Fronteiras (n.d.d) Motivation. See http://www.cienciasemfronteiras.gov.br/web/csf-eng/motivation (accessed 24 April 2017).

Chakma, A., Bisson, A., Côté, J., Dodd, C., Smith, L. and Wright, D. (2012) International Education: A Key Driver of Canada's Future Prosperity (report prepared by advisory panel on Canada's international education strategy for the Department of Foreign Affairs, Trade and Development Canada). See http://www.international.gc.ca/education/report-rapport/strategy-strategie/ (accessed 24 April 2017).

Chun, C. (2009) Contesting neoliberal discourses in EAP: Critical praxis in an IEP classroom. *Journal of English for Academic Purposes* 8 (2), 111–120.

Cruz, V. and Foreque, F. (2015, September 3) Programa 'Ciência sem Fronteiras' será congelado'. *Folha de S. Paulo*, newspaper article. See http://www1.folha.uol.com.br/ciencia/2015/09/1677170-programa-ciencia-sem-fronteiras-sera-congelado.shtml (accessed 4 September 2015).

Dardot, P. and Laval, C. (2013) *The New Way of the World: On Neoliberal Society* (G. Elliott, trans.). London: Verso (original work published 2009).

Davidson, A.I. (2011) In praise of counter-conduct. *History of the Human Sciences* 24 (4), 25–41.

Dean, M. (2010) *Governmentality: Power and Rule in Modern Society* (2nd edn). London: Sage.

Embassy of Canada to Brazil (2012) *Canada-Brazil Joint Committee for Cooperation on Science, Technology and Innovation: Inaugural Action Plan*. See http://www.canadainternational.gc.ca/brazil-bresil/bilateral_relations_bilaterales/STIActionPlan_PalnActionCSTI.aspx?lang=eng (accessed 24 April 2017).

Flores, N. (2014) Creating republican machines: Language governmentality in the United States. *Linguistics & Education* 25 (1), 1–11.

Foreign Affairs, Trade and Development Canada (2014) *Canada's International Education Strategy: Harnessing our Knowledge Advantage to Drive Innovation and Prosperity.* See http://international.gc.ca/global-markets-marches-mondiaux/assets/pdfs/overview-apercu-eng.pdf (accessed 24 April 2017).

Foucault, M. (1988) Technologies of the self. In L. Martin, H. Gutman and P. Hutton (eds) *Technologies of the Self: A Seminar with Michel Foucault* (pp. 16–49). London: Tavistock.

Foucault, M. (1997) The ethics of the concern of the self as a practice of freedom. In P. Rabinow (ed.) *Michel Foucault, Ethics, Subjectivity and Truth: Essential Works of Foucault 1954–1984, Volume 1* (pp. 281–301). London: Penguin.

Foucault, M. (2007) *Security, Territory, Population: Lectures at the Collège de France 1977–1978* (G. Burchell, trans.). New York: Picador (original work published 2004).

'G1' (2013) *Portugal será excluído do Ciência sem Fronteiras, diz Mercadante*, newspaper article, April 24. See http://g1.globo.com/educacao/noticia/2013/04/portugal-sera-excluido-do-ciencia-sem-fronteiras-diz-mercadante.html (accessed 18 May 2015).

'Globo.tv: Bom dia Brasil', *Domínio de segunda língua será obrigatório no Ciências Sem Fronteiras*, video file, April 14, 2014. See http://globotv.globo.com/rede-globo/bom-dia-brasil/v/dominio-de-segunda-lingua-sera-obrigatorio-no-ciencias-sem-fronteiras/3279346/ (accessed 18 July 2015).

Harvey, D. (2005) *A Brief History of Neoliberalism.* Oxford: Oxford University Press.

Holborow, M. (2013) Applied linguistics in the neoliberal university: Ideological keywords and social agency. *Applied Linguistics Review* 4 (2), 229–257.

Johnson, D.C. (2009) Ethnography of language policy. *Language Policy* 8 (2), 139–159.

Johnston, D. (2012, April 24) Governor General Meets With the President of Brazil and Announces Canada's Participation in the Science Without Borders Program, news release. See http://www.gg.ca/document.aspx?id=14504&lan=eng (accessed 3 July 2015).

Johnson, D.C. (2013a) Positioning the language policy arbiter: Governmentality and footing in the school district of Philadelphia. In J. Tollefson (ed.) *Language Policies in Education: Critical Issues* (2nd edn; pp. 116–136). New York: Routledge.

Johnson, D.C. (2013b) *Language Policy.* New York: Palgrave Macmillan.

Kubota, R. (2009) Internationalization of universities: Paradoxes and responsibilities. *The Modern Language Journal* 93, 612–616.

Kubota, R. (2011) Questioning linguistic instrumentalism: English, neoliberalism and language tests in Japan. *Linguistics and Education* 22 (3), 248–260.

Li, T.M. (2007) Governmentality. *Anthropologica* 49 (2), 275–280.

Lloyd, M. (2014) 'Interview with Paulo Speller, Brazilian higher education secretary'. *Revista Ensino Superior: Unicamp.* Digital journal article. See https://www.revistaensinosuperior.gr.unicamp.br/entrevistas/interview-with-paulo-speller-brazilian-higher-education-secretary (accessed 18 June 2015).

McCarty, T.L. (2011) Introducing ethnography and language policy. In T.L. McCarty (ed.) *Ethnography and Language Policy* (pp. 1–28). New York: Routledge.

'O Globo' (2014) *CAPES manda 110 bolsistas do Ciência sem Fronteiras voltarem ao Brasil por nível baixo em ingles.* Newspaper article. See http://oglobo.globo.com/sociedade/educacao/capes-manda-110-bolsistas-do-ciencia-sem-fronteiras-voltarem-ao-brasil-por-nivel-baixo-em-ingles-12138918 (accessed 14 July 2015).

Olssen, M. and Peters, M.A. (2005) Neoliberalism, higher education and the knowledge economy: From the free market to knowledge capitalism. *Journal of Education Policy* 20 (3), 313–345.

Park, J.S-Y. (2010) Naturalization of competence and the neoliberal subject: Success stories of English language learning in the Korean conservative press. *Journal of Linguistic Anthropology* 20 (1), 22–39.

Pennycook, A. (2002) Language policy and docile bodies: Hong Kong and governmentality. In J. Tollefson (ed.) *Language Policies in Education: Critical Issues* (pp. 91–110). New York: Routledge.

Pennycook, A. (2006) Postmodernism in language policy. In T. Ricento (ed.) *An Introduction to Language Policy: Theory and Method* (pp. 60–76). Malden, MA: Blackwell.

Piovezan, S. (2015) 'USP é a instituição com mais bolsas do Ciência sem Fronteiras, diz balance', *G1*, newspaper article. See http://g1.globo.com/sp/sao-carlos-regiao/noticia/2015/07/capes-e-cnpq-apresentam-balanco-do-programa-ciencia-sem-fronteiras.html (accessed 24 July 20015).

Shannon, T.A. Jr. (2012) Brazil's strategic leap forward. *Americas Quarterly* 6 (4), 45–49.

Saudi Arabia Ministry of Education (2015) King Abdullah scholarships program. See http://he.moe.gov.sa/en/studyaboard/King-Abdulla-hstages/Pages/default.aspx (accessed 4 August 2015).

Shohamy, E. (2006) *Language Policy: Hidden Agendas and New Approaches*. New York: Routledge.

Stroud, C. and Wee, L. (2012) *Style, Identity and Literacy: English in Singapore*. Bristol: Multilingual Matters.

Urciuoli, B. (2008) Skills and selves in the new workplace. *American Ethnologist* 35 (2), 211–228.

Wee, L. (2008) Linguistic instrumentalism in Singapore. In R. Rubdy and P. Tan (eds) *Language as a Commodity: Global Structures, Local Marketplaces* (pp. 31–43). London: Continuum.

7 Neoliberalism in ELT Aid: Interrogating a USAID ELT Project in Southern Philippines

Honey B. Tabiola and Beatriz Lorente

Introduction

In 2009, the first Job Enabling English Proficiency (JEEP) project in Mindanao was inaugurated at the Western Mindanao State University (WMSU) in Zamboanga City. Among those who attended the launch of this English language teaching (ELT) aid project were: Kristie Kenney, the then US ambassador to the Philippines; Jon Lindborg, the mission director of the United States Agency for International Development (USAID); Joji Ilagan, president of the Philippine Call Center Alliance; Virgilio Leyretana, chair of the Mindanao Economic Development Council (MEDCO); Dr Emmylou Yanga, regional director of the Commission on Higher Education (CHED); Dr Grace Rebollos, WMSU president; and Zamboanga City Mayor Celso Lobregat. The attendees at the launch represented the alliance of key institutions involved in the JEEP project: the American government, more specifically, USAID, the business processing outsourcing (BPO) sector of the Philippines, local businesses, the tertiary education sector and local government.

Speaking against the backdrop of an old American colonial building and to an audience consisting mainly of university students, former US ambassador Kenney inaugurated the project. In her speech, she described the JEEP project as:

> A project of the United States to help you get jobs by learning English. We are investing in you, so it's up to you to use that investment [...] Never ever settle to [sic] being less than your best [...] (Learn English) so (when) people hire you for jobs they can pick you because you are the best that you can be. (US Ambassador Kenney Inaugurates WMSU's JEEP, 2009)

The jobs that the students could be hired for because of their English became clear in subsequent speeches. Leyretana, chair of the MEDCO, announced that BPO companies were planning to establish call centers in Zamboanga City and that the JEEP project was essential for developing the necessary workforce for the industry. Ilagan, the president of the Philippine Call Center Alliance, expressed gratitude and felt 'encouraged' by the community's effort to help develop the BPO industry which was 'doing great' and 'growing' (JEEP project in Zambo, 2009). Lobregat, the mayor of Zamboanga, stressed that the ability to communicate in English would be the 'key to the city's economic competitiveness'. Because Zamboangueños already spoke Chavacano, a Spanish creole, English could be their edge when applying for or attracting BPO companies who might prefer applicants who can understand and speak both Spanish and English.

In broad terms, this narrative illustrates how neoliberalism continues to animate foreign aid and how, with their focus on 'English learning', ELT aid projects are particularly potent instruments for transforming citizens into neoliberal subjects. Foreign aid has been criticized on many fronts especially for its role in promoting and ensuring that recipient countries adopt neoliberal free-market reforms (Petras & Veltmeyer, 2004). This aspect of foreign aid has been under-researched in the case of ELT aid, even as critical analyses of ELT aid have been made in relation to neocolonialism and gender (Appleby, 2010), language ideology and discourse (Seargeant & Erling, 2011) and language diversity and multilingualism (Phillipson, 1992; Widin, 2010). In this chapter, we attend to the ways in which the neoliberal rationality saturates the strategy of development in Mindanao and its production of human capital. In particular, we address the following questions: What are the contours of development initiatives in Mindanao and in the Philippines today? How might JEEP be situated within this developmentalist fantasy? What does it mean to invest in students' English language skills for economic and global competitiveness? What happens when students are responsible for using that investment?

Neoliberalism as State Policy and Subjectivity

In this chapter, neoliberalism is understood as a set of economic policies and a form of subjectivity. There is no settled definition of neoliberalism, but at its core it is 'a governing rationality extending a specific formulation of economic values, practices, and metrics to every sphere of human life' (Brown, 2015: 30). The term not only signifies the free rein of the market with minimal state interference (classical economic liberalism), it also names the conversion of *every feature of human life* into the image of the market and the transformation of every human conduct and activity, including previously non-economic spheres and endeavors such as statecraft, education, fitness, wellness and dating, among others, into the model of the market. This especially affects both the *state* and their *citizens* who are increasingly submitted to and interpellated by market metrics to construct themselves as entrepreneurs and investors who always strategize to improve their value and competitiveness.

Neoliberalism remakes the relationship of the state to the market. As an ensemble of economic policies, neoliberalism, among others, is characterized by the promotion of free markets which includes the privatization and outsourcing of public goods and services, the deregulation of industries and capital flows, the dismantling of state provisions and the replacement of progressive with regressive taxation and tariff schemes. It champions the view that the state is an inefficient economic player and that the unfettered market is the ideal and efficient social organization to achieve economic growth, all the while accepting that the state is a powerful broker and effective enforcer of capitalist policies and practices. Indeed, economic growth and taking care of the market has become a source of legitimacy for the state (Brown, 2015: 68). Reduced to being a market actor, the state ceases to become an entity that represents the public's best interests (e.g. providing the public with publicly funded goods and services and protecting them from the infelicities of the market). With neoliberalism, the state does not regulate the market anymore; rather, it regulates *for* the market by implementing policies that promote the unleashing of market forces.

Equally as important, neoliberalism remakes citizens' subjectivities by constructing and producing citizen-entrepreneurs who are supposedly self-reliant and who know how to invest in themselves. Endeavors such as training, leisure and internships are mere 'strategic decisions' to invite people to invest in themselves so they can further enhance the value of their present and future self. In this way, the state makes citizens responsible for the market and they are integrated into the project of macroeconomic growth of the state and the market.

Given the colonial history of the Philippines and the crucial role of the US in today's development aid, neoliberalism can be conceived as imbricated with neocolonialism. More specifically, neoliberalism could be considered to be neocolonialism's primary administrative form, the economic and political modality through which the neocolonial relationship of the Philippines and the US is constantly reproduced and maintained at the level of policy and the conduct of human subjects. By neocolonialism, we mean 'a continuing economic hegemony' where 'the postcolonial state remains in a situation of dependence on its former masters and that the former masters continue to act in a colonialist manner towards formerly colonized states' (Young, 2001: 45). Although in 1946, the Philippines was granted formal independence from US colonial rule, the Philippines continues to be tethered and subservient to the former imperial powers through economic means, with the national elite in complicity. As we shall see in the chapter, the continued colonialist behavior of the US continues to take the form of the deepening of neoliberal restructuring of the Philippine economy which began in the late 1980s. In Robert Young's (2001: 49) account of the operations of neocolonialism, in the early days of independence, the lure of 'development' facilitated the incorporation of formerly colonized countries into 'modernity' which is synonymous with the Western capitalist economic system. The sources of capital to achieve modernization were loans, foreign aid, trade agreements and the operation of US-backed international financial institutions such as the World Bank (WB) and the International Monetary Fund (IMF) to finance even unnecessary and dubious industrial projects (Nkrumah, 1965, as cited in Young, 2001: 47) to maintain economic control. The accumulation of debt since the 1970s has resulted in a debt crisis which was used as justification to start imposing neoliberal free-market policies on non-Western economies. This is the exact development path that the Philippines has taken since it gained political sovereignty. This chapter suggests that development plans in the country today iterate the neoliberal restructuring of the Philippine economy. While in the past, development and modernity required the shedding of traditional social attitudes of the formerly colonized, development today entails the production of neoliberal human subjects who are investors in and speculators of their own capital value, as shown in the case of investments in English language skills today.

The JEEP Project

The JEEP project was 'designed to help graduates of Mindanao colleges and universities compete successfully for jobs that require a high level of English proficiency in specific sectors' which include nursing and allied health services, the maritime sector, travel and tourism services, among others (GEM Completion Report, n.d.: 33). The two-year project subsidizes the replacement of the 'traditional' language teaching methodologies and instructional materials used by the partner tertiary institutions with a mixed method of task-based language teaching and computer-assisted language learning (CALL) software whose license must be renewed annually from a

US company. JEEP is part of the Growth with Equity in Mindanao Year 3 (GEM3), a $99 million flagship project of the USAID aimed at promoting development throughout Mindanao. Three years after its first launch in WMSU, 26 colleges and universities in Mindanao have implemented JEEP, having graduated approximately 55,000 students.

Situating JEEP within the axis of Mindanao's local history, the island's previous colonial experience under the US, and its general distrust with the capital Manila's politics helps illuminate the reasons for the local population's widespread embrace of JEEP and the Philippine government's endorsement of the project. Mindanao, which lies at the southern part of the Philippines, has been viewed as an unstable frontier which 'stands for mystery, volatility, and darkness' (Abinales, 2010: 154), an island not living up to its potential despite its rich natural resources. Its people still have memories of the US military who they consider to be 'good imperialists' even as they view the Christian Filipino leaders in the Filipino capital of Manila with enmity and suspicion. The island is home to 'special groups' composed of supposed 'wild tribes' and the Muslim minority who must be 'enlightened' through educational, legal, economic and political systems (Abinales, 2010: 155). In the first decade of American occupation, Mindanao was put under army rule, opposite to the civilian rule practiced in most parts of the country. It became a laboratory of progressive-type state-building by its governing military officers whose administration was centralized and successful in pacifying, integrating and taxing communities (successes unaccomplished under Spanish rule). The military officers, who tended to despise Hispanized Filipino leaders and their patronage politics, also shared the separatist aspirations of the local Muslim leaders and fought every effort by the colonial capital in Manila to submit Mindanao under its direct control. However, in 1914, the military turned over power to civilian rule and Filipino leaders, resulting in the unification of Mindanao with the rest of the Philippines under the Filipinization program (Abinales, 2010: 30). This was worked out by Manuel Quezon as he ascended to power in Philippine politics, backed by the newly elected democratic president Woodrow Wilson who favored tutelage training of Filipinos for their eventual independence. Muslim leaders eventually submitted to Filipinization after being convinced by Quezon that their interests were better protected under Filipinization.

Today, this imaginary of Mindanao as a backwater colony remains an important premise of every development project in the region. For the Philippine state, the US development efforts are not only aligned with its own development goals, they are also aligned with its most cherished cultural goals in Mindanao – the consolidation of the fragmented nation state and 'the civilization of a part of its citizenry that has yet to join the majority on the road to full modernity' (Abinales, 2010: 155). Today, Mindanao has been a laboratory of some neoliberal experiments which attempt to transform not only policy but also human subjects.

JEEP within the neoliberal constellation of the Philippines

To better understand JEEP is to locate it within the three larger development initiatives of the US government and the Philippine government. What this framing reveals is that the three seemingly disparate development interventions, namely Growth with Equity in Mindanao III (GEM3), the Partnership for Growth (PFG) and the Philippine Development Plan (PDP), are contoured to and by the same neoliberal vision of development. In a nutshell, these development interventions are geared towards ensuring that private sector-led industries are competitive and attractive enough to local and foreign investors which necessarily tasks the government with making sure the business climate is inviting enough by addressing the 'constraints' to growth characterized by the following coordinates: export orientation, trade liberalization, state deregulation, privatization and the accumulation of foreign investment. Getting rid of the 'constraints' to growth is synonymous with lessening restrictions on foreign investment, reducing tariffs for importers, reconsidering protectionist paradigms that 'distort competition', establishing solid infrastructure, harmonizing procedures for doing business, making sure the judicial system has enough teeth in deciding and prosecuting financial crimes and developing the 'human capital' of the population by providing healthcare and education for the workforce. In this thinking, economic competitiveness needs to be secured first for development to spontaneously follow. Good governance, anti-corruption and an efficient judiciary system are considered to be inseparable from the goal of business competitiveness and economic efficiency.

A 'more stable, prosperous and well-governed nation' is the purported goal of the development initiatives of the US in partnership with the government of the Philippines (GPH). The compass that guides this venture is its 'development hypothesis' which is spelled out this way:

[...] if USAID improves economic competitiveness (by strengthening weak governance and expanding fiscal space) and strengthens human capital (through improved health and education), USAID's strategy will contribute substantially to accelerating and sustaining broad-based and inclusive growth in the Philippines . . . combined with enhanced peace and stability in conflict-affected areas of Mindanao. (USAID/Philippines Country Development Cooperation Strategy, n.d.: 11)

There is an implicit admission in the document that the intervention is not going to solve the problems of the Philippines. It only hopes to lay the groundwork for a sustained broad-based and inclusive growth facilitated and accelerated by two things: economic competitiveness and the strengthening of human capital. The three development interventions sketched below have the same programmatic content in terms of their neoliberal vision and strategy of development as captured by the PDP's statement of macroeconomic policy:

> It is the private actors – from the smallest self-employed entrepreneurs to the largest conglomerates – that create productive jobs and incomes. Government's responsibility however – through fiscal and monetary policies – is to create an environment for vigorous economic activity, as well as to ensure that enough gains from growth are set aside for larger social purposes. (PDP, 2011: 36)

All of these interventions are justified by the idiom of 'inclusive growth' which is treated as synonymous to development. However, a closer look at the contours of these interventions reveals that the use of 'inclusive growth' is not benign but actually facilitates and secures particular transformations in policies.

First, GEM3 concretizes a neoliberal developmentalist fantasy with four components: the *infrastructure development component* which spawns community and regional projects (e.g. airport runways and roadway upgrades); the *governance improvement component* which entails providing incentives and technical assistance to local governments to improve revenue generation, and internships for 200 young leaders to the Philippine House of Congress (PHC) to equip them with policy know-how; the *business growth component* which includes assistance to Chambers of Commerce, producers and business support organizations (BSOs) to facilitate sales in international exports and domestic out-shipments of various commodities such as fruit products, vegetables and seafood which amounted to $86 million (GEM3 Evaluation Reports, n.d.: 42); and a *workforce preparation component* designed to supposedly improve the quality of education in schools by providing computers and internet access to elementary schools, providing internships in national and multinational firms to recent college graduates, providing financial support to students in careers where Mindanao is under-represented and lastly, improving the English proficiency of this workforce through JEEP.

The same set of concerns – infrastructure, efficient governance structures, revenue generation and exportation – animate the vision of PFG, a five-year enhanced bilateral agreement between the US and

GPH to 'address the most serious constraints to economic growth and development in the Philippines' (Partnership for Growth, 2011: iii). In the PFG, key economic officials from both governments concluded that the two binding constraints to growth and competitiveness in the Philippines are *weak governance* and *narrow fiscal space*. Thus, the PFG Joint Country Action Plan (JCAP) proposed three inter-related areas of intervention, informed by the results of benchmarks and indicators like the investment climate diagnostics and global competitiveness rankings. First is *regulatory quality* which 'seeks to promote an environment attractive for investment, trade, and private sector growth' (Partnership for Growth, 2011: iii) by easing foreign restrictions to Philippine market entry, reducing the cost of doing business, ensuring that GPH import regulations are in line with international standards and enhancing human resources. Second is *judicial efficiency* which seeks to enhance the ability of the justice sector to resolve cases, 'particularly those that significantly undermine the trade, the investment climate and business confidence' (Partnership for Growth, 2011: iii–iv). Initiatives include assisting the GPH in resolving commercial disputes and financial crimes. Third is the *expansion of fiscal space* by addressing insufficient revenue generation, enforcing of anti-tax evasion and anti-smuggling laws and improving budget and expenditure management.

The same set of concerns characterizes the 2011–2016 PDP. It is the government's 'social contract with the people' and its blueprint for development. To achieve inclusive growth, the PDP (2011: 26–31) has five key programs and strategies, namely boosting industry competitiveness, improving people's access to credit, investing massively in infrastructure, maintaining good governance and developing human capital. PDP cites the various competitive indicators like the World Economic Forum (WEF) Global Competitiveness Ranking and International Finance Corporation/World Bank's (IFC/WB) Doing Business Report which the country has been using to describe its business climate and discover its weaknesses in major development aspects. These measures of competitiveness reveal the inadequate state of the country's infrastructure, the expensive cost of doing business and its unsatisfactory economic performance in terms of investments, exports and competitiveness (PDP, 2011: 63–64). To save resources, many of these projects are to be carried out through the private sector through public-private partnerships (PPP) which, according to an analysis paper by the Ibon Foundation, allows the private sector to profit from the provision of public goods and services (PDP, 2011: 5).

Certainly, weeding out corruption and bureaucratic inefficiency, improving revenue generation and improving some capacities of the justice system do have beneficial consequences. However, the point here is that these benefits serve as an alibi for securing and revitalizing the more crucial and problematic policies that accompany these initiatives, such as further export orientation, trade liberalization, accumulation of foreign investment, state deregulation and privatization; in other words, these initiatives occlude deep structures of the country's underdevelopment and facilitate the deepening of the neoliberal restructuring of the Philippine society. These policies build on and strengthen the neoliberal revolution that began in the country in the late 1980s (Bello et al., 2009: 9) that make up the 'accumulated structural weaknesses' of the 'political economy of the permanent crisis' in the Philippines. These structural weaknesses were brought about by phases of structural adjustments which began in the late 1980s during the Marcos administration until the late 1990s during the Ramos administration (Bello et al., 2009: 12–17) and were motivated by the economic success of the country's East Asian neighbors which were attributed to free-market policies.

In many ways, today's development interventions are recodings and rearticulations of the myths and myopia of the recent but continuing development story of the country. Bello et al. (2009: 22) write that the tragedy of the Philippines is that despite nagging realities, Filipino technocrats continue to pin their faith on the unfettered market and its entailments as the key to development. On governance, the Ibon Foundation (2011: 3) argues that the emphasis on improving governance is myopic as the interventions are preoccupied with facilitating business competitiveness and attracting investors and 'not in the direct interest of the majority of Filipinos, especially the poor'. These policy directions are not surprising. After all, the US remains the top buyer of Philippine exports, the biggest source of the country's imports and its net foreign direct investment (FDI) (Padilla, n.d.). On export-oriented industrialization, as early as 1984, Ofreneo (1984: 489) had already argued that this official industrial policy of the country is risky, faltering, antagonistic to local industries and renders the country 'highly vulnerable to global economic fluctuations'. The concern about narrow fiscal space or the focus on revenue generation as a solution, while important, distracts attention away from addressing the major reasons for the country's deficit problems which are the tariff reductions (deregulation) and the continued prioritization of foreign debt repayment. Lastly, for Bello et al. (2009: 24), the idea of the 'economic miracles' of the Association of Southeast Asian Nations (ASEAN) neighbors which are perceived to be linked to their free-market policies, has constantly ignored the important policy differences between the strategic protectionism and selective liberalization implemented by Malaysia and Thailand and the directionless, indiscriminate liberalization pursued by the Philippines.

JEEP and the speculative value of English

The JEEP project then can be seen as an active effort by the donors and the students themselves to invest in English language skills to enhance the latter's capital value. GEM3 and schools invest in students by putting up JEEP laboratories and purchasing imported language learning courseware while students invest in their own human capital by paying additional school fees for enrolling with JEEP and by investing 30 hours every semester studying the courseware. Students also submit themselves to optimizing technologies such as entering the air-conditioned 'state-of-the-art' JEEP laboratories and regulating the space and their bodies for optimal productivity through *technolog(ies) of subjection* (Ong, 2006: 6). The laboratory is solely dedicated to studying the JEEP courseware using the CALL method and is governed by rules such as an English-only language policy, reinforced by the teacher and two student assistants. At any given time, students can occupy cubicles where they can log into their own JEEP account which keeps records and monitors all their work, test scores, ratings and class rankings.

Furthermore, in the JEEP laboratory, students develop their social body as 'a kind of capital-ability machine' (Tadiar, 2013: 20) by engaging in activities and practices of investment in the form of acquiring skills and dispositions. For example, they are supposed to acquire the necessary 'workplace communication skills' by imitating a native speaker and answering the phone, attending to the front desk at a hotel and many others. They are supposed to plan and strategize their time so they can balance learning the courseware, beating the 30-hour time requirement every semester and complying with the requirements in their other subjects. In the JEEP laboratory, taking the time for classroom discussions or exploring questions that pique the students' interest in the courseware can be seen both by the students and the teachers as a waste of time and a distraction from beating the 30-hour time quota or from studying the topics in the courseware that need to be covered in the semester. This has important implications for what gets taught and how time should be spent.

These investments in money, time and labor in learning English are often made in the hopes that these efforts will pay off in the future by increasing the students' chances to land a job. However, these efforts do not always pay off. Park (2011) attributes the elusiveness of the economic promise of English to the constant recalibration of the standards of the linguistic market to defer access to economic and social advancement even as the market keeps the promise alive and lucrative. Meanwhile, Kubota (2011) suggests that, given that English is not always used in workplaces, the purpose of learning English today seems to be to nourish an aspiration for (imagined) upward career mobility for workers; English serves as a convenient indicator, not of language proficiency but of the effort exerted by the workers toward staying adaptable. While both emphasize the interpellation of the neoliberal subject to strive to learn English as an effort to stay competitive and survive in precarious job markets, each differs in the way they identify the ruses of inequality – for Park, it is the ever-changing language standards induced by the market while, for Kubota, it is the notion of English as a requirement for job success and its accompanying imaginary of upward mobility, coupled with the stratifying effects of gender and race differences.

We want to contribute to the discussion of the nature of investments in English today and complicate further the link between English and economic success by suggesting that the financialization of the economy or the ascendance of shareholder capitalism has shaped how human capital (the skill set included) is valued today (Davis, 2009). Kubota's suggestion of the (imagined) mobility nourished by English as a 'learning capital' is now a fundamental feature of today's economy. In the age of financialization, an important goal of today's human capital is the need to *self-invest to attract future investors*. This version of human capital is not just a creature of exchange in which a person learns English language skills that can be eventually traded as a resource for salary or increase in income. Instead, the human capital is a creature of investment and competition whose preoccupation is not just (immediate) monetary gains but attraction and successive competition for the attention of future investors who appreciate the 'stock value' associated with workers in general and with English in particular. In the case of JEEP, studying English through an aid project would appear to be potentially attractive to the students' potential investors. As evidence of this investment, a certificate of completion is given to students upon finishing the JEEP courses, a selling point that the project uses to convince the students to avail of it. This document is marketed as one which the students' potential employers can speculate on based on the perception of the 'stock value' of the students, especially as the language aid project is associated with the use of 'modern' methodology (e.g. CALL) donated by a foreign aid agency, and especially funded for the students of the Southern Philippines.

In this picture, USAID and the state invest in English language skills as a way of investing in the present and future value of the students. Specifically, for the students, it is an attempt to manage risk in an uncertain future they are told to confront and an active effort to attract future investors to bet on their potential. Akin to corporations who are anxiously attracting investors to fund their endeavors, students are also busily figuring out how to enhance their 'stock value' through various conducts and behaviors, in this case learning English, so they can convince potential investors that they are worthy investments. If the purpose of today's investments in English is not just immediate income but attracting investors, how might we describe English as capital?

Investment in English language skills today might be described as *speculative capital*. The term names the relation between the subjects and the investment they make in their human capital which is self-appreciating, often non-monetized, non-possessive and conjectural. At its core, the nature of this investment is *speculative* in that its goal is not just monetary gain but the appreciation of the student's human capital, measured primarily in partial estimates and holding no guarantee of future return. It is this speculative dimension of this investment that contributes further to the elusive promise of English. There are various features of the speculative value of English.

First, as seen in the JEEP project, investment in English skills today is not just about the desire to gain immediate income but, more importantly, an effort to enhance their human capital (Feher, 2009: 27), that is, the 'stock value' of the person or the future value of investments associated with the person. While money and increase in income still remain important motivations in learning English, enhancing the capital value attached to the person so that more investors would be attracted is a paramount concern. Indeed, in some cases, even if an investment will not lead to immediate monetary gain, one still makes the investment as long as it appreciates human capital. In some way, even if the investment in English does not yield an immediate benefit, the students or workers still invest in English if it means increasing their chances of getting the job in the future, being promoted, increasing their social prestige and being offered other opportunities (e.g. internships) that further maximize their value. Indeed, the *dividends* (the types of returns on investments) that one gets from his or her human capital cannot be limited to monetization but may also include gains in the form of favors, positive regard from peers or more opportunities for self-development. English skills are seen as a valuable addition to the *portfolio* of conducts and assets the student has. On the part of the employers as investors, a job applicant who has undergone language training supported by a USAID project appears to be a better investment and seems to hold more potential compared to someone who has not.

Second, the speculative nature of investments in English language today is also brought about by its corollary scheme of 'stock market valuation'. Akin to the valuation of corporations based on a range of tangibles and intangibles, today's human capital is also valuated in a speculative manner. How do we measure the enhancement of the human capital of a person? How do we measure the increase in the stock value of a person? For Feher (2009: 28), the answers of the neoliberal policies and discourses are an actor's *bankability*, a worker's *employability* and a person's *marketability* which are 'alleged', 'partial estimates of the value of human capital', 'crude speculations insofar as they are based on income'. No 'objective' algorithm is available or used for measuring the human capital of a person; it is based on tangibles such as a person's present income as much as it is depends on its speculator's guesses, beliefs and perceptions about the value of that human capital. In the case of JEEP, the stock value of a JEEP student may be perceived as increasing insofar as JEEP is seen from the outside as an important investment in the students' capital value. What is clear is that it is perceived as an English language teaching aid project with cutting edge CALL technology, designed and offered altruistically in the name of development in Mindanao. Conceived as an investment, JEEP could contribute to the employability of the students as perceived by the latter's future investors. Considering that the valuation of English today is done in rough estimates, this suggests that we might reconsider, if not give up, the idea that gains from English skills are always determined by objective criteria or measurements, because determining value in today's (stock) market is reduced to guesses, even reduced to child's play (Martin, 2002: 1).

Finally, there are no guarantees of return on investments in human capital. Feher (2009: 34) writes, 'neoliberal subjects do not exactly own their human capital; they [only] invest in it'. The relationship of the person to his or her human capital should be considered as one of speculation rather than ownership. Students can alter their human capital by enhancing it through various conducts and behaviors but they can never really sell it because there is never really a capital that can be sold. They just benefit from it by gaining dividends from their investments by other (indirect) means such as access to income, gaining additional opportunities for further training, gaining more friends and acquaintances and expanding their social networks. Nevertheless, they cannot sell their human capital because they do not own it. This makes return on every investment in English always speculative – that is, there are no monetary or non-monetary guaranteed gains from an investment because the rewards will be up to investors if they put their money, time and resources in the potential (the future value) of the person. Unlike selling or trading skills for wages in an exchange economy, the human capital – the capital value associated with the person – is not translatable to a specific monetary figure but is primarily meant for its speculators to see, perceive and make guesses about. Because there is no guarantee of return, investments in human capital and in English skills today is, in this sense, considered a risk. The students are betting on the future value of their English language skills in the hopes of achieving future gain. They spend on them and invest in them even if there is no guarantee of return and even if the possible gains depend on the people who will bet on their future value, their investors.

The contemporary neoliberal subject is not just morally burdened with the survival of the self but also the survival of the national economy. As Brown (2015: 37) writes, 'we are human capital not just for ourselves, but also for the firm, state, or post-national constellation of which we are members'. That is, today's human capital invests and works hard not just out of pleasure or self-interest but out of responsibility for the health of the economy and for contributing to the economic aspirations of the state. Within JEEP, students are made conscious that their self-investment needs to be viewed within the wider context of supporting economic growth and peace-building in Mindanao. For instance, on one occasion, US Undersecretary Burns told the students 'the JEEP Program strengthens the spirit of the US and Philippines to push for education as a means to improve the peace and development needs of your country' (US Undersecretary visits Cotabato, 2010). This linking of JEEP with the country's development also finds echoes in the screensaver of every JEEP computer unit in the lab collocating the logos of JEEP, USAID and the Mindanao Development Authority (MinDA), reminding students everyday of their moral burden to contribute to development. By virtue of being called 'human capital', the students have been effectively inserted and integrated into the development agenda of the state, private firms and the USAID.

The point here is not that students should never be integrated into the larger purposes of the state in pursuit of development, peace or any other worthy cause. Rather, what is regrettable is the integration of the students into the kind of development strategy chosen by the state: that of a neoliberal order where the survival of the individual depends on how well he or she invests and competes with others for the jobs that the private sector provides. This binding of the individual into this model of neoliberal development is what facilitates the tethering of the individual to the maneuvering of the state or the firms (Brown, 2015: 84). So, for example, massive layoffs, the defunding of other social services and other forms of austerity policies are easily justified by the state's 'mandate' to save the economy, say, by bailing out the banks and other financial institutions. In the process, an individual's well-being can be easily tossed aside. In short, citizen subjects easily become a *sacrifice*.

This is the tragedy of the speculative nature of investment in human capital: people are easily sacrificed to 'neoliberal capitalism as a life-sustaining sacred power' (Brown, 2015: 220). At present, this order narrowly means development pursued through the restoration of economic and state fiscal health. And like all sacrifice, it entails 'a destruction or deprivation of life in the name of sustaining or regenerating that order' (Brown, 2015: 215). At this point, students – now converted into human capital – lose their protection as citizens, the most important constituents of the state. Education and employment cease to become rights and are reduced to matters of prerogative for the state and the market depending on whether they contribute to the larger (economic) goals. As the state delegates its most important function (i.e. to take care of its citizens) to the market, the survival of the students, who would eventually become workers, is now tethered to the whims and exigencies of the market and to the current national purposes of the state which include economic growth, competitive positioning, credit rating and the management of fiscal constraints.

Historically, the Philippine state has sacrificed the welfare of its citizens to maintain its national economic goals: maintain its creditworthiness, ensure the flow of transnational capital into the country and attract foreign investments. First, since former President Corazon Aquino's administration, in the name of creditworthiness before its foreign lenders, the state has been prioritizing the repayment of its foreign debt resulting in the defunding of the physical, technical and educational infrastructure of the country. Second, the Philippine state has mainly relied on exporting its (English-speaking) citizens who are the drivers of the country's 'economy of sacrifice' which 'seeks to perpetuate the inward flow of transnational capital through the systematic and sustained deployment of productive economic agents' elsewhere in the world (Bautista, 2014: 3). The image of the overseas Filipino workers conveniently invokes the discourse of modern-day heroism and martyrdom when Filipino overseas workers suffer from dislocation or even death due to abuses in foreign shores. Third, consistent with its tendency to sacrifice the welfare of its citizens, in the early 1960s, the Philippine state brought down wages (the lowest in Asia) so Filipinos could compete with one another for already scarce jobs and so as to force more people to work for much lower compensation, a step designed to attract foreign investors into the country (Ofreneo, 1984: 488). Finally, what is more worrisome today is the same lack of interest in the protection of the citizens/workers shown by the private sector which is counted on most to provide jobs. In terms of job security, Ofreneo (2013: 435) claims that the already narrow Philippine job market ahead of the students is a continuously 'flexibilizing' one characterized by 'short term and unprotected temporary hiring arrangements', suggesting that Filipino students today are investing in a context replete with risk and uncertainty, more prominently in the service sector such as the call center-BPO sector which development initiatives such as JEEP are targeting.

Conclusion

The JEEP project shows how, in the Philippines today, the anxious investments in English language skills are driven by the need to compete for already scarce jobs. While these endeavors may lead to tangible immediate income in some circumstances, inherent in these investments today is their speculative nature: their preoccupation not just with income but with the enhancement of one's present and future value to attract investors whose decisions on whether to invest are based on conjectures rather than concrete tangible measurements. These partial estimates do not guarantee returns of investment for the subject and are, therefore, considered a risk. These investments can be further considered risky because the state can legitimately offer them as sacrifice to 'save the economy' such as in the case of austerity politics, a process consecrated by the moral burden that the state disseminates to its citizens and its citizens willingly accept when they signify themselves as human capital.

As long as ELT initiatives traffic under the sign of competition and are justified as preparation for a world where students need to invest just to compete, *inequalities* will always be generated. As Brown (2015: 64) reminds us: 'inequality is the premise and outcome of competition'. As ELT aid participates in the discourse of competition by invoking global competitiveness as justifications for language instruction, it is helpful to remember that in any competition some learners will triumph and some will not as a necessary and legitimate consequence. The thriving of some requires the shedding of many. And those who will not be able to compete will often come from the social classes who do not have the resources and time to (self)-invest (Park, 2011: 453).

With the admission by a few economists of the disaster that neoliberalism has wrought, a growing body of scholarship within applied linguistics has also started puncturing the ways in which neoliberalism has saturated the field and the ways in which it might be resisted. More generally, this offers an occasion for applied linguists to reflect on the theoretical and conceptual resources that the field borrows and inherits from other disciplines, foremost of which is the (neoliberal) social order that the field finds itself in. Any struggle against inequalities facilitated by English should put on its agenda the recognition that ELT, in general, and ELT aid, in particular, participates and even promotes this discourse of (global) competitiveness. This awareness of the field's imbrications should be the start of resistance and a cultivation of an opening to an alternative – whether it is the critical analysis of the mechanisms of the linguistic market to reproduce social inequalities (Park, 2011: 455) or the exploration of critical discourses in ELT such as the knowledge and dispositions for democratic citizenship (Kubota, 2011: 258). With the current speculative nature of English, one also needs to imagine new ways of valuing English or even perhaps ways of imagining the non-necessity of valuation itself, in an alternative social order where individuals do not need to compete and busily invest just to thrive.

References

Abinales, P. (2010) *Orthodox and History in the Muslim-Mindanao Narrative.* Quezon City: Ateneo de Manila University Press.

Appleby, R. (2010) *ELT, Gender and International Development.* Bristol: Multilingual Matters.

Bautista, J. (2014) An economy of sacrifice: Roman catholicism and transnational labor in the Philippines. *ARI Working Paper No. 218.* See www.ari.nus.edu.sg/pub/wps.htm (accessed 26 February 2014).

Bello, W., Docena, H., de Guzman, M. and Malig, M. (2009) *The Anti-Development State: The Political Economy of Permanent Crisis in the Philippines.* Manila: Anvil Publishing.

Brown, W. (2015) *Undoing the Demos: Neoliberalism's Stealth Revolution.* New York: Zone Books.

Davis, G. (2009) The rise and fall of finance and the end of the society of organizations. *The Academy of Management.* See http://webuser.bus.umich.edu/gfdavis/davis_09_AMP.pdf (accessed 19 April 2014).

Feher, M. (2009) Self-appreciation; or, the aspirations of human capital (I. Ascher, trans.). *Public Culture* 21 (1), 21–41 (original work published 2007).

GEM Completion Report January 2008 to December 2013 (n.d.) See http://www.louisberger.com/sites/default/files/GEM3_CompletionReportMagazine_Web-fnl.pdf (accessed 19 July 2015).

GEM3 Development Activity Approval Document (2006). See https://www.fbo.gov/index?s=opportunity&mode=form&id=10534c2d80c98909f492b53bd23464c6&tab=core&_cview=1 (accessed 27 July 2015).

Government of the Republic of the Philippines (2011) *Philippine Development Plan 2011–2016.* See http://www.neda.gov.ph/wp content/uploads/2013/10/pdprm2011-2016.pdf (accessed 27 July 2015).

Ibon Foundation (2011) *The Philippine Development Plan (PDP) 2011–2016: Social Contract With Whom?* See http://www.ibon.org/includes/resources/IBON_pdp2011-2016.pdf (accessed 27 July 2015).

JEEP Project in Zambo (2009) JEEP project in Zambo to improve English proficiency in key industries. News article, July 6. See http://balita.ph/2009/07/06/jeep-project-in-zambo-to-improve-english-proficiency-in-key-industries/ (accessed 25 February 2014).

Martin, R. (2002) *Financialization of Daily Life.* Philadelphia, PA: Temple University Press.

Ofreneo, R. (1984) Contradictions in export-led industrialisation: The Philippine experience. *Journal of Contemporary Asia* 40 (4), 485–495.

Ofreneo, R. (2013) Precarious Philippines: Expanding informal sector, flexibilizing labor market. *American Behavioral Scientist* 57 (4), 420–443.

Ong, A. (2006) *Neoliberalism as Exception: Mutations in Citizenship and Sovereignty.* Durham, NC: Duke University Press.

Padilla, A. (n.d.) US-PH 'Partnership for Growth': Greater economic intervention. Blog post. See https://arnoldpadilla.wordpress.com/2013/10/09/us-ph-partnership-for-growth-greater-economic-intervention/ (accessed 29 July 2015).

Park, J.S. (2011) The promise of English: Linguistic capital and the neoliberal worker in the South Korean job market. *International Journal of Bilingual Education and Bilingualism* 14 (4), 443–455.

Partnership for Growth (2011) Joint Country Action Plan. See http://photos.state.gov/libraries/manila/19452/pdfs/Philippines_PFG_JCAP_public_final_11-29-11.pdf (accessed 29 July 2015).

Petras, J. and Veltmeyer, H. (2004) Age of reverse aid: Neo-liberalism as catalyst of regression. In J. Pronk *et al.* (eds) *Catalysing Development? A Debate on Aid* (pp. 63–75). Malden, MA: Blackwell.

Phillipson, R. (1992) *Linguistic Imperialism.* Oxford: Oxford University Press.

Seargeant, P. and Erling, E.J. (2011) The discourse of 'English as a language for international development': Policy assumptions and practical challenges. In H. Coleman (ed.) *Dreams and Realities: Developing Countries and the English Language* (pp. 248–267). London: British Council.

Tadiar, N. (2013) Life-times of disposability within global neoliberalism. *Social Text* 31 (2), 19–46.

US Ambassador Kenney Inaugurates WMSU's JEEP (2009) News article, July 7. See http://wmsu.edu.ph/index-v09.php?news=159 (accessed 25 February 2014).

US Undersecretary visits Cotabato, leads in turnover of JEEP materials to government school (2010) News article, July 21. See http://balita.ph/2010/07/21/us-undersecretary-visits-cotabato-leads-in-turnover-of-jeep-materials-to-government-school/ (accessed 25 February 2014).

USAID/Philippines Country Development Cooperation Strategy 2012–2016 (n.d.). See http://www.usaid.gov/sites/default/files/documents/1861/CDC_Philippines_FY2012-FY2016.pdf (accessed 27 July 2015).

Widin, J. (2010) *Illegitimate Practices: Global English Language Education.* Bristol: Multilingual Matters.

Young, R. (2001) *Postcolonialism. An Historical Introduction.* Oxford: Blackwell Publishing.

8 Enterprising Migrants: Language and the Shifting Politics of Activation

Alfonso Del Percio and Sarah Van Hoof

Introduction

Foreign workers, especially so-called unskilled or low-skilled migrants (Vigouroux, 2015), have been greatly affected by the increase in unemployment caused by the current crisis of capitalism, and in many countries more so than native-born residents (OECD & European Union, 2015). Migrants are therefore a prime target of the politics of activation that has been central to labor market policies in many Western states (Demazière & Glady, 2011; Dermine & Durmont, 2014). 'Activation' can be conceived of as a cover term for the techniques of government (Foucault, 1994), deployed by local employment agencies and other actors, to get the unemployed off benefits and into work (Clasen & Clegg, 2006; Psacharopoulos & Schlotter, 2010). These techniques often take the shape of training or course programs, designed to equip the unemployed enrolled in them with sets of skills and norms of professional conduct that, once internalized and automatized, are supposed to help them raise their employability in a changing labor market (Allan, 2013, 2016; McHugh & Challinor, 2011). Language and communication training are typical ingredients in activation schemes for migrants, as the cause of their unemployment is often seen to reside in insufficient competence in the local or national languages of their host societies (Collett, 2011; Collett & Sitek, 2008; Demazière & Glady, 2011; Flubacher, 2014; McHugh & Challinor, 2011; Vigouroux, 2015).

Traditionally, activation schemes aim at activating people as waged workers. But recently, European states, encouraged by the supranational organizations that inform and influence their labor policies, such as the European Union (EU), the Organization of Economic Co-operation and Development (OECD), the World Bank and the International Labor Organization, seem to be increasingly investing in self-employment as a strategy for fostering macro-economic growth and job creation (see e.g. BMAS & OECD, 2010; European Commission, 2012; IDOS, 2014; OECD, 2006, 2015). Also for furthering migrants' professional integration into their host societies, entrepreneurship is increasingly seen as key, and states have therefore devised activation programs to promote and facilitate entrepreneurship among this group.

The aim of this chapter is to investigate how this increased investment in the activation of migrants through entrepreneurial education takes place on the ground. We do so by focusing on an entrepreneurial training scheme organized for unemployed migrants in Italy, where unemployment rates in general and migrant unemployment rates in particular, are among the highest in the EU (OECD & EU, 2015).[1] The specific case we discuss here is a training scheme organized by an Italian social cooperative, Legame,[2] which is located in the city of Rome and is mandated by the Italian state to support refugees and other migrants in their professional integration. This training scheme was designed specifically for migrants who wanted to become entrepreneurs in the agricultural sector and was followed closely by the first author of this chapter when it was implemented for the first time, from the summer of 2014 until the summer of 2015. The data we report on in this chapter consist of ethnographic observations of the training; semi-structured as well as casual conversations conducted with the actors designing, giving and receiving the training; and institutional and legislative documents entextualizing the forms of expertise that the training drew on.

This chapter is structured as follows: We first discuss the role of entrepreneurship in current active labor market policies and document the ways in which the EU and the Italian state have invested in entrepreneurial education for migrants. Second, we look into the way in which Legame has put this policy into practice, by focusing on the different interests associated with this entrepreneurial training, the rationales defining the way it was conceptualized and the tensions that Legame's strategic focus on entrepreneurial education caused. Third, we will describe the knowledge that the migrants participating in this training were asked to internalize and the role that language and communication assume for turning migrants into agricultural entrepreneurs. Finally, we inquire into who profited from the training and highlight the circumstances and logics determining the convertibility of the acquired knowledge into forms of professional integration.

Activating Entrepreneurs

The investment in entrepreneurship as a key strategy for the insertion of unemployed migrants into the labor market needs to be interpreted within a gradually changing politics of labor. The preceding three to four decades already saw a transition from a Keynesian welfare politics, aimed at social well-being through full employment and a welfare system that guaranteed equitable distribution of opportunities and wealth, to a deregulated, neoliberal model counting on market competition and individual freedom to deliver individual and collective well-being (Allan & McElhinny, 2016; Del Percio & Flubacher, this volume; Harvey, 2005). The activation schemes that many nation states have since developed are part of a labor policy urging and in many cases obliging unemployed individuals to engage in a constant active search for employment and to upgrade their skills through continuous education and vocational training (Wrana, 2009). Such activation schemes assume that professional inclusion is the workers' choice, i.e. it is dependent on their willingness to continuously optimize and flexibilize their work capacities through the acquisition and internalization of the tokens of knowledge and attitudes demanded by a changing capitalism (Duchêne, 2016; Flubacher et al., 2016). Indeed, the constant self-regulation of the professional body has been said to be the only viable way for the individual to remain competitive in an unstable and precarious labor market (Sennett, 1998), i.e. to get access to employment, promotion and pay raises as well as to be reallocated and reeducated in case of unemployment (Fraser, 2003; Psacharopoulos & Schlotter, 2010). Activation schemes have therefore often been identified as textbook cases of neoliberal governmentality: they address individuals as entrepreneurial selves, who should actively create and seize opportunities for their own self-care, and invest in the enhancement of their human capital, for their own benefit as well as that of society at large.

The current crisis of capitalism does not seem to have led policy makers to question the neoliberal rationalities underpinning the politics of activation, but only seems to have intensified these neoliberal rationalities, as the current investment in activation into entrepreneurship marks a further shift from a politics of *employability of the self* to a politics of *self-employability*. The neoliberal maxim of the entrepreneurial self (Foucault, 1994; Martín Rojo, 2015) now emerges not just as a disciplining technology projecting the logics of flexibilization and efficiency that have characterized post-Fordist businesses onto the body of the unemployed worker. Rather, unemployed individuals are now not metaphorically but practically interpellated (Althusser, 1970) as entrepreneurs in activation schemes set up to stimulate self-employment.

Activation into entrepreneurship has become one of the central goals in the labor market policy recommendations that have in recent years been formulated by several supranational organizations, among which is the EU. In 2012, the European Commission, the executive body responsible for proposing legislation and implementing decisions in the EU, defined a new economic agenda, the Europe 2020 Strategy, in which entrepreneurship was seen as a crucial means to bring the continent back to sustainable growth and higher levels of employment after the economic crisis (European Commission, 2012). Alongside the categories of 'women', 'seniors' and 'unemployed, in particular young people', migrants were considered to represent an underexploited entrepreneurial potential that member states should capitalize upon in their efforts to revitalize their national economies (European Commission, 2012). The Commission therefore developed guidelines for integrating entrepreneurial training into the curricula of its member states' educational systems and provided funds for the development of training activities preparing 'people to be responsible and enterprising individuals' and 'to develop the skills, knowledge, and attitudes necessary to achieve the goals they set out for themselves', all this in order to be 'more employable' (European Commission, 2012) and thus to contribute to the 'well-being and prosperity of European societies' (European Commission, 2009).

The Italian state has used these European funds for entrepreneurial education to set up activation programs in several sectors, including the food and restaurant industry and the telecommunications and IT sector. One of the most significant entrepreneurial initiatives sponsored by EU funding was a project called 'Support, Orientation, Training, Entrepreneurialism for Migrants in Agriculture' (SOFIIA [Sostegno, Orientamento, Formazione, Imprenditoria per Immigrati in Agricultura]), intended to support young unemployed migrants motivated to launch a business in the farming industry. In Italy, access to agricultural entrepreneurship is regulated by Confagricultura, the cooperative organization that represents the interests of the Italian farming industry in national and local state institutions, certifies the quality of Italian agricultural products and issues the obligatory professional certificates required for establishing oneself as a self-employed farmer. SOFIIA's objective was to provide aspiring migrant farmers with the knowledge and competence necessary to meet Confagricultura's standards and to enable them to acquire the obligatory certificate.

Italy's investment in the activation of migrants in the domain of agricultural entrepreneurship was intended to simultaneously address several problems and concerns. First and foremost, it was a response to the phase of economic uncertainty that the Italian agricultural sector is currently going through. Agriculture was seen as an ideal site for experimentation with migrant entrepreneurialism, given the difficulty of the Italian farming industry to compete in increasingly deregulated global markets, the aging of the farming community (with 64% of farmers currently over 65, see INEA, 2013) and the lack of enthusiasm of young Italians for working in an industry that is usually associated with hard labor, low wages and isolation from modernity and urban life. The experiment would moreover most likely be acceptable to that part of the voting public which is averse to devoting resources to migrants. These voters would probably have disapproved of similar measures in other sectors, which would have been more likely to create a new elite of migrant entrepreneurs and thus to challenge the relations of domination between Italians and migrants in Italian society. In the context of its integration policy, Italy's investment in migrant entrepreneurialism was at the same time a way of showing to the migrant communities, the Italian population and international humanitarian organizations that the state was genuinely concerned about furthering the socioeconomic emancipation of newcomers. Finally, if these educational programs were said to help migrants in their professional integration, they could also be seen as strategies to control and discipline migrants, to guarantee security and public order and as such, to counter the perceptions of illegality and insecurity that the presence of migrants is usually associated with in dominant discourses in contemporary Italy.

The Italian state administration did not itself develop the entrepreneurial training. In line with its policy of outsourcing its welfare (Muehlebach, 2012), the state issued a call for projects, asking Italian non-governmental organizations (NGOs), social cooperatives and other private corporations to propose entrepreneurial training programs that could be financed through SOFIIA. In 2014, Legame, a social cooperative supporting migrants and refugees' professional integration in Rome, was granted part of the SOFIIA funds to conduct entrepreneurial training in 2015 in Lazio, the region hosting the largest number of migrants in Italy. The cooperative's project consisted of a three-phase program. In the first phase, suitable candidates were recruited for the training program; during the second phase, the selected unemployed candidates went through a series of theoretical and practical training modules; in the third and final phase, a selected number of participants were supported in the creation of a business. Alfonso closely followed all three phases of this program from July 2014 until August 2015. The following sections present some of his ethnographic findings.

Turning Migrants into Agricultural Entrepreneurs

Legame has been developing activities to support migrants' integration in the Italian labor market for over a decade now. The cooperative provides job orientation services, information on qualification and recognition of credentials, information on locally available vocational training opportunities and support in writing CVs and job applications and in interacting with public and private job placement services. Supported by national and European funds, Legame has also organized vocational training and internships for migrants in the tourism and healthcare sectors. Until recently, the training and internships were addressed to recently arrived migrants from sub-Saharan Africa, the Middle East, North Africa, Pakistan and Bangladesh, and oriented to jobs as dish washers, servants, nannies, construction workers or cleaners. These forms of so-called low-skilled or unskilled employment are seen to be the most easily accessible for migrants in the job market. In one of the first conversations that Alfonso had with Susanna, Legame's director, she explained that this focus on low-skilled or unskilled employment was in her view the organization's main weakness. She feared that by exclusively focusing on these low-wage and highly precarious jobs, Legame would contribute to reproducing the positions of socioeconomic subalternity that it wants to challenge.[3] The management had therefore recently decided that the organization would continue to provide the orientation and information services it had been offering for many years and would still finance internships, but would from now on invest more in projects promoting migrant entrepreneurialism, which, according to her, would create the conditions for social mobility and professional emancipation.

Many of the migrants that Legame was working with already had extensive experience in the farming industry, both in their home countries, where many of them had been running a farm or had been employed in farming, and in Italy itself, where many had been employed as seasonal workers, often under conditions of severe labor exploitation. According to Susanna, training migrants as agricultural entrepreneurs would allow them to capitalize on their skills, become their own employers and escape the precarious conditions under which they were currently often forced to work.[4] However, not all members of the team of project officers mandated with the design and planning of the training were as optimistic about the project as Legame's management. Antonella, a senior project officer who had contributed to the design of the training, argued that it was 'a mission impossible', given the migrants' lack of financial resources, their lack of professional networks and connections, their scarce linguistic competence and their poor knowledge of the Italian bureaucratic system.[5] She was convinced that for the Italian authorities the politics of entrepreneurialism was a way to avert responsibility for the integration of newcomers, which under the current economic crisis and the scarce availability of employment was difficult to manage. The investment in entrepreneurship, Antonella argued, was to make the migrants as well as the Italian public believe that if the migrants tried hard enough they would succeed in their entrepreneurial projects, thus rendering the migrants themselves responsible for their potentially failed integration.[6]

Despite these tensions and the officers' low confidence in the actual emancipatory power of this investment, Legame decided that it was at least worth trying to develop an entrepreneurial program. Indeed, as Susanna put it, even if SOFIIA helped just one or two migrants to start a business, the cooperative would consider the project a success. For those migrants who would not be able to start up an entrepreneurial project, Legame would find another solution, such as an internship or a job on one of the farms in the region or in another economic sector. The training, she argued, would in any case provide the migrants with skills that would help them work on their professional selves and render them more flexible and desirable on the Italian labor market. Finally, Susanna explained that, for an organization like Legame that relies on public funding and hence on every call for projects that national or European authorities launch, boycotting SOFIIA because of ideological and moral reasons would endanger the organization's financial stability. Given that national and supranational sponsors would currently mainly invest in entrepreneurial education, her organization had to follow this trend in order to secure its own long-term survival, its services and projects and the positions of its own employees. But this did not imply that Legame merely executed a policy of economic integration dictated by Rome or Brussels. Once awarded, Susanna explained, these national and European projects could always be adapted to Legame's agenda and to participants' needs.[7]

From Manual to Intellectual Work

In January 2015, Legame launched its first SOFIIA training for 30 migrants interested in agricultural entrepreneurship. The training was held on the cooperative's premises located in the working-class peripheries of Rome. It lasted for six months until the end of June 2015 and was given partly by Legame's coaches and partly by external experts who were collaborating with Legame or working for other cooperatives active in the domain of agriculture. These experts had been selected by Legame's director because of their experience with teaching future agricultural entrepreneurs. They were to provide the participating migrants with the knowledge and competence necessary to successfully launch an entrepreneurial project in agriculture and to help them meet the standards imposed by Confagricultura that certified the training and provided the diplomas. In addition, the training needed to comply with EU guidelines (European Commission, 2009), in order to be eligible for European funding. On the basis of these guidelines, pertaining to both the structure and the content of the training, Legame devised a program consisting of the following eight (one- or two-week long) training modules:

Module 1 – Civic education and EU law [Educazione civica e diritto del UE]
Module 2 – Technical terminology of the agricultural sector in Italian [Terminologia tecnica in lingua italiana del settore tecnico-agricolo]
Module 3 – The agricultural business and its stakeholders [L'impresa agricola e il contesto di riferimento]
Module 4 – Management of an agricultural business [La pianificazione dell'impresa agricola e la Multifunzionalità]
Module 5 – Bookkeeping and budgeting in an agricultural business [Contabilità e bilancio dell'impresa agricola]
Module 6 – Workplace safety in agriculture [La sicurezza sul lavoro in agricoltura]
Module 7 – Promotion of agricultural products [La promozione e valorizzazione dei prodotti agricoli]
Module 8 – National and European public funds [Finanziamenti pubblici nazionale e comunitari][8]

These modules reflect the fact that agriculture is one of the many professions where physical labor has become increasingly intertwined with immaterial labor (Boutet, 2001a, 2001b; Del Percio & Duchêne, 2015; Dlaske et al., 2016; Duchêne, 2009; Duchêne, in press; Duchêne & Flubacher, 2015; Gee et al., 1996; Heller, 2003, 2010; Kraft, 2015; Urciuoli & LaDousa, 2013). Being a self-employed farmer not only requires the traditional practical skills but also knowledge of the administrative procedures for starting a company, the ability to draft a business plan, insight into the principles of accounting, commercial law and tax law, a marketing instinct and awareness of business ethics and social responsibility. Such skills (Urciuoli, 2008) in turn require advanced linguistic proficiency levels, including high-level literacy skills. The training was conceptualized accordingly: while it was presupposed that the migrants already had sufficient knowledge of agricultural techniques and had mastered the necessary practical skills to apply them, it was knowledge of the legislative and bureaucratic aspects of farming and the communicative habitus necessary to handle those aspects that these migrants were seen to lack. As a consequence, the training program, which would be taught entirely in Italian, was highly theoretical in nature, comprised a lot of administrative, legal and technical jargon and aimed at familiarizing participants with highly specialized, abstract and complex communicative genres and registers. This had palpable consequences for the selection of participants for the training.

Initially, the project officers feared that most of the migrants they normally targeted would not be able to successfully complete an educational program that required such advanced proficiency in Italian. As Antonella explained, normally Legame would first have informed all unemployed migrants in its database about the training and then have mobilized its vast network of NGOs, reception centers and employment agencies serving migrants in order to identify suitable candidates.[9] However, in this specific case, the organization decided to recruit a number of unemployed South American migrants – mainly from Peru, Chile and Ecuador – who had used the services of Legame in the past and who had been employed in the agricultural industries around Rome. In addition, Legame recruited a dozen laborers from India, Pakistan and the Middle East, all of whom had worked as seasonal workers in the South Italian tomato industry. Not only did these candidates have experience in the agricultural sector and the motivation to run a farm, but they were also imagined to have acquired the communicative competence necessary to follow this training in the years that they had spent in Italy. Their linguistic competence was tested in recruitment interviews, during which migrants were asked to speak about their work experience in their home country and in Italy. These accounts were considered reliable indicators of their linguistic proficiency levels.

The focus on agricultural entrepreneurship implied targeting a specific audience, and by implication, excluding a considerable section of Legame's usual audience from admission to this activation program. In addition to experience in the agricultural sector, the main criterion for participation or exclusion was linguistic: the newly arrived, often socially and economically marginalized migrants who had not yet had the opportunity to acquire enough linguistic skills to be competitive on the formal or informal labor market were excluded from the forms of visibility and capital that entrepreneurial education was promised to come with. No recently arrived migrants from sub-Saharan Africa were accepted, their linguistic competence being estimated too low for this training. In addition to language, other criteria were used in the selection process. No women were recruited for this specific activation program because it was assumed they would be more suitable for participation in activation schemes preparing for (traditionally feminized) work in care, cleaning or tourism. Finally, no one over the age of 45 was accepted into the program, since the European funding that SOFIIA drew on was mainly directed to young aspiring entrepreneurs between the ages of 25 and 40. In sum, although Legame's new focus on a type of professional activation demanding high literacy skills may have been intended as an ambitious strategy, setting the bar high in terms of achieving emancipation and empowerment, in practice it contributed to legitimizing the production of new forms of difference as well as of existing gendered and racialized hierarchizations within the community of migrant workers that Legame was working with, as the new focus excluded newly arrived, illiterate, female and elderly migrants.

This created new tensions in the team of project officers that had designed and organized the training, since the redefinition of the target audience meant renouncing the organization's original mission to support those members of the migrant community who were considered most vulnerable on the job market. Still, project officer Laura deemed the choice justified. As she explained, the admission of participants with limited competence in Italian would have been frustrating for the participants themselves, who would have hardly been able to follow the class and would have had little chance at acquiring the certificate of agricultural entrepreneurship necessary for starting up an agricultural business. Furthermore, she explained, having to teach in front of an audience of learners unable to understand or reproduce the provided knowledge would have been equally frustrating for the instructors.[10] Finally, jeopardizing the program's chances for success would also threaten Legame's position as a beneficiary for funding, as the SOFIIA grant came with an obligation to produce results. Indeed, as Legame's director Susanna explained, the agreement with the Ministry of Agriculture and Food, the Italian ministry responsible for SOFIIA, included Legame's guarantee that participants would regularly attend the training sessions and be able to profit from the acquired knowledge. If these criteria were not met, Legame would have to reimburse part of the funds to the ministry and would lose credibility for future public calls.[11]

In sum, the recruitment of participants was governed by a rationale going beyond the mission and values of the social cooperative. Migrants' conditions of access to the entrepreneurial training were rather at the intersection of political-economic interests and practical necessities: the politics of integration and economic development pursued by the EU and the Italian state, the logic of accountability and profit maximization governing the subcontracting of SOFIIA funds, the professional protectionism conducted by Confagricultura through the attribution of professional diplomas and certificates and the interests of the appointed instructors, who preferred to be able to have a stimulating conversation with the participants.

Learning How to Communicate

In the preparatory meetings preceding the training program, coaches were instructed to take into account the fact that participants, although they were thought to speak and read Italian fluently, still had less than native-like proficiency in the language. While presenting the list of candidates participating in the training activities to the instructors, Antonella explained to them that they needed to pay extra care to 'make sure that every participant would be able to follow the content of the classes'. She added that their task was to work on that proficiency with a focus on sector-specific linguistic skills.[12] As a consequence, the training in practice largely amounted to familiarizing the participants with normative, codified registers and communicative practices and teaching them to adapt their own communicative practices accordingly.

In Module 2, for instance, focusing on Italian agricultural terminology, instructor Giacomo provided the participants with a handout containing a list of 'difficult but important words and their definitions' related to the topic of irrigation. It contained 24 items, including terms like *hydrometeors* [idrometeore], *pedogenesis* [pedogenesi], *surfactants* [tensioattivi] and *formulation* [formulazione]. Giacomo was an anthropologist teaching the history of scientific terminology at one of the major Italian universities, and had contributed to the compilation of a larger multilingual glossary on irrigation in agriculture for the World Food Organization. He had based the handout he distributed to the participants on this glossary but had deliberately chosen not to use glossaries in the migrants' mother tongues, even though there were versions of the document available in most of the native languages of the participants. Instead, he had chosen to provide them with the Italian document, albeit in a shortened and simplified version, 'because the original glossary [was] very long and technical and [did] not suit the linguistic competence and agricultural knowledge of these migrants'. Giacomo considered knowledge of the Italian terms crucial, he told Alfonso, because 'learning the Italian language of agricultural business makes sure that participants speak and sound like a professional Italian agricultural entrepreneur'.[13] Within this line of reasoning, mastery of the words listed in the above-mentioned handout indexes proficiency in the register of 'Italian agricultural speech' and becomes iconic of professionalism and expertise, recognizable to the public of Italian agricultural entrepreneurs and of stakeholders. Proficiency in this register was, in other words, imagined to lead to recognition as a legitimate member of an imagined community of Italian agricultural entrepreneurs and to facilitate access to professional inclusion. In order to practice their proficiency in this register, the migrants did exercises in class to help them memorize the different concepts. Giacomo encouraged them to test each other's capacity to use these terms in conversations about agriculture and irrigation, urged them to practice the pronunciation of the terms at home or during breaks and provided them with the web addresses of Italian agricultural magazines. Reading those would help them to develop a sensitivity for the idiomatic use of these concepts 'by [native] Italian agricultural entrepreneurs'.[14]

Along the same lines, Module 4 was dedicated to the functioning and management of a business. Luca, the business consultant in charge of this module, provided the participants with instructions for communicating and selling their business idea to sponsors and stakeholders. Considerable attention was paid to the production of a business plan, which, Luca explained, ought to make explicit the entrepreneur's capacity to formulate clear and realistic entrepreneurial objectives, to allocate resources in an efficient and sustainable way, to identify entrepreneurial risks and to understand the conditions of the market in which he or she would operate. Therefore, participants were taught to structure their plan on the basis of the following questions which were displayed on a slide that Luca projected on the wall of the training room:

(1) What are your personal aims or those of your family? [Quali sono i vostri scopi personali e familiari?]
(2) What is the vision of your enterprise? (Definition of the mission) [Quale vision avete della vostra azienda? (Definizione della missione)]
(3) What are the objectives of your enterprise? How do you want to pursue these objectives? [Quali sono i vostri obiettivi aziendali? Come pensate di conseguire tali obiettivi?]
(4) What is the strategy that you want to pursue? At which point are we at the moment? Where do we want to get? How do we want to get there? [Qual è la strategia che intendiamo seguire? A che punto siamo? Dove vogliamo arrivare? In che modo intendiamo arrivarci?]
(5) What is the financial investment that we have to provide, where will we get the necessary financing and how do we plan to reimburse the

financing? [Qual è l'impegno finanziario che dobbiamo prevedere, da dove intendiamo prendere i finanziamenti necessari e in che modo intendiamo restituire tali finanziementi?]

For every component in this architecture Luca summed up the elements it needed to contain and the criteria it needed to fulfill. The vision, for instance, needed to 'provide information, but also be a source of inspiration; be precise, but not too limiting; be realistic, quantifiable, flexible and adaptable; take into account the clients and other stakeholders interested in the enterprise, such as the staff, the investors and other possible co-participants; identify a defined period of time; and be easily comprehensible' [fornire informazioni, ma essere anche fonte d'ispirazione; essere abbastanza particolareggiata, ma non eccessivamente limitante; essere realistica, quantificabile, flessibile e adattabile; prendere in considerazione i client e altri operatori interessati all'azienda, quali il personale, gli investitori e altri eventuali copartecipanti; individuare un periodo di tempo definito; essere facilmente comprensibile].

The assumption underpinning this module was that 'linguistic clarity, argumentative structure, textual cohesion, and, more generally, the way such a document is written' would 'say a lot about the consistency and feasibility of the ideas and projects' represented by a business plan. Hence, learning to write a convincing business plan, Luca explained to the participants, is not only a way to 'order one's ideas about a future entrepreneurial project' but also to indicate that 'behind a business project stands an entrepreneur that is prepared, professional and trustworthy'.[15] Thus, in Luca's line of reasoning, similar to Giacomo's in Module 2, a 'well-written' business plan becomes an icon of the solidity of both the business idea it entextualizes and of the person who has produced it (see Irvine and Gal [2000] for a detailed explanation of these semiotic processes). 'Expert discourse' stands for 'professional agricultural entrepreneurship' and is thus considered to greatly increase one's chances of success in front of an audience of creditors or investors.

In order to practice these skills, groups of participants were asked to draft a fictitious business plan using the textual components provided by the instructor. Excerpts from their drafts were discussed and commented on in class. Fellow participants were asked to express their opinions about the quality of the proposed projects and to suggest alternative, more convincing ways of formulating these ideas. For each plan, Luca gave suggestions for rendering it textually more coherent, argumentatively more solid and linguistically and terminologically more appropriate to the genre of a business plan.

Also migrants' ability to orally communicate about their product to an audience of consumers was trained. According to instructor and marketing expert Maria Elena, a common cause for migrants' business failure is the entrepreneurs' incapacity to orally perform expertise in their everyday interactions and negotiations with stakeholders. She explained that since migrants have often been socialized in cultural contexts with different value systems, learning how to communicate not just verbally but also nonverbally would help to avoid misunderstandings and potential conflict in interactions with business partners, employees, sponsors and clients.[16] In the module dedicated to the acquisition of marketing and promotional skills, future entrepreneurs were therefore asked to become aware of their body language, in order to better be able to control it. Special attention was paid to facial expressions that according to Maria Elena 'were often the cause of intercultural misunderstandings that could disturb the business interaction and lead to failure and conflict'. She had prepared a set of practical exercises that would help 'to better and more readily understand these types of body signals'. In one of the exercises, she asked the participants to describe a number of pictures, drawn from works of art that – according to Maria Elena – are widely known in Italian society (see Figure 8.1) and represented different smiles.[17]

In this task, the participants had to reflect on what emotions these smiles would express and to attribute to these pictures one of the following feelings: 'sympathy, neutrality, detachment, hate, resentment, curiosity, joy, sadness, rage, pain, bitterness, serenity, indifference, love' [simpatia, neutralità, freddezza, odio, rancore, curiosità, gioia, tristezza, rabbia, dolore, amarezza, serenità, indifferenza, amore]. Then, they were to discuss in groups which emotions they had attributed to which picture and why. Finally, Maria Elena asked the migrants to practice their own facial

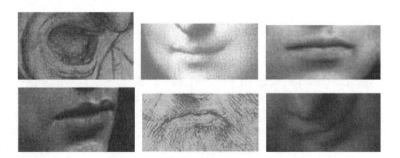

Figure 8.1 Exercise on facial expressions distributed to participants

expressions by performing these types of emotions and to give each other feedback about the communicative effects of their smiles and laughter.

The lists of words that the migrant had to memorize, the instructions for writing a business plan and the reflections on non-verbal communication were all part of a larger set of training activities providing learners with bits and pieces of pre-structured discourse or behavioral scripts, intended to support these individuals in their performance of a professional self (Cameron, 2000; Del Percio, 2016; Lorente, 2010, 2012). These aspects of the training modules drew heavily on academic knowledge about intercultural communication that, according to the instructors, is a default part of the training that social workers or vocational teachers nowadays receive. All of them were familiar with different communication models, like the Shannon–Weaver model and Jakobson's model, and now tried to integrate these models in the training activities for the migrants. The aim, they explained to Alfonso, was to sensitize the migrants to the cultural differences between their home countries and their Italian host society as well as between the different social and professional contexts they would move through. The training thus implicitly entertained the assumption that all migrants shared one common 'foreign' cultural background, erasing the potential cultural differences within this group. All the modules described above hinged on the rationale that by internalizing the registers and forms of conduct that the organizers considered iconic of expertise, seriousness and cultural appropriateness, these migrants would learn to speak and act like credible, professional, Italian-like entrepreneurs. Acquiring this communicative habitus would prevent the migrants from stigmatization on the basis of their foreign background and different skin color and would further their acceptance as legitimate members of the Italian agricultural community.

The migrants themselves quickly internalized this logic. Most of them tried hard to acquire the instructed communicative competence and techniques. They took notes of the technical concepts and tried to find a corresponding term in their own language, sometimes with the help of dictionaries that they had brought from home. Some took pictures of the slides presenting the structure of a good business plan. They repeatedly asked the coaches for help to linguistically and stylistically improve the business plan that the coaches had asked them to develop at home. They also participated actively in role plays, in which they simulated sales conversations between producers of organic vegetables and potential consumers and they eagerly commented on each other's body language and facial expressions. Most of them still complained regularly about the tough job market and the difficulty in getting access to services, certificates and information from the municipality and other state authorities. Many of them had already tried to secure funding for micro-entrepreneurial projects such as stands at fairs or markets and had experienced difficulties in doing so. But none of them overtly contested the assumption that improving their communicative competence would help them to get access to entrepreneurship and socioeconomic independence. On the contrary, in the short evaluation statement that they were asked to produce at the end of the training, most of the migrants highlighted the usefulness of the acquired communicative skills and stressed the importance of having learned the techniques to produce an appealing and professional business plan.

To be clear, we do not want to dispute that mastery of sector-specific registers and genres would be an asset for anyone wishing to become an agricultural entrepreneur, just as the knowledge of the local networks of distribution and the insight into the bureaucratic requirements, regulations and procedures that the training provided to the migrants would most likely prove useful to them. Nor do we want to contest the fact that certain forms of speech are considered more prestigious than others and are icons of specific qualities, personae and positions, and that the mastery of those prestigious registers will most likely facilitate speakers' access to the positions of expertise that these tokens of speech are associated with. But our ethnographic data show that such immaterial resources are not the only condition regulating these migrants' access to self-employment. In the Legame case, moreover, these could be compensated for, as we will see in a moment. Much less easy to remedy or circumvent, however, is the lack of access to the necessary material resources: seed capital, loans, agricultural equipment and an infrastructure where production can take place and products can be stored.

Indeed, at the end of the entrepreneurial training, all 30 candidates who had been accepted into the program received the diploma allowing them to start up their own agricultural business. Admittedly, some of the migrants had had serious difficulties following the training activities and coaches acknowledged that their graduation was more a way to reward their attendance and motivation than a certification of their actual knowledge and skills. But the participants could count on the continued support of the coaches, who had agreed to support these projects in their first phase of development and to help them overcome the challenges posed by the Italian bureaucracy. Some interesting entrepreneurial ideas had emerged during the training, and two or three teams of migrants were particularly motivated to transform their vision into a concrete business project. Still, almost a year after the end of the entrepreneurial training none of these projects had been launched. As a Legame officer explained, the creation of the businesses had been delayed because of a lack of financial resources and difficulties in getting access to public or private funds. In times of financial crisis, banks and public sponsors were not willing to invest in start-ups they considered too risky, because they lacked seed capital and did not have any material assets (machines and tools) available to them, nor did they have the necessary network within the community of local farmers. Therefore, sponsors did not consider the migrants' projects eligible for financing. In addition, the city of Rome and the region of Lazio did not keep the promise they had made at an early stage of the SOFIIA trainings, to provide the future entrepreneurs with public land that they could cultivate and to give them access to public infrastructure that they could use for their projects.

Clearly, the main objectives of SOFIIA – enabling migrants to create the conditions for their own employment – had not been met. One might expect that the parties involved would see this as a failure of SOFIIA and of the entrepreneurial rationale it drew upon. But this did not seem to be the case. In the final meeting, where Legame's directors met with representatives of the Ministry of Agriculture and Food in order to take stock of this educational experiment, the governmental authorities expressed their satisfaction with the training activities and the achieved results. They explained that at this point of the process it would be the migrants' responsibility to capitalize on the knowledge and skills acquired. They acknowledged that at this specific moment of crisis, banks and other funding bodies would be reluctant to invest in such high-risk enterprises but were convinced that a better conjuncture and the further development of their communicative and entrepreneurial skills would help them to get access to funds and realize their entrepreneurial ideas in the future. The representatives of Legame were equally convinced that activation programs such as this need to be judged not just on the basis of immediate success or failure of an entrepreneurial project but as part of the continuous self-improvement that these migrants need to do, in order to become independent and emancipated members of Italian society. Finally, the state authorities and Legame's representatives argued that the program would help the migrants not to give up hope for a better future, despite their difficulties in getting access to employment. In this view, schemes such as this are pre-emptive measures: busying the migrants with useful training would keep them from taking on informal or illegal labor, as well as prevent them from falling prey to depression, alcoholism or drug abuse.[18]

None of the migrants interpreted the fact that no enterprise had been launched yet as a failure either. To the contrary, after the end of the training module, most of them explained to Alfonso that they had not expected that their participation in this training would immediately lead to an entrepreneurial project in the first place. Most of them saw the training and the acquired certificate as a way to become more desirable on the job market. In a context in which work opportunities are scarce, one of them explained, having an additional diploma increases the possibility of employment. In other words, many had internalized the value of cultural capital in Italian society and saw the training not as an avenue for entrepreneurship, but as an avenue for employment in the formal labor sector. For others, the participation in a vocational training was a way to demonstrate their willingness to actively integrate into Italian society which they hoped would help them to get recognized as good citizens. Some also hoped it would help them get access to further subsidies and support – and in this way endorsed a rationale entirely at odds with the activation logic. Still others explained that the training module was a good way to meet people and to get access to forms of social contact and conviviality. None of the migrants openly expressed their disappointment for not having been able to launch an entrepreneurial project.

In sum, rather than completely erasing the existence of structural impediments to entrepreneurship, organizers as well as participants acknowledged that the present economic climate rendered starting up a business extremely difficult. Nevertheless, to a large extent, all parties involved still reproduced the logic of entrepreneurial activation, subscribing to an 'investor ethos', as Allan (2016) calls it, a logic of continuously investing in one's human capital in order to increase one's chances at (self-)employment, if not immediately, then in the future – even if the actual future return on investment is highly uncertain.

Conclusion

In order to understand the social and political meaning of entrepreneurial activation and the role that language and communication play in such practices, we need to anchor them in the multiple, and sometimes contradictory, logic, interests and rationales entertained by the different actors investing in, organizing, conducting and consuming these trainings. Among them are authorities' interests in presenting an image of humanitarianism, progressiveness and a genuine care for the integration of underprivileged groups on the one hand, and the necessity to guarantee security and public order by taking the migrants off the streets and providing them with useful activities on the other hand. These state concerns intersected in our case study with a social cooperative's wish to foster forms of social mobility and empowerment, within the limits of the existing funding schemes and political agendas imposed by the Italian state and the EU, and with migrants' desire for socioeconomic inclusion, independence and access to networks and forms of social capital that would help them overcome the challenges posed by the fluctuating labor market.

Within this context, language and communication, and more particularly specific forms of speech enregistered (Agha, 2007) as entrepreneurial talk, were conceived of as resources that would lead to inclusion, independence, freedom, participation and emancipation. Indeed, in a context in which structural impediments were perceived by the institutional actors involved as 'given', i.e. as currently immutable conditions, learning to speak like a professional entrepreneur was constructed by both the social cooperative and the state authorities as the only possible domain of intervention and agency. Linguistic and communicative competence were not only seen as resources that would help the migrants jump through the bureaucratic hoops that come with the institutionalization of small-scale entrepreneurialism but were also considered necessary forms of cultural capital, enabling migrants to present professional, desirable and acceptable selves that would get recognized as legitimate members of an imagined community of Italian entrepreneurs and as reliable beneficiaries for loans or financial investment.

In light of the absence of immediate results, however, the activation program could ultimately be seen to boil down to a tactic of appeasement: useful activities contributing to their self-improvement would make migrants feel like they were moving forward and would create temporary fulfillment in the absence of work, in the hope that at a certain moment in their professional lives they would eventually be able to exchange the acquired entrepreneurial speech habitus if not with self-employment, then at least with waged employment. Although structural barriers to (self-)employment were not erased, they were considered temporary, so that the activation scheme was conceived of as a future-oriented investment, the return on which was considered migrants' individual responsibility.

The neoliberal investment in language and communication for self-employment therefore seems to be similar to other politics of social and professional inclusion that have historically been put forward by liberal nation states (see e.g. Bauman & Briggs, 2003; Gal, 2006; Heller, 2011; Hogan-Brun *et al.*, 2009; Weber, 1976) and that have defined language as a means of participation and citizenship. Becoming a speaker, in this case of a highly specialized register, has historically been seen by liberal governments as a *sine qua non* for political, social and professional integration and has, as such, been used as a justifying and legitimizing principle for forms of social exclusion and marginalization. In this sense, investing in language and communication for self-employment is only the last event in a chain of state investments in language that are conducive to reproducing a liberal illusion of equality, meritocracy and freedom, justifying a capitalist model that produces subalternity, and keeping those occupying these subaltern positions in check.

Acknowledgment

This work was partly supported by the Research Council of Norway through its Centres of Excellence funding scheme, project number 223265. We would like to thank Beatriz Lorente, Luisa Martín Rojo, Cécile Vigouroux and Mi-Cha Flubacher for their feedback on earlier drafts of this chapter. All remaining shortcomings are, of course, our own.

Notes

(1) In 2012–2013, unemployment among native-born Italians amounted to 11%; the unemployment rate among foreign-born persons in Italy was 15.3% (OECD & EU, 2015).
(2) The name of the organization and those of all individuals mentioned in this chapter are pseudonyms.
(3) Field notes (3 July 2014).
(4) Field notes (11 October 2014).
(5) Field notes (17 October 2014).
(6) Field notes (17 October 2014).
(7) Field notes (19 October 2014).
(8) All translations are ours.
(9) Field notes (8 February 2015).
(10) Field notes (11 February 2015).
(11) Field notes (11 February 2015).
(12) Field notes (28 February 2015).
(13) Field notes (21 March 2015).
(14) Field notes (21 March 2015).
(15) Field notes (7 April 2015).
(16) Field notes (8 May 2015).
(17) Field notes (8 May 2015).
(18) Field notes (22 June 2015).

References

Agha, A. (2007) *Language and Social Relations.* Cambridge: Cambridge University Press.
Allan, K. (2013) Skilling the self: The communicability of immigrants as flexible labour. In A. Duchêne, M. Moyer and C. Roberts (eds) *Language, Migration and Social Inequalities. A Critical Sociolinguistic Perspective on Institutions and Work* (pp. 56–78). Bristol: Multilingual Matters.

Allan, K. (2016) Self-appreciation and the value of employability: Integrating un(der)employed immigrants in post-Fordist Canada. In L. Adkins and M. Dever (eds) *The Post-Fordist Sexual Contract. Living and Working in Contingency* (pp. 49–69). Basingstoke: Palgrave Macmillan.

Allan, K. and McElhinny, B. (2016) Neoliberalism, language and migration. In S. Canagarajah (ed.) *The Routledge Handbook on Language and Migration.* London: Routledge.

Althusser, L. (1970) Idéologie et appareils idéologiques d'État. *La Pensée* 151, 3–38.

BMAS and OECD (2010) From employment to self-employment: Facilitating transition in the recovery. See http://www.bmas.de/SharedDocs/Downloads/ DE/PDF-Publikationen/a809e-unemployment-to-self-employment.pdf?__ blob=publicationFile (accessed 8 March 2016).

Bauman, R. and Briggs, C.L. (2003) *Voices of Modernity. Language Ideologies and the Politics of Inequality.* Cambridge: Cambridge University Press.

Boutet, J. (2001a) La part langagière du travail. *Langage & Société* 98, 17–42.

Boutet, J. (2001b) Le travail devient-il intellectuel? *Travailler* 6, 55–70.

Cameron, D. (2000) Styling the worker. *Journal of Sociolinguistics* 4 (3), 323–347.

Clasen, J. and Clegg, D. (2006) Beyond activation. *European Societies* 8 (4), 527–553.

Collett, E. (2011) *Immigrant Integration in Europe in a Time of Austerity.* Washington, DC: Migration Policy Institute.

Collett, E. and Sitek, K. (2008) Making migration work. *EPC Working Paper* 30.

Demazière, D. and Glady, M. (eds) (2011) Les discours de l'accompagnement: Nouvelles normes du retour à l'emploi. *Langage & Société* 137 (3).

Dermine, E. and Dumont, D. (eds) (2014) Activation policies for the unemployed, the right to work and the duty to work. *Work and Society* 79.

Dlaske, K., Barakos, E., Motobayashi, K. and McLaughlin, M. (eds) (2016) Languaging the worker. *Multilingua* 35 (4).

Del Percio, A. (2016) The governmentality of migration: Intercultural communication and the politics of (dis)placement in Southern Europe. *Language and Communication.* DOI https://doi.org/10.1016/j.langcom.2016.07.001

Del Percio, A. and Duchêne, A. (2015) Sprache und sozialer Ausschluss. In A. Schnitzer and R. Mörgen (eds) *Mehrsprachigkeit und (Un)gesagtes: Sprache als soziale Praxis im Kontext von Heterogenität und Differenz* (pp. 194–216). Weinheim: Juventa.

Duchêne, A. (2009) Formé-e pour servir! La part langagière de la formation professionnelle dans la nouvelle économie. *Bulletin Suisse de Linguistique Appliquée* 90, 125–147.

Duchêne, A. (2016) Investissement langagier et économie politique. *Langage & Société* 157, 73–96.

Duchêne, A. and Flubacher, M. (2015) Quand légitimité rime avec productivité. *Anthropologie et Société* 39 (3), 173–196.

European Commission (2009) *Entrepreneurship in Vocational Education and Training.* Brussels: EC.

European Commission (2012) *The Entrepreneurship 2020 Action Plan.* Brussels: EC.

Flubacher, M. (2014) *Integration durch Sprache – die Sprache der Integration: Eine Kritische Diskursanalyse zur Rolle der Sprache in der Schweizer und Basler Integrationspolitik 1998–2008.* Göttingen: V&R Unipress.

Flubacher, M., Coray, R. and Duchêne, A. (2016) Language, integration and the labour market: The regulation of diversity. *Multilingua.*

Foucault, M. (1994) Technologies of the self. In P. Rabinow (ed.) *Ethics: Subjectivity and Truth. Essential Works of Michel Foucault, 1954–1984.* Vol. 1 (pp. 221–251). New York: The New Press.

Fraser, N. (2003) From discipline to flexibilization? Rereading Foucault in the shadow of globalization. *Constellations* 10 (2), 160–171.

Gal, S. (2006) Contradictions of standard language in Europe. *Social Anthropology* 14 (2), 163–181.

Gee, J., Hull, G. and Lankshear, C. (1996) *The New Work Order.* Boulder, CO: Westview.

Harvey, D. (2005) *A Brief History of Neoliberalism.* Oxford: Oxford University Press.

Heller, M. (2003) Globalization, the new economy, and the commodification of language and identity. *Journal of Sociolinguistics* 7 (4), 473–492.

Heller, M. (2010) The commodification of language. *Annual Review of Anthropology* 39, 101–114.

Heller, M. (2011) *Paths to Post-Nationalism. A Critical Ethnography of Language and Identity.* Oxford: Oxford University Press.

Hogan-Brun, G., Mar-Molinero, C. and Stevenson, P. (2009) *Discourses of Language and Integration. Critical Perspectives on Language Testing Regimes in Europe.* Amsterdam: John Benjamins.

Irvine, J.T. and Gal, S. (2000) Language ideology and linguistic differentiation. In P. Kroskrity (ed.) *Regimes of Language. Ideologies, Polities, and Identities* (pp. 35–83). Santa Fe, NM: School of American Research Press.

INEA (2013) *I giovani e il ricambio generazionale nell'agricoltura italiana.* Rome: Ministero delle politiche agricole, alimentari e forestali.

IDOS (2014) *Rapporto Immigrazione e Impreditoria 2014.* Rome: IDOS.

Kraft, K. (2015) Constructing risk and responsibility: The instrumentalisation of language and communication in a building site. Presentation in the Panel Language, Work and Political Economy at the AAA Annual Meeting, Denver, Colorado.

Lorente, B. (2010) Packaging English-speaking products: Maid agencies in Singapore. In H. Kelly-Holmes and G. Mautner (eds) *Language and the Market* (pp. 44–55). London: Palgrave-MacMillan.

Lorente, B. (2012) The making of 'workers of the world': Language and the labor brokerage state. In A. Duchêne and M. Heller (eds) *Language in Late Capitalism. Pride and Profit* (pp. 183–206). New York: Routledge.

Martín Rojo, L. (2015) Five Foucauldian postulates for rethinking language and power. *Working Papers in Urban Language and Literacies* 176.

McHugh, M. and Challinor, A.E. (2011) *Improving Immigrants' Employment Prospects through Work-Focused Language Instruction.* Washington, DC: Migration Policy Institute.

Muehlebach, A. (2012) *The Moral Neoliberal. Welfare and Citizenship in Italy.* Chicago, IL: The University of Chicago Press.

OECD (2006) *OECD Employment Outlook.* Paris: OECD Publishing.

OECD (2015) *Entrepreneurial Education in Practice.* Paris: OECD Publishing.

OECD and European Union (2015) *Indicators of Immigrant Integration 2015: Settling In.* Paris: OECD Publishing.

Psacharopoulos, G. and Schlotter, M. (2010) Skills for employability, economic growth and innovation. *EENEE Analytical Report* 6.

Sennett, R. (1998) *The Corrosion of Character: The Personal Consequences of Work in the New Capitalism.* New York: W.W. Norton.

Urciuoli, B. (2008) Skills and selves in the new work place. *American Ethnologist* 35 (2), 211–228.

Urciuoli, B. and LaDousa, C. (2013) Language management/labor. *Annual Review of Anthropology* 42, 175–190.

Vigouroux, C.B. (2015) Néolibéralisme, mobilité transnationale et catégories migratoires. Plenary talk at the Colloque Réseau Francophone de Sociolinguistique, Hétérogénéité et changements: Perspectives sociolinguistiques. Grenoble, France.

Weber, E. (1976) *Peasants into Frenchmen*. Stanford, CA: Stanford University Press.

Wrana, D. (2009) Economizing and pedagogizing continuing education. In M. Peters, A.C. Besley, M. Olssen, S. Maurer and S. Weber (eds) *Governmentality Studies in Education* (pp. 473–486). Rotterdam: Sense Publishers.

9 Assembling Language Policy: Challenging Standardization and Quantification in the Education of Refugee Students in a US School

Jill Koyama

Introduction

A man and three women from Somalia, a woman from the Democratic Republic of Congo (DRC) and another from Burma sat with an English as a second language (ESL) teacher, a refugee resettlement caseworker and me in the basement of a small church, often a gathering place for refugees, in Wayside, New York. Different configurations of this group had sat together many times before – during adult refugee ESL classes at a resettlement agency, at 'diversity' celebrations held near the church and in various performances of dance, artistry and food-making. In the ESL classes, I was the volunteer teacher and the refugees from Somalia, Burma and DRC were designated as learners. In the other settings, such as weaving workshops, I was the learner and they were the teachers. On this cold February night in 2012, I was the researcher; they were emergent 'activists' and language 'experts'. I took notes on a blackboard and audio-recorded the meeting, as the rest of the group talked about language learning and pedagogy, although they did not refer to it as such. 'We are talking about what children learn … how they speak', explained Mohamed, a father from Somalia. 'Why they try to do this to our child, take her tongue is why we come', said Grace, a Somalian mother. Joan, the ESL teacher added, 'and we need to have more say in how the children learn English *and* keep their own languages'. The refugees, all parents of children attending the school, Harbor Middle

School (referred to also as Harbor) where the ESL teacher taught, nodded in agreement.[1]

The meeting was one of several, organized by Mohamed, his former caseworker from the refugee settlement agency, Abdi, and ESL teachers from Harbor. They did not support the school's recently adopted language policy and newly purchased language program which increased formal assessments and narrowed the curriculum. After Harbor failed to meet the adequate yearly progress (AYP) objectives in English language arts (ELA) for six years, it had bought a pre-packaged curriculum and training program from a for-profit educational support company, Educational Success. They intended to use the program to target the school's refugee and newcomer students, ages 13–16, in seventh and eighth grades, who were deemed 'responsible' for the failure. The program, which was devoid of adequate language supports for refugees, followed what was best described by Tim, another ESL teacher at the school, as a 'drill and kill English-only set of curricula'. In response, a handful of ESL teachers, refugee parents, community activists and refugee caseworkers engaged in 'productive policy play', which Koyama and Varenne (2012: 158) describe as the selective maneuvering or appropriation of policy 'as policy directives move from administrative centers to diverse local contexts of implementation' that extend into, but well beyond, classrooms.

In this chapter, I draw on data collected between January 2011 and March 2013 as part of an ethnographic study of immigrants and refugees' social networks in Wayside, a mid-sized city in Western New York State. Within that larger ethnography, I conducted case studies of two schools, one elementary (Koyama, 2014) and one middle school, which the majority of the city's refugee students attended. This chapter centers specifically on the middle school, Harbor Middle School (Harbor), where all of the school's 158 English language learners (ELLs), who comprised 18% of the total student population, were refugees the year I began my study, a year in which 56,384 persons were admitted to the US as refugees. New York State received nearly 6.3% or 3529 of the refugees (Martin & Yankay, 2012); Wayside has resettled 1000–1500 refugees annually since 2005; however, due to the implementation of more stringent screening policies by international institutions, fewer refugees were resettled in 2011.[2] Wayside's immigrant and refugee community is 7%, or approximately 18,291 people, of the overall population of the city. Defined as those who have been forced to flee their countries of nationality due to persecution or fear of persecution based on race, religion, political opinion or membership of a particular social group, refugees are a heterogeneous, if not disparate, subpopulation of immigrants. These refugees originate from countries as diverse as Burma,

Somalia, Colombia and Iraq, and speak greater than 100 languages and regional dialects. At the time of the study, the school district in which Harbor is located identified 73 languages that were spoken by students and their families.

In this chapter, I trace what happens when the new language policy and its associated curriculum and program are introduced at Harbor. I apply the notion of assemblages (Latour, 2005) as presented in actor-network theory (ANT) which explains how disparate people, their material objects and their discursive ideas are linked in a network, even temporarily, to get something done – in this case to implement and challenge a language policy. Specifically, I examine the controversies and contestations that emerge as the educational support company aims to establish its authority and legitimacy of ideas and practices for educating the school's student population of refugees – most of whom speak languages other than English and have had prolonged interruptions in their formal education – refugee parents, resettlement caseworkers and ESL teachers challenge the company's expertise and demand changes in the language program. These new policy actors mobilize themselves to resist the school district's regulations, to challenge the company's expertise and to demand changes in the language program. I pay particular attention to the ways in which they resist the practices produced by authorized policy actors, including school administrators and the professional development team of Educational Success.

I utilize this particular case to illuminate how language education policy, including its inextricable practices, pedagogy and curricula, has taken a neoliberal turn in US schooling. It has increasingly become technical, rational, comparative and quantified, reflective of the characteristics of neoliberal-driven education reform. Language policy has become more and more standardized even as the languages spoken by students, and their previous schooling experiences, have become more and more diverse. As noted by Ross and Gibson (2007: 4), such 'neoliberal educational reform policies focus on the creation of curriculum standards (where the state define the knowledge to be taught)' and in this chapter, we see how accountability strategies are linked to these curriculum standards. The programs developed, the curricula demanded and the practices implemented to meet the demands of language policy have narrowed as they have been 'outsourced' to a handful of for-profit companies (Burch, 2006, 2009; Koyama, 2010). Here, one such company, Educational Success, and their subcontractors, which have been bolstered by the neoliberal focus on choice and privatization in an educational marketplace, are hired by a public school to improve test scores. This kinds of outsourcing, as noted by several scholars (including Hornberger, 2005; McCarty, 2003; Menken, 2008; Menken & García, 2010; Valdiviezo, 2009), undermines the work of educators, who are local policymakers, interpreting and selectively appropriating policy into daily practices.

The commodities and services – curricula, testing products, tutoring and teaching training materials – developed and sold to schools and school districts by educational support companies offer 'one-size-fits-all' solutions. This is even the case, as we see in this chapter, for teaching students identified as English language learners (ELLs) under No Child Left Behind (NCLB)[3], the United States' most recent federal education policy which has been well documented as replete with a neoliberal undergirding (for a detailed review of NCLB and neoliberalism, see Koyama, 2013). Particularly salient to this chapter are the ways in which learning and teaching are quantified and made commensurable in NCLB. With its directives for increased standardization, high-stakes testing and accountability, NLCB and its related policies, like the language policy introduced at Harbor, are embedded with the necessity of assessment, legitimization, comparison and competition – all characteristic of neoliberal ideology in schools (Saunders, 2015).

In this chapter, I interrogate the emphasis on the quantification and standardization of Harbor's adopted language policy and program for ELLs, who I refer to as 'emergent bilinguals' (García, 2009, 2011) – children who are acquiring English through schooling and are also continuing to use their home language, thus becoming bilingual (or multilingual). First, I briefly discuss language policy under the broader NCLB. From there, I present my findings, critiquing the ways in which language policy under the weight of NCLB categorizes and compares children as numeric units. I demonstrate how refugee parents and ESL teachers push back against the numeric categories used to label students' English proficiency levels, and ultimately get them removed from school-related policy reports sent to parents. I also highlight the ways in which these parents, ESL teachers and refugee resettlement caseworkers disrupt notions of language learning experts by creating their own tutorial programs that do not follow the purchased curricula. Finally, I conclude with a recommendation that we challenge quantification that, in education, narrows our interpretations of learning to sets of numbers and standardization that restricts and regulates behaviors (Lampland & Star, 2009).

Language Policy Under NCLB

In the United States, education policy mandates standardization and increased accountability that generates comparable schooling data, making it possible to situate 'educational achievement as a mimetic of global capitalist competition' (Stronach, 2009: 19). The United States' NCLB reflects a larger neoliberal trend, in which education is based on a transnational capitalist model. It operates through a range of state-level comparative instruments and enacts progressively substantive sanctions for schools that fail to improve – that is, which do not meet adequate yearly progress (AYP). Central to NCLB is a focus on numeric and comparative accounts of academic achievement which are discursively justified in the name of international competitiveness and presented as benefiting the public. The national narratives surrounding NCLB tie schooling standards and accountabilities in the United States to 'a narrative of global competitiveness, economic dominance, and nationalist pride' (Foster, 2004: 179). Through NCLB, the US government engages in market-driven and sanctions-laden reforms that perpetuate competition, privatization and deregulation (Apple, 2010; Au, 2009; Hursh, 2007). NCLB makes an official contribution to the 'global spectacle' (Stronach, 2009: 9), in which hegemonic hyper-narratives link accountability and educational effectiveness to the advancement of transnational capitalism.

NCLB, the latest United States' federal policy solution to academic 'failure', mandates states to 'develop and administer an accountability system that assesses students annually, in reading/language arts and mathematics, and, based on those tests, determines whether schools and districts are making adequate yearly progress (AYP)' (Sunderman & Orfield, 2008: 125). In its current form, NCLB overemphasizes accountability and compliance and moves federal policy from its historical focus on creating equitable education to regulating and evaluating day-to-day school practices (NCSL, 2009: 3). Nowhere is this exemplified more acutely than in accountabilities and progress targets assigned to language learners.

While all children are affected by NCLB's emphasis on high-stakes testing, standardization and increased accountability, the impact on emergent bilinguals is compounded in three ways. First, NCLB mandates that these learners be placed together in a separate accountability subgroup. Specifically, emergent bilinguals are tested in academic content areas, as well as in English language proficiency. Each state sets annual performance goals based on complex calculations for individual schools and for up to 40 demographic subgroups, including emergent bilinguals, within each school's student population. According to NCLB, each demographic group is assigned performance targets based on standardized test scores. Schools that miss any single subgroup target for two consecutive years face a series of sanctions, the most severe of which include reorganization and closure. Because emergent bilinguals, in the aggregate, score lower on the standardized tests, especially in ELA, schools serving above average numbers of emergent bilinguals are more likely to be penalized under NCLB for not meeting the AYPs. By 2011, Harbor Middle School had missed the ELA target for emergent bilinguals for six years, placing them into a category of 'persistently low achieving' schools. Emergent bilinguals (referred to as ELLs in official policy documents) were the only subgroup in 2008–2011 not to meet its AYP objectives. This, according to the vice principal, caused the entire school to be penalized. He stated: 'ELLs are a big drag on AYP, bringing us under [NCLB] sanctions right and left'. He was not alone in blaming the emergent bilinguals, as I will show in this chapter.

Second, states rely on tests administered in English to meet NCLB's demands for accountability. Thus, all tests are in reality language tests for emergent bilinguals (Menken, 2008, 2010). Further, emergent bilinguals as a group must always, by definition, be deemed 'low performing' by NCLB; when students acquire enough English to no longer be considered as ELLs, they are moved from the subgroup and newly arrived students are added to the subgroup, inevitably ensuring low overall performance (Abedi & Dietel, 2004; Menken, 2008, 2010). Not surprisingly, emergent bilinguals score an average of 20–50 percentage points below other students on ELA state assessments and other content-area subjects. As pointed out by Koyama and Menken (2013: 85): 'In New York, as elsewhere across the U.S., emergent bilinguals and the schools that serve them are being disproportionately penalised for their performance on tests administered in English'. At the beginning of this study, only 4% of the state's eighth-grade emergent bilinguals achieved a proficient score on the ELA examination, a percentage that indicates that these students are in the process of learning English and are not yet fully proficient in academic English (New York State Education Department, 2010). At Harbor Middle School, just 6% of the refugees, according to the state test scores, reached proficiency in reading and writing (portions of the ELA assessment, along with listening and speaking) during 2011–2012; 35% exhibited proficiency in listening and speaking, reflecting the students' abilities to first grasp conversational aspects of English.

Third, 'the impact on emergent bilinguals is compounded by the larger political neoliberal discourses surrounding immigration that perpetuate inequalities for these students' (Koyama & Menken, 2013: 83). When resettled in the United States, refugees, a subpopulation of immigrants who are not easily located in broad American categories of race and class, become embedded in broad narratives of risk in which there is a precarious and often contested balance between losing and gaining something. In these narratives, their experiences are portrayed as those of hope, resilience, risk-taking and perseverance, which tidily align with often-cited American values. Yet, along with other immigrants, they are also positioned as potential risks to working class and poor American citizens with whom they might compete for increasingly limited jobs and social services. Even though they are net contributors to the US economy (Potocky-Tripodi, 2004), refugees, in the latter narrative, are seen as threats to the American economy and way(s) of life. They can, in more extreme framings, fall under a 'pathologisation of uprootedness' (Malkki, 1992: 32) and be depicted as potentially harmful, immoral and terroristic. Refugee children, because they often enter US schools with little formal education, disrupted education and a lack of English proficiency, are seen as a drain on schools' resources and a threat to schools' abilities to meet their NCLB accountabilities.

Putting Assemblage to Work in the Study of Language Policy

Assemblage thinking, which centers on how human actors, their material products and their discursive practices come together to form dynamic associations to produce agency and perform actions, is particularly useful in the study of the enactment of language policy which is 'made up of uncertain, fragile, controversial, and ever-shifting ties' (Latour, 2005: 28). My analysis draws on the conceptual resources of material semiotics associated with actor-network perspectives, which are particularly useful in studying controversies (Venturini, 2010), in which various groups struggle to establish authority, expertise and legitimacy. Because ANT has no prior categories or prioritized roles, multiple perspectives, such as those in controversy, are simultaneously examined. I am interested in the ways in which 'policy phenomena emerge as contingent effects of socio-material practices, how certain policy ideas come to cohere as more-or-less durable assemblages or networks and how they are mobilised, challenged, defended and strengthened' (Gorur & Koyama, 2013: 635). How, for instance, do refugee students become constructed as the 'problem' in Harbor Middle School's attempt to meet NCLB accountabilities? How do refugee parents, with minimal formal education, become language learning 'experts' who resist the construction and further aim to change the official language policy?

In ANT, there is a focus on material objects, in addition to human actors. Semiotically, ANT insists on symmetry between human and non-human things; however, I agree with Pickering (1993) who acknowledges that humans have intentions that set them apart from material objects.

Objects with subjective investments can, in this thinking, still mediate resettlement practices and 'shape intentions, meanings, relationships, routines' (Fenwick & Edwards, 2011). I examine the interactions between human (e.g. ESL teachers and refugee parents) and non-human (e.g. test reports, curricula and video tutorials) policy actors by examining the emergent human and material entities as they 'engage in a means of a dialectic of resistance and accommodation – the mangle' (Pickering, 1993: 559) or what Latour (2005) refers to as 'translation' – a process in which different actors come together, exert force on one another, 'changing and being changed by each other' (Fenwick & Edwards, 2010: 3) to create linkages that eventually form a network of action and material. Following Heimans (2012: 314), I focus on 'researching the entanglements of the material and discursive in education policy enactment'. Specifically, I look at the contestations between the technical and standardized curricula and pedagogy offered by Educational Success and supported by the school administrators, and the values, motivations and resources of the ESL teachers and parents.

To study assemblages or networks, one begins either by following people or by following objects and then builds an ethnography from the interactions those initial people make with other people, with material objects and discourses; I began my ethnographic study of refugee networks in Wayside by following people, specifically the executive directors of two refugee resettlement agencies I met at a conference/workshop focusing on refugee education. I traced the linkages between the resettlement agencies, and other agencies and organizations that provided services to refugees for nearly three years. I became immersed in the refugee networks: I interviewed refugees, resettlement agency staff, service providers, employers, religious leaders, Wayside officials, school administrations and faculty and community members; I observed and participated in the career readiness and career/workforce programs offered at the refugee resettlement agency and in four different ESL programs. I also attended multiple community and school meetings, events and activities in which refugees participated, and a variety of government meetings and forums in which issues associated with the Wayside refugee population were discussed. I visited refugees at home and came to know their families and friends. I conducted case studies on two public schools in which the majority of refugee children attended. Below are some findings from the case study of Harbor Middle School that illuminate how the power of achievement data to define and regulate learning can, and should be, challenged in schools – especially by those who, like refugee parents, are not necessarily recognized as educational policy experts.

Challenging Categorization

In the summer of 2011, as a persistently low achieving school, Harbor was mandated to submit and then implement a comprehensive education plan (CEP), an accountability between the state and school. Two objectives in the CEP had a near immediate impact on the teaching of emergent bilinguals in the school: The first stated that the school leader and teachers would develop a data-driven culture based on student needs, assessments and analysis. The second promoted the effective use of evidence-based curricula and pedagogy to improve student achievement. Based on these objectives, the school principal and assistant principal revised the school's language learning policy to include the implementation of educational supports targeted at the students who tested at the high end of the intermediate level of English proficiency, a high Level 2 on a 1–4 scale. These students were referred to as 'on the bubble' or 'bubble students' because they were just points shy of being in Level 3. Moving them from Level 2 to Level 3 was seen as the easiest and most efficient way of satisfying NCLB accountabilities and reaching AYP objectives.

Several teachers opposed the focus on high Level 2 students, the 'bubble students', noting that all the students in ESL classes needed attention. Liz, an ESL teacher, argued that: 'All the ELLs need our attention, especially the level 1s ... not only the high level 2s who will probably get to 3 within the year, without additional help' (Field notes, Harbor faculty meeting, September 12, 2011). Another ESL teacher, Tim, added that he was tired of using numerical labels for children. At the same meeting, he said: 'Look, I'm sick of hearing kids called 1s and 2s and high 2s and 3s ... Memo: They're kids, not numbers'. The assistant principal replied: 'C'mon, Tim, don't be so difficult. We all know we're talking about students, but numbers are just our short-hand for talking about groups of test scores'. Debate ensued but the meeting ended with the principal stating that they 'had to do something about the kids whose test scores were keeping the school in failure status'. She said that the numbers 'reflect the standards imposed by NCLB', that 'there's no way around them'. She reminded the teachers that their evaluations were also based on the students' achievement.

The 1–4 levels constructed objects out of the refugee children, and their teachers and the scores were interpreted and evaluated as part of the activities aimed toward a perceived educational problem – in this case, the low test scores of the emergent bilinguals at Harbor, all of whom were refugees during the study. The NCLB standards oriented relations and inflicted a classification system, forming boundaries between learning, teaching, test scores and emergent bilinguals. At schools like

Harbor, such classifications of children are 'both conceptual (in the sense of persistent patterns of change and action, resources for organising abstractions) and material (in the sense of being inscribed, transported, and affixed to stuff)' (Bowker & Star, 2000: 152). Over time, the numbers and the classifications become proxies for students. As I have argued elsewhere with Menken (Koyama & Menken, 2013), they discursively reframe emergent bilinguals as quantifiable data that prevent schools from meeting their AYPs.

Two weeks after the faculty meeting, the issue of numerical labels and achievement categories was revisited in an English department meeting. This time, it was not Tim who initiated the conversation, but Molly, the most veteran teacher at the school and the head of the department. She began:

> Like many of you, I am so tired of talking about our students as numbers to be raised or I guess, sometimes, celebrated ... but it is the ELLs who get the worst of it. Right now, they're seen as the limits to our school's achievement. You know, why we're still a C school that can't meet its ELA numbers ... I get it, and so do you, but there's changing coming down the pipeline that'll affect them big time ... (Field notes, September 28, 2015)

Some teachers nodded their heads in agreement, but one, the newest member of the English department, responded: 'Forgive me if I'm wrong here, but we need some way to talk about them ... and for me, being new, numbers are easiest. We've got to think about our AYPs'. Tim pounded his fist on the table and said: 'Easiest is not best, and if that's what you think, you're just buying into neoliberal propaganda!' Molly regained the attention and said they would need to move on to other topics but that she hoped they could return to this topic at another meeting or have individual conversations about it. Tim apologized for his outburst and they moved onto the results of the latest ESL assessments – which had been disaggregated according to the 1–4 category system, essentially taking the discussion back to numerical representations of children.

The material objects in the language policy assemblage mediated, if not demanded, action on the part of the human policy actors. The numbers had become something to be contended with; they had become matters of fact. Fenwick and Edwards (2010: 130) explain that '[m]atters of fact produce, and are a product of, very literal politics, that which we might associate with such notions as evidence informed policy and practice, as though facts are unassailable'. However, as seen in the English department meeting, they had also become 'matters of concern' (Latour, 2005) which do not distance people from objects, in this case, numeric labels of proficiency.

A conversation surrounding the 1–4 labels also emerged during an informational meeting between the ESL teachers and refugee parents. As the ESL teachers were showing the parents graphs of students' test scores and progress toward proficiency, a parent asked: 'Why numbers? 1, 2 means who?' Joan, the lead ESL teacher, explained the proficiency categories and the related 1–4 levels. One of the translators attending the meeting raised her hand and asked: 'Uhm, I should tell them that you are putting their children into groups by numbers? Is that right? Those numbers are numbers of kids, right?' Joan tried to explain the groups again and apologized for using numbers to talk about their children. There seemed to be confusion. Translators and refugee parents were simultaneously talking in small groups, aiming to understand the numbers. Joan tried unsuccessfully to get their attention back. Finally, one of the refugee resettlement caseworkers, Abdi, said: 'I will tell them that this is part of the American schooling system … Children must be sorted but there are many factors, not just numbers' (Field notes, April 27, 2012). Joan agreed, although she later admitted she was not sure if that was the right thing to say because she, too, saw the numbers – especially the 1s and 2s – as demeaning.

Creating formal representations of learning into quantitative data involves three processes according to ANT: 'First, relevant things are sorted, detached and displayed in single frame. Second, these entities are manipulated and transformed to show or create relationship between them. Third, a result is extracted such as a new thing, a ranking or a decision' (Fenwick & Edwards, 2010: 123). Callon and Law (2005) provide the concept of 'qualculation', in which things, both quantitative and qualitative, are manipulated into calculations. These things, some material and some human, must then qualify for calculation in a common frame. At Harbor, qualculations included some prejudice against the refugee youth who were blamed for the school's failure, the NCLB categorizing and sorting through the 1–4 levels and the district's push for more quantifiable data. They became part of the ongoing work of constructing and implementing sorting systems, masked as apolitical diagnostic tools (Fenwick, 2009; Lipman, 2004). They were ubiquitous and mostly taken for granted by many, not only at Harbor, but at schools across the US.

Yet, when I interviewed Grace, a Somalian refugee mother, the gravity of the qualculations became more apparent. Grace, through an interpreter, explained:

> In camps, always a number. Numbered tent and numbered people in a family in a tent ... The number tells where to go [where to be resettled], when to go ... I am a number. My son is a number .... No more numbers ... Here, everything numbers. My son is a number. His sister is a number. No .... Teacher show me pages of numbers to talk my children's learning English ...(January 6, 2013)

Grace clearly understood the power of numbers and comparison. Numbers and categories matter. They are not neutral labels. As the study ended, Grace had worked with Joan, the ESL teacher, to devise a different way of presenting information to the refugee parents, one that did not attach a numerical label to the children. However, reports in the school, the district and across the state still sorted information by the 1–4 levels.

Calculations in ANT do not reside in human actors who then project them; they are enacted through material practices and multiple translations. Translation, a key ANT process, refers here to the chain of actions and activities whereby dynamic, incongruous and complex parts of everyday schooling are quantified and become nearly unquestioned facts. The ELA test scores, through translations, become detached from their origins, and are made commensurate and analogous with other scores across the district, the state and the nation for the purposes of fitting into the ongoing activities of language policy under NCLB. They are compared and ranked. They are amplified and transported from location to location, school to district to state, and act at a distance from the experience from which they were extracted. The low test scores of the refugee students are then evoked as scientific evidence and authorized knowledge in support of targeted curricula, more testing and, ultimately, the raising of standards. They are used, as seen at Harbor Middle School, to talk about refugee students' lack of proficiency in English and to strategize about how to move those 'on the bubble' to the next level.

Entangling Expertise

Dependent on statistical expertise, the data produced through NCLB-mandated calculations narrow teaching and learning to technical accounts for which rational solutions are offered by educational support organizations, such as Educational Success (Gorur, 2013). Language learning programs, like the one offered by Educational Success and bought for emergent bilinguals by Harbor Middle School, are said to be 'evidence based'. According to the company's regional director of professional development assigned to provide training to Harbor's teachers, 'following the program exactly gets results because it's basically based on best practices, proven ones that can work for everyone'. As she describes it:

> We have the data, the numbers. We run the formulas and we know what works ....The hard part is getting ESL teachers who have their own ways, think they're right, to follow the program to the letter ... I know this sounds harsh, but this school needs to perform and the ELLs are the ones we are targeting. They're holding the school back and there's no reason for it when we have these programs. (Interview, November 8, 2011)

Through this director's narrow construction of academic achievement and pedagogy, and the accompanying construction of NCLB's demographic subgroups, knowledge about emergent bilinguals becomes exclusively framed by discourses based on quantitative formulas and the need to meet certain cut scores, with relatively little concern for the actual learners.

The principal admitted that yes, they were 'narrowing curriculum with the program for ELLs', but asserted that she would no longer 'let the school fail with solutions out there'. She explained:

> For years, we've been, since I got here anyway, we've been trying to fix things ourselves. The ESL teachers are determined to teach the way they were taught and most of them are good teachers, but it isn't working. And they can't accept it ... I've seen this [Educational Success] program get real results in other schools and so I put my foot down. Sure, it is formulaic, but we're going to use it and the teachers are going to have to get on board, fast. I'm not messing around any longer. These refugees need to learn English and we can get them there ... We've got NCLB strangling us and that doesn't help, but still we can teach them English ... (Interview, May 22, 2011)

The excerpts from both the Educational Success director and Harbor's principal reveal how powerful and taken for granted the discourse surrounding the technicization of teaching has become. The rationale: If the ESL teachers, who have been trained in methodologies particularly used when teaching emergent bilinguals, would only follow the 'rules' of the prescriptive language program, the students would learn English. This, of course, would require the teachers to concede their expertise and any autonomy they had left under NCLB and strictly follow a program developed and sold by a for-profit company that has no accountability to federal education policy.

Four of the six ESL teachers would not concede their expertise. As outlined in a letter they wrote to the principal, they did not agree with the new approach to teaching emergent bilinguals. The letter, a copy of which was given to me by Tim, an ESL teacher, was dated in September 2011, only one month after the principal had signed the contract with Educational Success and it had been approved by the district. It read:

> ... As you know, two of us were on the committee that reviewed potential language programs for our ELLs .... The committee was composed of nine members, six teachers, a reading specialist, the assistant principal, and you, the principal. Only four members rated the program offered by Educational Success the best program for our school. Why, then, was it chosen? We are left to assume that you decided that it was the best program, and with all due respect to your previous teaching experience, you have never taught ELA or ESL ...
>
> We will not implement the program in our classrooms. The curricula, which allows no room for SIOP [Sheltered Instructional Observational Protocol] or the use of creative and differentiated instruction, is not the best program for our students, who, as you know, suffer from long periods of no formal schooling, and the mental illnesses that follow years of violence and fear. Instructing them daily in rote memorization exercises and teaching to the test will not support them in learning English or in becoming proficient in American culture, which is part of what they need to become integrated into Wayside ...

At the end of the letter, the teachers requested a meeting, which was held on October 21, after school. The six ESL teachers attended, as did Harbor's principal and assistant principal. After the meeting, Joan, one of the ESL teachers who had written the letter, said that the principal had not budged from her position but that the teachers were going to see what else they could do, including talking to 'someone at the district' and forming a group to advocate for the refugee students' language learning.

The group included six refugee parents: Mohamed, Grace, Joy and Roda from Somalia, Mi Mi from Burma and Cesarine from DRC. Mohamed, who had worked as a teacher in the Kenyan refugee camp where he had previously lived for 12 years, volunteered as an aide at Harbor and invited the other refugee parents to join the group. Tim, Joan, Liz and Tami were also ESL teachers at Harbor. Joan, who worked as a liaison between the school and the resettlement agencies, and who lived near the school in a neighborhood populated by recently arrived refugees, invited two caseworkers, Abdi and Sang, from Wayside's largest refugee resettlement agency. The group began meeting in November 2011 with the aim of 'strategising ways to make sure the kids got good instruction despite the Educational Success program' (personal communication, Tim, December 11, 2011), which was to be implemented in January 2012, at the start of the spring semester.

At one meeting in early January 2012, the group discussed creating teaching materials for the refugee parents to use at home. From that meeting:

Liz (ESL teacher): I think we don't want to have just worksheets… We could create some online tutorials.

Joan (ESL teacher): I really like that idea. [To refugee parents] What do you think?

Mohamed: Computers are good but not all have at home …

Abdi (caseworker): We could, I think, set everything up at [name of the refugee resettlement agency]. We have the computer room and everyone could come there with their kids once a week.

Mi Mi: I teach at home?

Mohamed: We need to be at home for kids, for rest, for cooking …

Grace (Mohamed's wife): Who cooking? Me. [laughs]

Sang (caseworker): … but the kids need it every day and how can everyone get to us? They can't and we can't always be there either.

Tim: What about if I could check out some iPads from Harbor and upload the tutorials?

Joan: Yeah, we could do that and then no one would need to have internet at home …. Can we really do that?

Tim: Yes. I do it all the time.

Within a month of that meeting, the ESL teachers and Mohamed had created five tutorial videos. Abdi had created instructions in five languages for parents and Tim uploaded them onto iPads, so that the parents could use them at home with their children. All the tutorials, which were approximately 45 minutes in length, were based on the SIOP model. SIOP uses English to extend the time that ELLs have for language support while still providing subject content through the integration of eight interrelated components – lesson preparation, building background, comprehensible input, strategies, interaction, practice/application, lesson delivery and review and assessment.

As the refugee parents worked on the tutorials with their children, there was a decentering, not only of the teacher as the expert, but also as a human subject, as the role of the material – the iPads and the videos – and the roles of the refugee parents became integral to the group's language learning plan. Two of the refugee parents even attended a SIOP training to better understand the tutorials. Clearly, the tutorials had human investment; the ESL teachers created them and the parents would aim to guide their children through them. However, in the tutorials, the human actors were 'continually coming into being, fading away, moving around, changing places with one another, and so on' (Pickering, 1993: 563). The tutorials played on iPads became literal and semiotic 'devices and instruments that act, perform, and do things' (Pickering, 1993).

The group, with its multiple and lay voices, entered into what was positioned as a technicized educational problem with technical solutions. As the school's language learning policy became increasingly targeted at the emergent bilinguals through technical curricula and prescribed pedagogy, the members of the group challenged it with their actions. Not only did they create the electronic tutorials, but they also spoke at school board meetings and they worked with others in the refugee community to write letters to the district superintendent and elected Wayside officials. The caseworkers enrolled volunteer ESL teachers, like me, to offer Saturday and after-school tutoring to the refugee parents and their children. At school, the ESL teachers disrupted the curricula, often using expanded versions of the tutorials, again inviting new material elements into the assemblage of language learning at Harbor Middle School.

By late 2012, the technical and rational accounts of what was working at Harbor became muddled and eventually began to unravel as 'spaces of uncertainty' (Callon et al., 2001) emerged. Agency became distributed across the intertwining of human and material agencies which were 'mutually and emergently productive of one another' (Pickering, 1993: 567). When the principal learned of the group's work and their tutorials – and after Educational Success had failed to deliver curricula for the seventh and eighth grades – she set up a meeting with the group, where they showed her their tutorials and teaching materials. According to Liz, the principal seemed 'resigned' to let the teachers and parents do what they wanted, openly, as long as they covered the material that would be tested in the state assessment. When I asked the principal about her change of heart, she replied:

> Maybe I was over reactive to the test scores, to the pressure of the district … I wanted an easy way out, for once in education … I just wanted to believe that I could buy the answer, but that was not right, really. Honestly, it might have worked, but Educational Success didn't

deliver on its promises and we lost time….Well, we would have lost ground if the teachers and parents hadn't been doing all that behind my back to keep students up to speed … Of course, I'm angry that they did it behind my back. Who wouldn't be, but that's another matter … (Interview, January 31, 2013)

The principal admitted that if Educational Success had delivered the curricula – and 'if it had worked like it was supposed to' – she would not have been so willing to accept the teachers' videos. However, she also added that she did not have any faith that the 'homemade' tutorials taught by the refugee parents would help that much. 'It just pretty much goes against the intervention I think would work. You get what you pay for', she lamented.

Harbor's principal had accepted the federal government's interventions into language education and had resigned herself to the fact that they were inextricably bound to market-based reform, which is more accurately referred to as 'deform' and privatization (Apple, 2006; Ball, 2007, 2010; Burch, 2006). She was not alone. Language policy and language learning programs have become part and parcel of what Harvey (2003) refers to as the 'accumulation of dispossession', where everything from ideas to the human genomes are potential commodities and thus open to privatization. Language learning programs have become transformed as part of a market system that includes for-profit vendors, influential political officials and non-profit 'local' educational activists. These programs are situated within neoliberal preferences for increased charter (publically funded privately governed) schools, vouchers (public funding that students can use for private school tuition) and school choice (the ability of students in underperforming schools to transfer to another school). Outside vendors, such as Educational Success, are approved by districts across the US to provide tutoring, testing and curriculum development. Schools like Harbor have been enticed by their need to meet NCLB accountabilities to increase their reliance on products and services of for-profit educational support businesses and educational management organizations (Ball, 2010; Koyama, 2010).

Concluding Thoughts: Disrupting Neoliberalism in Language Policy

Menken and Garcia (2010: 1) call our attention to the lack of research that 'exists about the complex process of language policy implementation within educational contexts'. I would add that there is a need for more studies that examine language policy networks that extend beyond classrooms and schools. Language policy does not exist, and is not enacted, in bounded contexts, such as schools, nor is it neutrally transferred from one level of educational bureaucracy to another. As we see in this chapter, language policy assemblages can include parents at home and refugee caseworkers at resettlement agencies and volunteers at community centers. Language policy is embedded with incongruent histories, aims and resources and it is political. As the neoliberal turn in education persists, there is an urgent need for the study of policy assemblages that include the global and the local, not as contexts, but as integral entities in the complex material, social and ideological conditions of language policy and practices.

As shown through the contestations and challenges to language policy and practices at Harbor Middle School, language policy can be situated as a set of dynamic, complex and often contested relationships among actors, who are 'dialectically constituted by social relations' (Nespor, 2002: 368). Viewed in this way, language policy (and other education policy) can be understood, and studied, as 'assemblages' of heterogeneous materials, 'all of which can move educational practices across space and time' (Nespor, 2002: 369) through non-linear, often temporal linkages that do not necessarily represent or construct consensus, decentralization or democratic decision making. In fact, throughout the study, ESL teachers, administrators and refugee parents often found themselves at odds with one another, and coming to decisions was an arduous process that frequently extended over months, if not years. Assemblage thinking precisely extends the field of study to interactions that cross multiple sites and contexts and times to reveal the complexities and power embedded in policy processes (Fenwick, 2010).

So too does the ANT approach that I have utilized here reveal the ways in which neoliberal ideologies are materially enacted in schools through their insertion into policy, programs and curricula. Quantifying learning and teaching, especially as we have seen in this chapter, for linguistically diverse students becomes legitimized through policy and its associated ritualized programs and practices. At Harbor Middle School, this was made even more concerning as the program package was purchased from a for-profit educational support company, Educational Success, which focuses on excellence through achievement scores.

The examples offered in this chapter, however, also illuminate the ways in which individuals can push back against formal compliance with standards (and standardization) and quantification that have come to be cornerstones of neoliberal regulations and policy in schooling. The efforts of the refugee parents, the ESL teachers and the refugee resettlement caseworkers draw our attention to the ways in which we can challenge standards, which have become so naturalized through their reutilization in practice and their enforcement by government agencies and educational support companies approved by such agencies. Perhaps because many of the actors at Harbor who were concerned with whom and what was being standardized and quantified were not necessarily situated within schools or professions associated with the US education system, they were the ones to notice that something was not right. The undergirding of education with neoliberal policy and practices had not, from their somewhat outsiders' perspectives, become hegemonic or taken for granted. Their actions can serve as examples for those of us in the academy, and in the US education system, who are also deeply concerned about the enactment of neoliberalism in public education.

Notes

(1) Pseudonyms are used throughout this chapter, and the identifying characteristics of the school have been slightly altered in an effort to retain the confidentiality of the study participants.
(2) 'Resettlement' refers to the process through which individuals with legal refugee status are transferred to another country that agrees to admit them, and ultimately to grant permanent settlement.
(3) NCLB was reauthorized as Every Student Suceeds Act (ESSA) in 2015, but retains much of the neoliberal underpinnings of NCLB.

References

Abedi, J. and Dietel, R. (2004) Challenges in the No Child Left Behind act for English language learners. *Phi Delta Kappan* 85 (10), 782–785.

Apple, M.W. (2006) *Educating the 'Right' Way: Markets, Standards, God, and Inequality.* Abingdon: Taylor & Francis.

Au, W. (2009) *Unequal by Design: High-Stakes Testing and the Standardization of Inequality.* New York: Routledge.

Ball, S.J. (2007) *Education Plc: Understanding Private Sector Participation in Public Sector Education.* New York: Routledge.

Ball, S.J. (2010) Privatizing education, privatizing education policy, privatizing educational research: Network governance and the 'competition state'. *Journal of Education Policy* 24 (1), 83–99.

Bowker, G.C. and Star, S.L. (2000) *Sorting Things Out: Classification and its Consequences.* Cambridge, MA: MIT Press.

Burch, P. (2006) The new educational privatization: Educational contracting and high stakes accountability. *The Teachers College Record* 108 (12), 2582–2610.

Burch, P.E. (2009) *Hidden Markets: The New Education Privatization.* New York: Routledge.

Callon, M. and Law, J. (2005) On qualculation, agency, and otherness. *Environment and Planning D* 23 (5), 717–733.

Callon, M., Lascoumes, P. and Barthe, Y. (2001) *Acting in an Uncertain World: An Essay on Technical Democracy* (G. Burchell, trans.). Cambridge, MA: MIT Press.

Fenwick, T. (2009) Making to measure? Reconsidering assessment in professional continuing education. *Studies in Continuing Education* 31 (3), 229–244.

Fenwick, T.J. (2010) (Un)doing standards in education with actor-network theory. *Journal of Education Policy* 25 (2), 117–133.

Fenwick, T.J. and Edwards, R. (2011) Considering materiality in educational policy: Messy objects and multiple reals. *Educational Theory* 61 (6), 709–726.

Foster, W.P. (2004) The decline of the local: A challenge to educational leadership. *Educational Administration Quarterly* 40 (2), 176–191.

García, O. (2009) Emergent bilinguals and TESOL: What's in a name? *TESOL Quarterly* 43 (2), 322–326.

García, O. (2011) *Bilingual Education in the 21st Century: A Global Perspective.* Hoboken, NJ: John Wiley & Sons.

Gorur, R. (2013) My school, my market. *Discourse: Studies in the Cultural Politics of Education* 34 (2), 214–230.

Gorur, R. and Koyama, J. (2013) The struggle to technicise in education policy. *The Australian Educational Researcher* 40 (5), 633–648.

Harvey, D. (2003) *The New Imperialism.* Oxford: Oxford University Press.

Heimans, S. (2012) Coming to matter *in* practice: Enacting education policy. *Discourse: Studies in the Cultural Politics of Education* 33 (2), 313–326.

Hornberger, N. (2005) Nichols to NCLB: Local and global perspectives on U.S. language education policy. *Working Papers in Educational Linguistics* 20 (2), 1–17.

Hursh, D. (2007) Assessing No Child Left Behind and the rise of neoliberal education policies. *American Educational Research Journal* 44 (3), 493–518.

Koyama, J.P. (2010) *Making Failure Pay: For-Profit Tutoring, High-Stakes Testing, and Public Schools.* Chicago, IL: University of Chicago Press.

Koyama, J. (2013) Global scare tactics and the call for U.S. schools to be held accountable. *American Journal of Education* 120 (1), 77–99.

Koyama, J. (2014) When things come undone: The promise of dissembling education policy. *Discourse: Studies in the Cultural Politics of Education* 36 (4), 1–12.

Koyama, J. and Varenne, H. (2012) Assembling and dissembling: Policy as productive play. *Educational Researcher* 41 (5), 157–162.

Koyama, J. and Menken, K. (2013) Emergent bilinguals: Framing students as statistical data? *Bilingual Research Journal* 36 (1), 82–99.

Lampland, M. and Star, S.L. (eds) (2009) *Standards and Their Stories: How Quantifying, Classifying, and Formalizing Practices Shape Everyday Life.* Ithaca, NY: Cornell University Press.

Latour, B. (2005) *Reassembling the Social: An Introduction to Actor-Network Theory.* Oxford: Oxford University Press.

Lipman, P. (2004) *High Stakes Education: Inequality, Globalization, and Urban School Reform.* Hove: Psychology Press.

Malkki, L. (1992) National geographic: The rooting of peoples and territorialization of national identity among scholars and refugees. *Cultural Anthropology* 7 (1), 22–44.

Martin, D.C. and Yankay, J.E. (2012) Annual flow report. Refugees and asylees: 2012. See http://www.dhs.gov/sites/default/files/publications/ois_rfa_fr_2012.pdf (accessed 3 April 2013).

McCarty, T.L. (2003) Revitalizing indigenous languages in homogenizing times. *Comparative Education* 39 (2), 147–163.

Menken, K. (2008) *English Learners Left Behind: Standardized Testing as Language Policy.* Clevedon: Multilingual Matters.

Menken, K. (2010) NCLB and English language learners: Challenges and consequences. *Theory Into Practice* 49 (2), 121–128.

Menken, K. and García, O. (eds) (2010) *Negotiating Language Education Policies: Educators as Policymakers.* New York: Routledge.

Nespor, J. (2002) Networks and contexts of reform. *Journal of Educational Change* 3 (3–4), 365–382.

Pickering, A. (1993) The mangle of practice: Agency and emergence in the sociology of science. *American Journal of Sociology* 99 (3), 559–589.

Potocky-Tripodi, M. (2004) The role of social capital on immigrant and refugee economic adaptation. *Journal of Social Service Research* 31 (1), 59–91.

Ross, E.W. and Gibson, R.J. (eds.) (2007) *Neoliberalism and Education Reform.* Cresskill, NJ: Hampton Press.

Saunders, D.B. (2015) Resisting excellence: Challenging neoliberal ideology in postsecondary education. *Journal for Critical Education Policy Studies* 13 (2), 391–413.

Stronach, I. (2009) *Globalizing Education, Educating the Local: How Method Made us Mad.* New York: Routledge.

Sunderman, G.L. and Orfield, G. (2008) Massive responsibilities and limited resources. Holding NCLB accountable: Achieving accountability, equity, and school reform. See http://citeseerx.ist.psu.edu/viewdoc/download?doi=10.1.1.160.8562&rep=rep1&type=pdf (accessed 22 February 2016).

Valdiviezo, L. (2009) Bilingual intercultural education in indigenous schools: An ethnography of teacher interpretations of government policy. *International Journal of Bilingual Education and Bilingualism* 12 (1), 61–79.

Venturini, T. (2010) Diving in magma: How to explore controversies with actor-network theory. *Public Understanding of Science* 19 (3), 258–273.

10 The Games People Play: A Critical Study of 'Resource Leeching' Among 'Blended' English for Academic Purpose Professionals in Neoliberal Universities

Gregory Hadley

Introduction

Around the globe, university English for academic purpose (EAP) programs are increasingly being steeped in the practices of the neoliberal business world. Originally designed to improve the language proficiency of international students so that they could access universities where English is the primary language of instruction, today EAP is taught in universities of the 'outer circle' (Kachru, 1982), where English is becoming a primary medium of content instruction (Charles & Pecorari, 2016: 19–21; Hadley, 2015: 7–8). Although once part of university language and linguistics departments, many EAP programs are currently subcontracted to third-party corporations offering 'educational services', or have been relegated to what the University of London's Celia Whitchurch (2008, 2009) has called 'third space' organizations – departments within the neoliberal university that manage corporate services, talent development and global initiatives.

The regime of 'new managerialism' (Deem, 2001) tasked with implementing these changes fosters precarious work environments where the vocational identities of teachers of EAP (TEAPs) are steadily deconstructed and are recast into service personnel. TEAPs are required to quickly 'process' students, fix their language and to unquestioningly support new administrative initiatives aimed at providing educational 'experiences' for a wide variety of new 'clientele'. Out of the maelstrom of these changes, a new type of worker has emerged – one who is responsible for managing processes and leading TEAPs to accept their altered roles. Expected to produce results without positional power, these new workers in the neoliberal university are no longer completely TEAPs, but neither are they fully administrators. Eminently expendable and perilously placed between teachers and the new management, here we find the blended EAP professional, otherwise known as the BLEAP.

This chapter presents one of several strategies that BLEAPs use to satisfy the demands of the neoliberal university. Known as resource leeching, a concept recently highlighted in a critical grounded theory (Hadley, 2015) studying sociological processes taking place within American, British and Japanese university EAP programs, it is a theoretical term that explains how BLEAPs profit from the free labor and talents of others while offering only token rewards in return. This chapter presents an overview of how resource leeching works in neoliberalized EAP programs, and sheds light on some of the ways that top-tier universities providing educational experiences for international students avoid the leeching attempts of their 'feeder' universities. Possible responses to resource leeching will be couched within the question of whether it contributes to educational opportunities for students or if it is a strategy aimed at cutting costs during an era when human labor has been drastically devalued. Background concepts and important theoretical terms will now be considered.

Conceptual Underpinnings

While neoliberalism has long been a concern of critical scholars, it has only recently garnered the attention of applied linguists (e.g. Block, 2008; Holborow, 2013). This section considers how neoliberalism has affected universities and their incumbent EAP programs. Following an overview of this subject, I will briefly discuss the critical grounded theory within which the strategy of resource leeching is located. For those unfamiliar with grounded theory, a short explanation of the methodology has been provided.

Neoliberalism, universities and EAP

As a 'rascal concept' (Brenner et al., 2010: 184) neoliberalism has been notoriously difficult to pin down, partly because of its interconnected economic, political, social and cultural dynamics, and partly because those promoting it around the world prefer anonymity (Monbiot, 2016). Neoliberalism represents the resurgence of the 19th-century economic theory of liberalism, which views ideal economic markets as self-regulating and self-correcting. Drawing from Social Darwinism, the basis of human interaction in neoliberalism centers on competition. Members of a society improve each other for the greater good through struggle, rivalry and consumption. The strong survive by being more successful than their competitors; losers are worthy of their lot in life. Modern neoliberalism builds upon this idea from the intellectual foundation of thinkers such as Friedrich von Hayek (1944) and Milton Friedman (1962), who in the name of personal choice and freedom, called for the deregulation of national economies, the liberalization of trade and commerce and the privatization of post offices, government welfare services and state-supported education. Presented as a rational world view (Frieden, 2006; Harvey, 2005), the virtues of a global market, such as 'excellence' and 'expertise', the free flow of goods, flexible services, and cheap yet talented labor, are elevated by multinational corporations as they pursue their vision of a technologically advanced, efficient and more convenient world (Steger & Roy, 2010).

One common question within this discussion is whether neoliberalism differs from capitalism, or if it is essentially one in the same. Operative here is the mistake of viewing capitalism as monolithic. Capitalism, in general terms, refers to 'a system in which markets and commodity production are pervasive, [and which] is essentially a type of market system involving extensive private property, capital markets, and employment contracts' (Hodgson *et al.*, 2001: 4). Within this understanding, various forms of capitalism have been constructed. For example, 'Quaker Capitalism' in England during the 19th century prioritized the needs of workers and their communities over that of the shareholders. Profits were used to develop sustainable enterprises that would benefit society (King, 2014). Keynesian theory, with its emphasis on investment and the government's role in curbing the boom–bust market cycle, was another form of capitalism. Neoliberalism is also a distinct form of capitalism, especially in its emphasis on pitting people against each other as competitors for goods, and in its stratification of society into winners and losers. In addition, neoliberal policymakers reduce corporate taxes and curtail public funding for social services. Once these services begin to run inefficiently due to underfunding, they are targeted for privatization which, it is claimed, stimulates competition, innovation and growth, but which also stratifies services based upon one's ability to pay (Frieden, 2006; Harvey, 2005; Steger & Roy, 2010). Neoliberalism privileges 'the market' as a moral compass, and by using constant measurement, assessment and the desire for unlimited growth to spur further competition, it encourages the creation of a society that, according to Verhaeghe (2014: 174–175), rewards people who are articulate, flexible, impulsive and able to stimulate the emotions of others in order to satisfy their need for new challenges, skilled in manipulating people or systems, able to lie convincingly, capable of quickly shifting the blame for failure, rational in using goal-oriented violence and willing to take risks at the expense of others. Neoliberalism, in Verhaeghe's view, rewards psychopathic behavior: the strong profit off the weak because this is what they deserve. What one should or should not do to others gives way to what one can do with impunity, so long as it is profitable.

Over the past 30 years, neoliberalism, rather than democracy, has had significant influence on government policies, markets, cultural values and higher education. The steady imbrication of neoliberal policies in America and elsewhere has contributed to the development of the neoliberal university, which is defined as a self-interested, entrepreneurial organization offering educational experiences and research services to paying clients. Educators are construed as managed knowledge producers who require constant measurement in order to confirm their conformity to prescribed sets of organizational processes. Students become knowledge consumers who have a voice in determining how educational services are packaged and delivered (Castree & Sparke, 2000; Jarvis, 2001; Mckenzie & Scheurich, 2004; Steck, 2003).

Scholars are also studying how long-held humanistic beliefs and practices in university EAP programs have been replaced by corporate discourse (e.g. Block et al., 2012). Fairclough (2008), Phillipson (2008) and Mautner (2010) have studied the diffusion of business words and managerial jargon within the world of language education, while Duchêne and Heller (2012) and Block and Cameron (2002) note the degree to which English language education has been repackaged as a product that is commodified for delivery to knowledge consumers. Holborow (2013, 2015) has written extensively and persuasively on the existential threat posed by neoliberal thinking on humanistic values in EAP, such as the nurturing of students, respect for the vocation of teachers and the notion of equitable treatment. Hadley (2015) has written most directly on the effects of neoliberalism on EAP through a critical grounded theory developed over six years, and which was based on nearly 100 informant interviews at 18 universities located in Japan, the United Kingdom and the United States. It details how TEAPs became unwitting pawns in the spread of neoliberal policies across their campuses through a process described as *professional disarticulation*, which takes place when EAP teachers are divested of their traditional teaching roles, moved out of academic departments and put into isolated, ambiguous 'third spaces' where working conditions become increasingly precarious. Modern neoliberalism attacks vocational identities as inflexible and works toward the creation of a malleable workforce that quickly and uncritically accommodates the demands of its technocratic leaders. Professional disarticulation is a process by which one is forcibly pulled out and twisted from one's earlier sense of calling. Job titles may stay the same, but the blurring of traditional boundaries in the neoliberal university means that one's original skills as a TEAP are explicitly devalued. One finds over time that one's earlier duties become subsumed under new, more pressing expectations from above and are accompanied by growing feelings of insecurity, powerlessness and injustice. TEAPs in many universities around the world now serve as the reluctant foot soldiers of university global initiatives and administrative strategic plans, all of which are mediated through one who has been raised up to become a BLEAP. More than teaching, these new workers are expected to keep TEAPs under control while both hunting and gathering new students for the EAP program, which provides a significant amount of new money to the university. BLEAPs are in charge of weighing and measuring all aspects of work in order to demonstrate excellence, and they must mold and shape both international students and TEAPs into whatever role the neoliberal university requires. BLEAPs, especially those who are upwardly mobile and seeking to enter into higher levels of administration, are central to the neoliberal colonization of EAP and resource leeching, a process that will be discussed, is only one of several theoretical properties that make up the overall process described as 'hunting and gathering'.

Grounded Theory

The grounded theory methodology (GTM) was introduced over 40 years ago through the pioneering work of sociologists Barney Glaser and Anselm Strauss. Their book, *The Discovery of Grounded Theory: Strategies for Qualitative Research* (Glaser & Strauss, 1967/1999), challenged researchers to develop theoretical perspectives from direct interaction with people in the field. For Glaser and Strauss (1967/1999: 1), 'grounded' meant that findings were rooted in first-hand evidence – the problems, actions, symbols and aspirations of the people being studied – and 'theory' referred to an explanatory model that 'fits empirical situations. It should be understandable to sociologists and laymen alike. Most important it works – it provides us with relevant predictions, explanations, interpretations and applications'.

Grounded Theory is a bottom-up form of analysis of various levels of coding and the constant comparison of incidents found in interviews, field observations, inductive memos and pertinent scholarly literature. Out of this, an abductive theory is constructed to explain the interactions and solutions of people in specific social circumstances.

Today, several forms of GTM are available (Bryant & Charmaz, 2007: 11–12). While differences exist among theorists regarding methods of coding, stages of analysis and modes of theory construction, the end product is something more than a description of different themes lifted from the data. Good grounded theories have a central problem or social process, around which one finds an interconnected set of properties. These properties are often described through memorable metaphors that explain the various social interactions that revolve around the main problem or issue. Grounded Theory has grown to become one of 'the most widely employed interpretive strategy in the social sciences today' (Denzin & Lincoln, 1998: xviii). For those who appreciate the role of theory for studying complex, multilayered social dynamics, GTM offers a large body of literature featuring theories that predict social outcomes and offer insight into a wide range of contexts. Let us now turn our attention to one of the many social dynamics currently taking place behind the closed doors of EAP programs in neoliberal universities, that of resource leeching.

Resource Leeching

I have chosen to expand upon this property because of the rapid spread of corporate practices such as zero hour contracts, the so-called 'sharing economy', the use of bots for replacing frontline service personnel and the corporate acquisition of free student labor under the guise of internships (Tuchman, 2009; Washburn, 2005). What binds these practices are intertwining notions of increased profitability through reducing labor costs and of using customers to provide free labor as part of the process of receiving products or services. These and similar cost-saving strategies increase the sense of precariousness in society and devalues people in the names of expediency and profitability. Such values from the corporate world, it is believed, operate within neoliberal universities, so a study of social processes such as resource leeching has a certain salience for teachers and scholars. While resource leeching was observed to be widespread in EAP programs, I will focus primarily upon blended EAP professionals, since they have a pivotal role in encouraging this practice within their programs.

Context

Neoliberal university policies compel BLEAPs to work in a climate of constant austerity. With the same or slightly reduced levels of budgeting every year, the only increase they can expect is in their workload. Employing extra help is rarely an option. More often than not, BLEAPs are alone in their task of implementing initiatives that seek to exploit the talents and resources of the EAP program. Such austerity and organizational isolation set BLEAPs on a trajectory that eventually leads to resource leeching.

Initial stage

BLEAPs soon find that they struggle to 'carve out time' for the things that truly matter – a common, though unhealthy feature of professional life in neoliberal universities around the world (Anderson, 2006). Often, they will attempt to address all the tasks received from both above and below, hoping this will free up time later for research or strategic planning. To their rue, they soon discover that successfully finishing such tasks results in even more work, with burnout looming on the horizon:

Informant: (sighs wearily) I can ... sort of, recruit a little bit more for the EAP program. With a little bit of time ... try to, get something planned ... but when you, when you ... don't have more than 30 minutes in a day to devote to sitting down and doing something large and strategic ...

GH: Right, mm-hm.

Informant: ... and you can carve that out, but ... I'm tired. I can carve out three hours here, and I still get every phone call that filters back, 'oh he's in his office, yeah just a second'. You know, and that's training issues and stuff. But I, I would rather ... make an impact, with the EAP program, that's going to be innovative ... a good program that really truly benefits the university on a larger level. That takes, takes a lot of work.

GH: Sure does ...

Informant: It really is easy to just sort of ... sit back on your heels, and, and just, you know ... plug, plug the holes. It really is. And that's, and that's really sort of all that you can manage on a day to day basis, is that you, you make sure that things are running that need to be running, and that's what you're doing. (Interview, November 28, 2005)

BLEAPs continuing on this path become too exhausted and embittered to be effective. Successful BLEAPs, however, quickly learn that maintaining the EAP program is insufficient in the new neoliberal order: they need to demonstrate that they are entrepreneurial and strategic, even if this means transforming the EAP program, its people and its sources of external support, into something very different from before. It is at this point that resource leeching becomes an option for the upwardly mobile BLEAP seeking to survive.

Taking a page from modern corporate practices

The term 'resource leeching' was inspired by the internet term of 'leeching', which is when people use software to mine information from other sites while leaving only minimal returns. Resource leeching as used here describes the purposeful utilization of volunteers, co-workers, educators, students, talented individuals and even prestigious organizations, for accomplishing innovative projects, reducing the weight of increased workloads and improving the image of the BLEAP and/or institution. Token returns usually take the form of certificates of appreciation or equally inexpensive forms of recognition.

Started in the 1990s, resource leeching draws upon managerial ideas that valued notions of 'free-riding' and 'consumer manufacture'. These required consumers to assemble the product or provide any final services for themselves (Huczynski, 1992: 19). The evolution of this concept can be seen today in companies such as IKEA or in automated banking services, automated airline ticketing and retail stores such as WalMart and Tesco, where customers are urged to check out their own goods and to pay into a machine. The savings in labor costs to the corporations are significant, but there are little or no savings to the consumers providing the free labor.

With regard to EAP in neoliberal universities, BLEAPs who engage in resource leeching will be on the lookout for isolated individuals yearning to showcase their talent or who are searching for a sense of belonging. The need for community and social interaction is also a draw for those outside the university, but other tradeoffs include the public recognition given by the university or the social prestige gained in having an association with the university. International students within the university hope to link their studies to real-world experience. The benefits to BLEAPs and the university, however, are often more concrete, as in this interview with a BLEAP at an American institution, who is discussing new government rules for tracking international students:

Informant: Without getting really super boring, immigration regulations have been broadened so that they're more beneficial to some students in the United States, but the heightened reporting requirements that are placed upon international student services offices have basically taken us from one paradigm to another in terms of tracking and maintaining students. The new paradigm is that if those students stay, we track them through to the finish. So we track them through and we're responsible for reporting on their address, when they start and stop any jobs in that training and where those jobs are. We're required to report all of that.

GH: To the government?

Informant: To the ... to the CEVUS database, which is the government. And it's a one-by-one field that full-time, or ... well, which paid staff need to do. And it's taken a workload, and I've already gone to the board to request funding to go and move that position to a full-time position, and it was denied. And so we don't have that. So what's happened is, is that it's pulled me back into CEVUS and to maintaining CEVUS, and making sure that we're compliant with those immigration regulations, that we're keeping up with those students, and right now, because we don't have, we don't have the money to pay for a really fancy database, I'm working with a project team of Indian Masters of Applied Computer Science students to make a database for us so that we can keep up with all of this, and keep up with tracking students, and from the time that they apply all the way through. (Interview, November 5, 2008)

Facing a major work increase and a denial of resources to hire extra help, this BLEAP appropriates the expertise of a group of international students, who in turn create a database tracking system that would have cost a considerable amount of money had it been developed by professionals. Resource leeching at this level is almost always motivated by the need to find free labor solutions to solve increased work burdens. If successful, BLEAPs can impress administrative mangers with their ability to mobilize people in innovative, strategic programs without incurring large financial costs to the institution. One easy way of identifying where resource leeching is taking place is to calculate how much university administration would request in remuneration for the same level of work being provided free of charge by students or other volunteers. There are both internal and external aspects to resource leeching, both of which will now be considered in brief.

Internal resource leeching

Internal resource leeching takes place within the university, as highlighted in the last interview extract in the previous section. Both international students and TEAPs are targets for internal resource leeching. This is because TEAPs within neoliberal universities are often marginalized unless and until they can demonstrate some measurable benefit to their administrative managers. Many in upper-level administration spoke of EAP primarily in its potential for international student recruitment. EAP at cash-starved neoliberal universities becomes a means to an end, and so too are the people connected to its functions. The multicultural talents and communicative skills of TEAPs, which were acquired for the task of educating and training learners to succeed in their academic studies, are now leeched for the purposes of recruitment or other initiatives related to service learning or diversity.

BLEAPs watch for international students who have the potential to recruit other students able to pay high tuition fees. Although 'word-of-mouth' referrals from students have been around for as long as there have been universities (Klafter, 2008), the resource leeching of international students represents a more purposeful effort at engaging students in the recruitment of other students.

At one Japanese university in my earlier study (Hadley, 2015: 88–89), students returning from their overseas experience found it difficult to relate with classmates who did not go abroad. In response, an entrepreneurial teacher seeking promotion to an administrative position in the university developed a program similar to the World Expo program at the University of Lawrence in the United States, where recently recruited international students showcase traditional aspects of their national culture to local residents and publicly highlight the image of diversity to which the university aspires (Katz, 2006: 58). In the program developed at the Japanese university, however, groups of overseas students were sent to primary and secondary schools. Often, there was an effort to ensure that students went to the schools they attended when younger, which afforded them a measure of respect and rapport, since Japanese tend to maintain social contacts made at primary and secondary schools long into adulthood. During these visits, students would perform skits, give experiential lessons on global issues and talk to their younger peers about their adventures in the university-sponsored overseas program.

While the program provided fresh and engaging educational experiences for young students, discussions with the administrative managers at the university revealed that the program was developed primarily for student recruitment. Using university teachers was not seen as effective because of the generational gap, so the idea was to use the enthusiasm of university students to reach these young learners. In this way, the university's name could be planted in their minds before pupils had started seriously thinking about a university. In addition, by packaging the program as an educational experience, the university students provided their recruitment services free of charge, thus making the program very economical. The success of the program propelled the faculty member into administration, and the BLEAP at the university was put in charge of maintaining it thereafter.

In the United States, this form of resource leeching is also carried out through 'word of mouse' approaches (Darrup-Boychuck, 2007: 51). Study blogs are designed for international and domestic students to contribute stories about their countries and overseas experiences. Similar to the Facebook model, BLEAPs carefully monitor contributions and create a database of names and interests:

> the most successful campaigns are those that fully integrate all of a campus' marketing activities, from using the Internet to generate initial inquiries, to building a database from which counselors extract student names based on the geographic regions they intend to visit, and then sending special invitations to those selected students. (Darrup-Boychuck, 2007: 51)

At Suffolk University in Boston, when domestic students who have contributed to the university's international studies blog mention any interest of going abroad, this is flagged in the database and students are invited to become a 'country ambassador' for the university. If they agree, they are given the contact information of potential international students living in the country where the ambassador is going, and are urged to recruit them for Suffolk University. The same sort of ambassadorship is extended to graduating international students returning to their home country (Katz, 2006: 56). The returns are considerable, since students pay for their own transportation and recruit for the university without receiving a commission.

External resource leeching

External resource leeching uses community members or prestigious institutions to provide economical educational experiences for students. As an example, the following is from an interview with a senior administrator about an American cultural studies class, which for many years had been an integral part of an overseas program designed for Japanese students. The lecturer no longer found the class to be worthwhile, because it had been reduced to a one-hour course in order to mitigate other rising program costs. The Japanese university wanted to maintain access to the faculty member, as it helped in their own marketing purposes for recruiting new students. The American university, however, wanted to avoid being leeched:

Informant: It's possible that we could find other ways for providing that experiences, different from a one-hour course that (name redacted) would teach. For instance, *could* we do, you know, where you spend two weeks or three weeks with this person coming in and talking about X, and then two or three weeks twice a week where this person comes in and talks about Y. The way to approach it *might* be, is what are the *other* ways to meet that purpose? It wouldn't always have to be a faculty member. It could be a staff member. It could be a community member. If you're talking about doing some things with the culture, (name of a retired teacher in the community) coming and talking about something like that. He'd get a kick out of doing something like that.

GH: You can do that with a team of academics. A team of community academics.

Informant: That's right. Right. A team of cultural experts. And that's **anybody** who could tell you about what they do, and then they're an expert in that part of the culture. (Interview, October 29, 2007)

One growth area for external resource leeching is within the changing relationship between elite universities and lower-status universities, who have served for many years as what was often described as 'feeders'. When I began my sociological study of university EAP, such programs were small, exclusive, taught by academics and attended by students who already had relatively high levels of language proficiency. Overseas programs for short-term students were virtually non-existent, as were blended EAP professionals mediating multiple agendas in the ambiguous third spaces of the organization. Today, however, the situation has changed. One can find EAP language centers and short-term experiential programs at even the most famous of universities. These are often taught by short-term or contracted EAP teachers, and those seen as having the most experience or business acumen are being raised up to become BLEAPs.

Focusing now on the short-term overseas programs, for many years at the top-tier universities in my study, the relationship between these elite universities and their feeders was almost symbiotic. Sitting at the top of the food chain, elite universities received ample numbers of students, often during times when normal classes were out of session. Even when attending during sessions, these students rarely put a strain on university finances, since they rarely took advantage of the campus services normally used by full-time students, and because they often brought a level of enthusiasm to campus not seen among the long-term international students. In addition to the substantial fees paid to the university, these other features made them valued resource enhancements. The students were inspired by having the chance to study briefly at a famous university and would usually receive a certificate bearing the name of the university acknowledging the successful completion of the non-credit bearing, short-term program. In addition, the sending universities benefited greatly by marketing themselves as an access point for what would otherwise be an unattainable elite university.

Most of these overseas programs were designed with the Asian student in mind. Developments in Asia, however, have started to change the dynamics between prestigious universities and their feeders. Across the region, in countries as varied as Japan, Vietnam, China and the Philippines, educational ministries, acting at the behest of multinational corporations, are pushing universities into the implementation of English medium instruction (EMI) programs, with hopes that graduates will be able to gain a level of English proficiency suitable for working in the global job market. Kirkpatrick's (2014) survey of EMI in several Asian countries found that many universities see EMI as a means of recruiting international students. Because EMI-based initiatives are increasingly linked to future government funding, many Asian universities are trying to find ways of implementing EMI programs while avoiding either the enormous expense of hiring large numbers of expatriate native speakers or retraining current teachers (Brown & Adamson, 2014; Brown & Iyobe, 2014; Nha & Burns, 2014). Underfunded and overworked, many of these Asian universities are turning to external resource leeching. BLEAPs are being sent out on hunting missions, first to sign international partnership agreements with prestigious universities, and then to encourage the exchange of students who are native speakers of English, so that they might provide educational opportunities for domestic students.

The result is that BLEAPs at prestigious universities are currently receiving more requests for student and faculty exchange than that of hosting groups of students on campus for short-term programs. One recent interview with a focus group of three BLEAPs at a world-famous British university revealed that, on the one hand, such interest generates the possibility of making more money, which enhances their value to university management:

GH: Yes, they're hunting … they're hunting you.
Informant 3: (Nodding) Mm.
Informant 1: Yes.
GH: How do you handle that?
Informant 1: Well actually for us it's actually a good thing because the role of our department is to support the main role of college, which is teaching the undergraduates. We set up probably fifteen, sixteen years ago, very small in the eyes of other people in the college, and it's actually grown and grown, and we're very professional at what we do and we take a lot of care about it. When people come to us … that's good because it means people have heard about us and word of mouth's gone out … it's a two-way process but it's actually a result of our hard work that people are now coming round. (Interview, March 11, 2015)

On the other hand, such requests are also problematic:

Informant 1: Well, we see it really wherever we go, but there's a slight problem that we've had, because let's say when we visit Taiwan we go to the universities, pretty much nine out of ten of those universities will say to us, 'Oh, and we'd also like to arrange exchanges' and that's something we can't … we're not authorized to make the decisions on … so it's always a bit tricky for us because we are actually going because they're our partners and we go to promote the program and hopefully recruit quite a

Informant 3:

large group of students, but beyond that we don't have much of a remit to do anything else ... we don't want to give bad news, especially for us three because we are actually the people delivering that news to the likes of [redacted] University or [redacted] University, and so that sort of intake is 'Oh, how do we get around this issue without appearing rude?'

Informant 3:   So it's a matter of not offending people and also pointing out politely that it's not actually our prerogative to make decisions, and also being mindful of the fact that it's not anybody's fault. It's just something, it's just an incompatible system. It's almost like we go to another country, change plugs or something, it's just an incompatibility. (Interview, March 11, 2015)

From a business standpoint, an exchange of students from a high-status to a low-status feeder university is a bad deal. Strategies for dealing with aggressive feeders were discussed:

Informant 1:   What we tend to do, because we do face it nine times out of ten, is slightly sort of 'Aah, mm, well we're not so sure', and then we suggest well maybe you might want to contact the more modern universities, and basically anyone apart from [university name].

Informant 2:   Or sometimes we say, with the best will, if they're interested in a specific subject, get in touch with (name of a university administrative office).

Informant 3:   Another we find quite useful is that even though we say, 'Look, we're sorry, we can't' or 'that's unfeasible' we often say, 'However, we are very happy to promote your Chinese language programs over to our graduates' because we can't promote year exchange programs, we can advertise to our graduates, after they've graduated then they obviously can do what they want, it's not dependent on what the [redacted] says.

Informant 1:   It's also more unofficial, isn't it?

Informant 3:   Yeah, but it sort of shows them that we are taking their courses seriously and it's not because we don't want to...

Informant 1:   ... no, no. It is awkward for us ...

Informant 3:   ... and sometimes they don't get the message. I think (name of Asian university academic) asks us every year <laughs>.

These are examples of a contingency strategy in resource leeching labeled *dead-ending*. Through dead-ending, feeders are either offered a less valuable host or are encouraged to expend their energies on hunting and gathering in empty places among the most unattainable of people in the university. In time, the BLEAP can either redirect the focus of this errant feeder back to supplying the original overseas program or replace it with another more pliable school. In a world where even the most prestigious of universities are being reshaped by neoliberal values, the hunter must avoid becoming the hunted. A measure of guile is needed to survive.

For BLEAPs at feeder universities sallying forth at the behest of upper-level management to leech students, faculty or other prestigious resources from elite universities, the chances for success in gaining greater access to such prizes are slim, unless and until feeder universities band together to coordinate their approach. Similar to an apex predator on the savannah who looks up from feeding to find he is surrounded by a pack of hyenas grinning in silent expectation, such a prospect would be a nightmare scenario for BLEAPs at elite universities. Nevertheless, no examples of such cooperation were ever observed among feeder universities, since neoliberal thinking posits universities more as corporate rivals than as partners cooperating in the task of educating people to build a better world.

A Critical Response to Resource Leeching

With reference to the earlier discussion of the nature of neoliberalism within the wider development of capitalism, I would argue that strategies such as resource leeching, which privileges acquisition over any qualms of veering into the gray areas of ethical action, is a classic example of how neoliberal thinking manifests itself in daily institutional action. Before the diffusion of neoliberal beliefs into virtually every aspect of public life, a time when universities had a parental role in the task of educating learners, resource leeching would have been unthinkable. This is no longer the case, and this chapter has presented only a fraction of how others use resource leeching in EAP. In the case of TEAPs, for example, some have turned to utilizing international students as 'near-peers'. These are students with a higher level of language proficiency who have been recruited as unpaid teachers' aides. While presented publically as a means of inspiring their contemporaries to progress in their studies (Bernat, 2008; Craig, 2008;

Murphey & Falout, 2013), my study found that the original motivation stemmed from finding ways to deal with growing workloads and steadily increasing numbers of students in the classroom. In this and other observed cases of resource leeching, Van Maanen *et al.* (1982: 11), inspired by Murray Edelman (1964), poignantly express the power imbalance that I find to be at the heart of this problematic process: 'The powerful gain rewards of the material sort while the weak gain (at best) rewards of the symbolic kind. Ceremony may be difficult to digest but the celebrants may find themselves hungry'. As universities face steady decreases in public support, hiring freezes and workload increases for those who remain, the walls which once protected students and separated universities from the hunger games of the business world have now become more permeable; entrepreneurs of all types seek to access the talent and valuable resources from outside and within. While it may be possible for educational opportunities to arise from resource leeching, this is derivative, since it is used less as a means to nurture students, and more as a way to feed the institution. Starved of resources through forced austerity, neoliberal universities resort to eating their young. The rationality of neoliberalism, left unchallenged and unchecked, abandons the most vulnerable members of society to the whims of those with the most power – and often those with the least accountability. In an attempt to bandage the fiscal wounds caused by neoliberalism, deeper wounds are being inflicted upon our future through the 'invisible syllabus' – one that instructs students about how to get ahead through watching how things work in the university. Resource leeching teaches that success comes through manipulating the unsuspecting and through justifying one's ulterior motives after the fact with vague promises of benefits. The result of such lessons will be to lead future generations boldly toward a new Bronze Age – a world described by educational reformer and Cornell University president Andrew Dickson White (1904/2007: 326) as one which reduces higher education to 'that which enables a man to live by his wits and prey upon his neighbors'.

How should one respond to resource leeching? My reading of other critical studies dealing with power and inequality in language teaching finds that, regardless of one's opinion about this issue, it must be approached in an attitude of full disclosure (Cook, 2012; Harwood & Hadley, 2004; Olssen & Peters, 2005; Phillipson, 2008). Just as other parts of the neoliberal administration require educators to be ethical in their dealings with students and informants by providing a full description of the purpose, risks and expected outcomes of research participation, in like manner, BLEAPs and others in the neoliberal university administration should fully explain their initiatives to international students and other volunteers.

Too often this is not the case. In over six years of research on this subject, I repeatedly found resource leeching thriving in ambiguity. International students, TEAPs and other volunteers were tacitly allowed to fill in their own blanks for why they were approached, how they would benefit from participation and how the EAP program and the university profited from their contribution. Unless there is informed consent so that participants can make a free and independent decision, practices such as resource leeching are inherently unethical, and for those who do consent to participate in administrative initiatives, more research is needed into discovering what and how much students learn from these experiences.

Conclusion

As educators and stewards of the future, we must question the world view that is being foisted upon our discipline. With critical awareness and in a spirit of academic fairness, we must make our learners aware of issues such as those discussed in this chapter and teach them to transcend greed in order to make contributions to the greater good. In doing so, we contribute to creating a world that represents one of progress and hope. Given that practices such as resource leeching represent one of the games that people play in the neoliberal university, full disclosure is needed so that everyone will know the rules. Otherwise, resource leeching and similar practices will continue to contribute to the corruption of the curriculum, and foster an environment in which education is gained through exploitation.

References

Anderson, G. (2006) Carving out time and space in the managerial university. *Journal of Organizational Change Management* 19 (5), 578–592.

Bernat, E. (2008) Towards a pedagogy of empowerment: The case of 'impostor syndrome' among pre-service non-native speaker teachers in TESOL. *English Language Teacher Education and Development* 11 (1), 1–8.

Block, D. (2008) Language education and globalization. In S. May and N. Hornberger (eds) *Encyclopedia of Language and Education* (pp. 1–13). Philadelphia, PA: Springer Science+Business Media LLC.

Block, D. and Cameron, D. (eds) (2002) *Globalization and Language Teaching*. London: Routledge.

Block, D., Gray, J. and Holborow, M. (eds) (2012) *Neoliberalism and Applied Linguistics*. London: Routledge.

Brenner, N., Peck, J. and Theodore, N. (2010) Variegated neoliberalization: Geographies, modalities, pathways. *Global Networks* 10, 182–222.

Brown, H. and Adamson, J. (2014) Localizing EAP in light of the rise of English-medium instruction at Japanese universities. *On Cue Journal* 6 (3), 5–20.

Brown, H. and Iyobe, B. (2014) The growth of English medium instruction in Japan. In N. Sonda and A. Krause (eds) *JALT2013 Conference Proceedings* (pp. 9–19). Tokyo: JALT.

Bryant, A. and Charmaz, K. (2007) Grounded theory research: Methods and practices. In A. Bryant and K. Charmaz (eds) *The Sage Handbook of Grounded Theory* (pp. 1–28). London: Sage Publications.

Castree, N. and Sparke, M. (2000) Professional geography and the corporatization of the university: Experiences, evaluations, and engagements. *Antipode* 32 (3), 222–229.

Charles, M. and Pecorari, D. (2016) *Introducing English for Academic Purposes.* Abingdon: Routledge.

Cook, G. (2012) British applied linguistics: Impacts of and impacts on. *Applied Linguistics Review* 3 (1), 25–45.

Craig, R. (2008) Time for a change – Back to the 70s: Language across the disciplines revisited. *International Journal of Learning* 14 (9), 249–257.

Darrup-Boychuck, D. (2007) Apropos of e-recruitment. *International Educator* 16 (1), 50–51.

Deem, R. (2001) Globalisation, new managerialism, academic capitalism and entrepreneurialism in universities: Is the local dimension still important? *Comparative Education* 37 (1), 7–20.

Denzin, N. and Lincoln, Y. (1998) Introduction to this volume. In N. Denzin and Y. Lincoln (eds) *Strategies of Qualitative Inquiry* (pp. xi–xxii). London: Sage Publications.

Duchêne, A. and Heller, M. (eds) (2012) *Language in Late Capitalism: Pride and Profit.* New York: Routledge.

Edelman, M. (1964) *The Symbolic Uses of Politics.* Urbana, IL: University of Illinois Press.

Fairclough, N. (2008) *Language and Globalisation.* London: Routledge.

Frieden, J. (2006) *Global Capitalism: Its Fall and Rise in the Twentieth Century.* New York: W.W. Norton and Company.

Friedman, M. (1962) *Capitalism and Freedom.* Chicago, IL: University of Chicago Press.

Glaser, B. and Strauss, A. (1967/1999) *The Discovery of Grounded Theory: Strategies for Qualitative Research.* New York: Aldine de Gruyter.

Hadley, G. (2015) *English for Academic Purposes in Neoliberal Universities: A Critical Grounded Theory.* Heidelburg: Springer.

Harvey, D. (2005) *A Brief History of Neoliberalism.* Oxford: Oxford University Press.

Harwood, N. and Hadley, G. (2004) Demystifying institutional practices: Critical pragmatism and the teaching of academic writing. *English for Specific Purposes* 23 (4), 355–377.

Hayek, F. (1944) *The Road to Serfdom.* London: Routledge Press.

Hodgson, G., Itoh, M. and Yokokawa, N. (2001) Introduction. In G. Hodgson, M. Itoh and N. Yokokawa (eds) *Capitalism in Evolution: Global Contentions – East and West* (pp. 1–18). Cheltenham: Edward Elgar.

Holborow, M. (2013) Applied linguistics in the neoliberal university: Ideological key words and social agency. *Applied Linguistics Review* 4 (2), 229–257.

Holborow, M. (2015) *Language and Neoliberalism.* London: Routledge.

Huczynski, A. (1992) Management guru ideas and the 12 secrets of their success. *Leadership & Organization Development Journal* 13 (5), 15–20.

Jarvis, P. (2001) *Universities and Corporate Universities: The Higher Learning Industry in Global Society.* London: Routledge.

Kachru, B. (1982) *The Other Tongue: English Across Cultures*. Urbana, IL: University of Illinois Press.

Katz, E. (2006) Recruiting international graduate students today. *International Educator* 15 (4), 54–58.

King, M. (2014) *Quakernomics: An Ethical Capitalism*. London: Anthem Press.

Kirkpatrick, A. (2014) English as a medium of instruction in east and southeast Asian universities. In N. Murray and A. Scarino (eds) *Dynamic Ecologies* (pp. 15–29). Dordrecht: Springer.

Klafter, C. (2008) University internalization: Dreaming of a bygone age. *International Educator* 17 (4), 56–59.

Mautner, G. (2010) *Language and the Market Society: Critical Reflections on Discourse and Dominance*. London: Routledge.

Mckenzie, K. and Scheurich, J. (2004) The corporatization and privatization of schooling: A call for grounded critical praxis. *Educational Theory* 54 (4), 431–443.

Monbiot, G. (2016) Neoliberalism – the ideology at the root of all our problems. *The Guardian*, 16 April. See https://www.theguardian.com/books/2016/apr/15/neoliberalism-ideology-problem-george-monbiot (accessed 21 November 2016).

Murphey, T. and Falout, J. (2013) Individual differences in the classroom. In C. Chapelle (ed.) *The Encyclopedia of Applied Linguistics* (pp. 2650–2654). Oxford: Wiley-Blackwell Publishing.

Nha, T.T.V. and Burns, A. (2014) English as a medium of instruction: Challenges for Vietnamese tertiary lecturers. *The Journal of Asia TEFL* 11 (3), 1–31.

Olssen, M. and Peters, M. (2005) Neoliberalism, higher education and the knowledge economy: From the free market to knowledge capitalism. *Journal of Education Policy* 20 (3), 313–345.

Phillipson, R. (2008) The linguistic imperialism of neoliberal empire. *Critical Enquiry in Language Studies* 5 (1), 1–43.

Steck, H. (2003) Corporatization of the university: Seeking conceptual clarity. *The ANNALS of the American Academy of Political and Social Science* 585 (1), 66–83.

Steger, M. and Roy, R. (2010) *Neoliberalism: A Very Short Introduction*. Oxford: Oxford University Press.

Tuchman, G. (2009) *Wannabe U: Inside the Corporate University*. Chicago, IL: University of Chicago Press.

Van Maanen, J., Dabbs, J. and Faulkner, R. (1982) *Varieties of Qualitative Research*. Beverly Hills, CA: Sage Publications.

Verhaeghe, P. (2014) *What about Me? The Struggle for Identity in a Market-Based Society*. Melbourne: Scribe.

Washburn, J. (2005) *University, Inc.: The Corporate Corruption of American Higher Education*. New York: Basic Books.

Whitchurch, C. (2008) Shifting identities and blurring boundaries: The emergence of 'third space' professionals in UK higher education. *Higher Education Quarterly* 62 (4), 377–396.

Whitchurch, C. (2009) The rise of the blended professional in higher education: A comparison between the United Kingdom, Australia and the United States. *Higher Education* 58 (3), 407–418.

White, A.D. (1904/2007) *Autobiography of Andrew Dickson White, Volume One*. Charleston, SC: BiblioBazaar.

11 Win-Win?! Language Regulation for Competitiveness in a University Context

Martina Zimmermann and Mi-Cha Flubacher

Introduction

It has often been argued that in times of neoliberalism and late capitalism, communicative skills and language competence have become a resource and a veritable work instrument (see for example Boutet, 2008; Cameron, 2000; Heller, 2003), which in turn is linked with the increasing tertiarization of labor and services (Duchêne & Heller, 2012; Spilker, 2010). Apart from being the main instrument for communication and client services, language competence is also used by companies to reach new markets and/or to target specific (linguistic) populations (Kelly-Holmes, 2006; Piller, 2001). In displaying competence in the customer language, certain companies can sell themselves as 'different' within a globalized labor market in which the majority of companies oftentimes only fall back on the most widely used lingua francas. On the other hand, individuals competent in these languages can sell this competence to employers and companies, thus turning them into their personal marker of distinction (Bourdieu, 1979) in the process of a job application, for example. Specific language competence thus allows both individuals and companies to create a marker of distinction for themselves and, thus, to become veritable symbolic capital (Bourdieu, 1979). In this case, this symbolic capital (i.e. linguistic profiles) can ideally be converted into economic capital (a job, more salary or revenues, more market shares etc.). It is this convertibility of different forms of capital that Bourdieu (1979) regarded as the most important aspect when referring to 'capitalization'.

Increasingly, the trend to treat languages and language competences based on their potential economic capitalization is not restricted to the private economic sector but has also become perceptible in the public sector. The division between the private and public sector has in any case become less clear, for example due to the introduction of new management structures that are related to the introduction of neoliberal policies. Similarly, higher education has undergone a variety of structural reforms and has had to adopt its own marketization in order to brace the (inter-)national competition (cf. also Hadley, this volume and Park, this volume). As part and parcel of this process, there has been a drastic change in how language is seen, chosen and used by different educational actors and in how it is marketized (cf. Urciuoli, 2003).

It is the aim of this chapter to investigate empirically how the neoliberal paradigm plays out in higher education in Switzerland on two different levels, i.e. in the management of universities in the form of policies promoting competition and marketization (Holborow, 2012a, 2012b; Saunders, 2010; Wilkins, 2012, 2014) and in the lives of students, manifesting as specific forms of technologies of the self (*sensu* Foucault, 1988; cf. also Gershon, 2011; Urciuoli, 2003, 2008, 2010). We will address how, in this context, language is (1) used as a means for marketization and (2) as an element in the choice of the location of study. In both instances, language is discursively constructed as a marker of distinction – but with different consequences for universities and students.

Even if tertiary education is offered in all the language regions in multilingual Switzerland, where the three official languages, French, German and Italian, are spoken, the power asymmetries between the regions cannot be ignored. Against this background, we will argue that Italian-speaking students enrolled at a university in German-speaking Switzerland are caught in a double bind between national language hierarchies and neoliberal policies of higher education. Before turning to the specificities of the Swiss higher education system, we will try to formulate our understanding of neoliberalism and its impact on linguistic practices in the tertiary educational sector. Drawing on ethnographic data collected in German-speaking universities, an analysis will follow that bridges the marketing discourse of the university on the one hand and the narrated experience of the students on the other. In the concluding section, we critically contemplate if the current situation at Swiss universities can be considered 'win-win', as is implicitly proposed in their marketing discourse – or, if not, who can be considered as winners and losers in this respect.

Neoliberalism and Higher Education

> Students originating from the French-speaking part of the country have a rather vast local study offer unlike the students from the Italian-speaking part. This is why it is beneficial for us to invest in language measures attracting the latter student population. (Marketing manager, at a university in central Switzerland, Summer 2014; our translation)

As this statement exemplifies, higher education institutions have adapted structures and strategies from the private economic sector. First of all, the interlocutor of the interview from which this statement was taken is a marketing manager of a university in central German-speaking Switzerland (henceforth: UCS). Management and marketing have become commonplace in today's universities as a result of the reforms and restructuring programs that draw on new public management, i.e. on the guiding principle that the public sector must be as efficient as any private company. Secondly, we can see that the vocabulary and strategies commonly assigned to the economic sector have been adopted by the public sector and, in this case, by higher education institutions. The manager thus explicitly states, 'This is why it is beneficial for us to invest in language measures attracting the latter student population', which hardly differs from the managerial talk of a company expanding into new target markets. In this vein, even people are reconfigured in this economic perspective as market actors, i.e. as targets, and are thus reduced to a veritable *homo oeconomicus*, permanently and ubiquitously (Brown, 2015).

This adaptation of a market logic into spheres where profit has not been the primary orientation is characteristic of what is considered the neoliberal paradigm. The universalization of the economic logic can be observed very markedly in the social sphere (Lemke, 2001) which had already prompted Polanyi (1944: 60) to make the following statement about what he read as a changed order: 'Instead of economy being embedded in social relations, socials relations are embedded in the economy'. The social domain of education is not exempted from this influence. Different aspects, levels and fields of education have been affected by policy reforms that are conditioned by a neoliberal paradigm. It is the aim of this chapter to investigate under which conditions and with which consequences neoliberal values are implemented in the tertiary education sector. For this, we will analyze the discourses both of universities and students by drawing on one particular case study on the marketing discourse and language regulation of UCS, a university in central Switzerland.

Neoliberalism is an elusive concept that has gained a lot of traction in public and academic discourse over the last few decades. Even if elusive, it is normally used to critique specific ideologies, policies and developments considered as neoliberal, while the proponents of the policies and practices generally prefer to use a different terminology (or euphemisms?). For example they prefer to speak of the 'free market' or of the 'limited' or 'minimalist' state (Sparke, 2017) when addressing specific conditions that neoliberalism pushes forward. However, even when 'neoliberalism' is the term used, there are several, often conflicting conceptualizations that might be inferred (cf. also Biebricher, 2012; Bourdieu, 1998; Holborow, 2012a or the discussion by McGroarty, this volume). We still believe that it is a useful and analytical term in order to understand what is going on, why and with which consequences. Yet, in order to use the term coherently, it is helpful to highlight the historical implication and development of neoliberalism which is basically an advancement from liberal market ideals that were spread in the 18th and 19th centuries and have led to a renewed (hence the 'neo') but slightly different rejection of the interventionist state and redistributive ideals of welfare-state liberalism in the 20th century. The emergence of neoliberalism can be read as a specific reaction to late capitalism, i.e. 'as an antidote to threats to the capitalist social order and as a solution to capitalism's ills' (Harvey, 2005: 19). Harvey (2005) locates the rise of neoliberalism in the period after World War II and, particularly, in the crisis-ridden 1970s and 1990s in Europe and North America. In this period, Adam Smith's competitive model was resuscitated by a number of economists and thinkers (most prominently, Friedrich von Hayek, Milton Friedman and his Chicago boys) who assumed that the unregulated market works for the benefit of each and everyone if only individual competition is allowed and if nation states create the legal framework that is productive for individual competition (Stiglitz, 2002: 74). This idea was primarily defended by the elite who already cherished privileged access to resources and to the means of production (cf. Holborow, 2012b). Concurrent with the Marxist reading of ideology as ideas of the ruling class that are 'nothing more than the ideal expression of the dominant material relationships, the dominant material relationships grasped as ideas' (Marx & Engels, 1974: 64), neoliberalism can be understood as the current expression of the dominant material relationship. This is seen to affect all (private and public) spheres, to which the public employment and service sector as well as higher education are no exception.

Yet, even if the degree of impact of market logics on education contexts is recent, education has always been interlinked with 'the economy'. The introduction of compulsory formal education across Europe in the

19th century was less an achievement of democratic and democratizing efforts than a way of responding to pressures exerted by the industry that was in need of specific skills (Holborow, 2012b). While universal education allowed the socialization of children into the societal roles and structures of industrial capitalism, it also cushioned the different blows resulting from the social changes induced by industrialization (Bowles & Gintis, 1976: 27; Gonon, 1997; Holborow, 2012b). Over the course of the 20th century, education has become even more closely aligned with the economy: educational processes were reconfigured in ways that were coherent with corporate structures and interests, as Spring (1998) pointed out. Education thus aims to increase the profit of national markets (Kellermann, 2009). On an individual level, education has become an investment that primarily serves to increase one's earning potential. If an individual fails to succeed in the labor market, however, it is clear that the individual has failed at appropriately marketing his/her skills. By extension, then, the individual has always been in charge of his/her education as well as economic success while society is not to be held responsible (Holborow, 2012b: 102; Rossiter, 2003). While individual responsibility is not in itself a brand-new phenomenon, it has become further accentuated under the neoliberal paradigm which is firmly anchored in the idea of individuals as self-branding entrepreneurs, who are in charge of their success (Lessenich, 2008; Spilker, 2010). In drawing on such meritocratic principles, universities have furthermore consistently contributed to the replication of class divisions (Bowles & Gintis, 1976; Foster, 2011). Nowadays, higher education institutions are one of the primordial sites where a future (elite?) workforce is formed in their preparation for the labor market (Urciuoli, 2010). It is also the site where the needs of the capital are met with corresponding 'technical education and job training' (Saunders, 2010: 54).

In the wake of reforms realized under neoliberal political regimes in the 1980s and 1990s, higher education institutions have had to come to terms with fundamental changes. While public funding of (social) services and the accomplishments of post-war social welfare systems have been dismantled, universities have also had to face cuts in funding, while forced to implement forms of new public management which is based on a culture of audit and evaluation and, in turn, aims to guarantee public accountability (cf. Brown, 2015; Giroux, 2014; Wilkins, 2012, 2014). Under the guise of maintaining institutional and structural 'autonomy', universities have been forced to activate private or industrial sources for funding and to generate additional revenue through the intensification of applied research or through the creation of re-sellable teaching material, etc. (Saunders, 2010). As a result of these neoliberal reforms and structural changes, universities have had to embrace the entrepreneurial mantras of 'competition', 'efficiency', 'innovation' and 'flexibility' (Wilkins, 2012). They have become entrepreneurs that offer a specific service and are expected to produce 'bundles of skills' (Spilker, 2010; Urciuoli, 2008), i.e. graduate students suitable for or needed by the market. In a further step, universities have by now implemented their own marketing strategies and departments. In other words, they operate their own 'marketization', a term which basically denotes the adoption of marketing principles and practices in education contexts (Mok & Tan, 2004: 15). Finally, then, the marketization is aligned with the business and corporate sector which is why in the following this process of alignment is labeled 'corporatization'.

Students, on their side, are redrawn as clients who buy a specific product, i.e. an education that will guarantee them a job, a salary and, finally, social mobility. In order to be successful, they are conditioned to adhere to the neoliberal dogma of 'corporate individualism' (Gershon, 2011: 543) which conceptualizes individuals as enterprises as well. Consequently, neoliberal notions of 'self-care' and/ or 'self-responsibility' become deeply entrenched with concepts of 'agency'. Paradigmatic of the neoliberal project, students are thus rethought as entrepreneurial selves who make rational choices, e.g. with regard to their location and subjects of study, fully aware of the possible risks and consequences that their respective choices might incur (Gershon, 2011; Wilkins, 2010). Reconfigured as self-responsible *homines oeconomici*, the (hypothetical and real) differences between students, i.e. their social backgrounds, their financial possibilities and/or linguistic abilities are erased from the discourses circulating in the neoliberal paradigm as everyone is considered to have equal chances in order to succeed (Rossiter, 2003).

We can conclude that adapting a critical approach to recent neoliberal trends will help us understand what is actually going on in higher education (Holborow, 2012b). Further, an investigation into how neoliberal values are implemented and reproduced in the context of higher education seems of particular relevance when we identify neoliberalism as a specific ideology that serves the capitalist class. It is thus no coincidence that several scholars around the world have focused on manifestations of neoliberal ideology within higher education (cf. also contributions in this volume). Holborow (2012b) for instance sheds light on how education policy has developed under neoliberal conditions in the Irish economic post-crash context. She argues that higher education has become an adjunct of the economy. Focusing on the United States, Saunders (2010) describes the neoliberal ideology and its impact on higher education there, while teasing out meaningful changes to the funding, finances, priorities and governance of universities, etc. Several other scholars show how neoliberalism has impacted on higher education from Australia and New Zealand (Marginson, 2004), to North and South America (De Korne, this volume; Giroux, 2013; Seaman, 2005; Spring, 1998; Torres & Schugurensky, 2002; Urciuoli, 2010, 2014), to Western Europe (Hill, 2003; Hill & Kumar, 2009; Olssen & Peters, 2005; Spring, 1998; Wilkins, 2012) and, finally, to Asia (cf. contributions in this volume on Japan, China and South Korea by Hadley, Gao and Park, respectively; Spring, 1998). Many parallels can be drawn in these different contexts that concern the manifestation of neoliberalism in higher education. However, the specific political-economic conditions of each country have led to particular forms of neoliberal materialization within tertiary education contexts. This chapter concentrates on the specific context of higher education in Switzerland.

Higher Education in Switzerland: Between Federalism, Multilingualism and Neoliberal Competition

National landscape and policies of higher education

As mentioned in the introduction, tertiary education is offered in Switzerland in each of the three linguistic regions (French, German and Italian). This has not always been the case due to the uneven distribution of the languages across the Swiss territory – and to the existing uneven distribution of political-economic power between the language groups. While in 2014, 63.3% of the Swiss population declared their main language to be German, 22.7% chose French and only 8.1% chose Italian (Federal Statistical Office, 2014). On the Swiss labor market, German is the most important language, followed by French and English. Of the companies based in the Italian-speaking part of the country, 70% use German at least on a weekly basis which reflects the Italian-speaking region's economic dependence on the German-speaking part (Andres et al., 2005; Grin, 1999). In contrast, in the German-speaking part, only around a quarter of the companies use Italian on a weekly basis (cf. Lüdi & Werlen, 2005). For the Ticino, the national market is economically more interesting than Italy, its economically struggling neighbor to the South, which gives additional value to German language competences. In addition to the already marginal occurrence of the Italian language across Switzerland, it is rather regionally restricted as an official language. Only the canton of Ticino and a few municipalities in the canton of Grison bordering on the Ticino use Italian as their official language.[1]

Thus, it comes as no surprise that the oldest university in today's Switzerland was founded in the 15th century in Basel, the German-speaking economic, cultural and political center of its region then and today. Even if most other tertiary institutions were established at a significantly later point, i.e. in the 19th and 20th centuries, they were once again restricted to the German- and French-speaking parts of the country. It was only in 1996 that a university was established in the Ticino, the Italian-speaking canton.

Today, there are 12 institutions of tertiary education across all language regions in Switzerland. Swiss universities are generally open to any Swiss student with a Matura (diploma of the gymnasium, the highest secondary education) at a cost of a few hundred Swiss Francs per semester (only a few programs warrant an entrance exam, e.g. medical studies). Ten universities are administered by one of the 26 cantons, while two are entirely funded by the Swiss state. While the 10 regular universities were originally administered and funded by the cantons alone, an agreement was implemented in 1874 that cantonal universities could also be entitled to financial support by the federal state. Yet, federal support for cantonal universities was ensured only as late as 1969, covering as much as 20%–30% of the cost (Gerbert, 1971; Herren, 2008). Several political movements had advocated for financial support by the state, arguing with the lack of a qualified workforce in science, technology, medicine and humanities sorely needed in the economic boom-years after World War II (Herren, 2008). In 1999, in light of the increasing internationalization and globalization of education and science and as a consequence of the neoliberal turn of the political economy, the state finally declared two aims: First, to enhance competition between Swiss universities and, second, to establish a mandatory collaboration between the state and the cantons in questions of tertiary education (Fritschi & Spycher, 2003; Universitätsförderungsgesetz [Law on the promotion of universities], 2013). In the end, this new national policy led to a shift from *cost*-based financial support (e.g. related to the amount of enrolled students) to an *achievement*-based support (i.e. based on the evaluation of the quality of teaching and research and/or the acquisition of external funds). To date, cantonal universities receive 10%–20% of their finances from the state, while the Swiss national science foundation allocates up to 12%. The principal funds (30%–70%) are provided by the university cantons themselves as well as by those cantons without universities that send their students to other cantons and transfer corresponding sums (OECD, 2004). The remaining finances are generated via third-party funds, a strategy, which again can be understood as resulting from the neoliberal paradigm of competition and marketization that turns institutions of higher education into enterprises. Concurrent with the political-economical transformations around that time, several inter-cantonal conventions were established in the 1990s that explicitly pushed direct competition between the different tertiary institutions. While competition between the universities had already been increasing, the founding of two new universities intensified this trend. These universities had been planned locally for centuries, but a variety of political, religious and financial reasons had prevented their founding earlier on.

Enter the two new universities of Ticino and Central Switzerland

In 1996, the very first university in the Ticino, the Italian-speaking part in the south of Switzerland, was established. Its opening suddenly offered students from that region the opportunity to follow tertiary education within their own linguistic region. Before this, they had to enroll in a university in Italy if they wanted to study in Italian, their language of schooling. Otherwise, they used to have the choice between Swiss universities either in the French- or in the German-speaking part, where tertiary education was mainly offered in the corresponding official language. The second (and, to date, last) university was founded soon thereafter. Located in central German-speaking Switzerland, UCS opened its doors in 2001 after centuries of unsuccessful attempts, due to confessional and political conflicts.

There are several parallels and ties between the two cantons with the newest universities. To begin with, both cantons have always been predominantly catholic. While different surveys have shown that religion is no longer a primary factor for the choice of study location (e.g. Altermatt, 2009: 173), the religious factor still plays a role, though maybe more in terms of tradition than confession (Metzger, 2010). If one looks at the current figures of the UCS, the majority of the non-local student body comes from catholic regions within Switzerland. It thus seems that UCS can still profit from the confessional ties with other catholic cantons, among them the Ticino.

Besides the religious factor, there is another connection between the two cantons. From the 13th century on, trade across the mountain 'Gotthard' contributed to the economic situation in the regions on either side of the pass (Carbonazzi, 1845). First, with the aid of a mule track across the Alps and several centuries later thanks to a tunnel through the mountain, trade was facilitated between the southern and central part of Switzerland. To date, it takes approximately two hours by train from central Switzerland to the Ticino. Summing up, the effects of the common historical ties, related to catholic connections and transport itineraries, linger on to this day (Ceschi & Mittler, 2003; Mattioli & Ries, 2000). We will see that these ties – crossing language regions – facilitate the recruiting of Italian-speaking students from the Ticino for the UCS.

Ties of this nature are particularly relevant since both of these newly founded universities cannot rely on an established traditional flow of students from specific regions. In this context, marketization and marketing strategies become fundamental, with language emerging as a useful and important element of marketization, especially when addressing potential students from other language regions within Switzerland. This particular marketization was making use of the dominant discourse that learning an additional national language would improve one's chances on the labor market, which, in fact, was one of the main reasons for studying in a different language region (Altermatt, 2009; Dubach & Schmidlin, 2005; Streckeisen, 1996).

In empirically unpacking the discursive capitalization of language by universities, in the following, we will focus on the marketization discourse and practices of one of the two new universities, UCS, which is based in central German-speaking Switzerland. It is not only the most recently founded, but also the smallest Swiss university, limiting its study offer to law, theology and social and cultural sciences. As argued in the following section, in order to increase its student body, UCS makes use of specific language regulations with the aim of attracting Italian-speaking students, thus entering into direct competition with the newly founded university in the Ticino.

Language as a Marketization Argument: An Ethnographic Approach

Every year, UCS organizes an information day designed for potential newcomers. The aim of this event is to present the university as a whole as well as the individual faculties. For the whole day, student advisers and students are on-site, ready to answer questions informally. Additionally, flyers, brochures and information material are distributed. In our understanding, these information days provide insight into the marketization of the university and into the materialization of the discourses that emerge in this context. For this reason, Martina Zimmermann carried out an ethnography on the site of the information day at this specific university. She paid special attention to the faculty of law, which is the first faculty to use language for its marketization. In the tradition of participant observation, she collected institutional documents by the university, took field notes and interviewed students from the faculty of law. This research can be further recontextualized in the framework of a larger ethnographic project (cf. Zimmermann, 2014, 2017), which in the end strives for a better understanding of capitalization strategies as well as of niche marketing that draw on language both as an added value and as a marker of distinction in saturated markets (Duchêne & Heller, 2012; Heller, 2010).

Prototypically, then, UCS invests in marketization that targets the Swiss Italian-speaking student population – for several reasons. First of all, with the range of courses offered at the 10 cantonal Swiss universities overlapping, each institution is carving out its own niche in order to increase its (inter-)national appeal and to become or remain competitive in the higher education market. Second, since the 10 Swiss universities are financed by the government on the basis of their student numbers, they try to attract students from other cantons or even from other language regions within Switzerland. As we will see, they do this by offering language regulatory programs such as introductory courses in their language, special examination rules, etc. Studying in another language region is (in theory) possible for students due to the Swiss education practice that puts emphasis on the learning of another official Swiss language in high school (German, French or Italian). As has been mentioned before, UCS is in special need of 'recruiting' a student body due to its recent formation. Furthermore, even if it has been shown that Swiss students mainly choose a place of study close to their hometown (Denzler & Wolter, 2010), the students originating from central Switzerland have become used to leaving the area, which makes it even more pressing to attract students from other cantons.

On the morning of the information day at the faculty of law, the dean gives an official welcome to all potential students. He produces half of his welcome speech in Swiss-German and half in German (the former for greetings and the latter to present the day's program). He then focuses on a special information session for the 'Ticinesi', the students from the Ticino and highlights (in Italian) that this session will be held fully in Italian. After the welcome, two law students distribute information material from behind a table laid out with two sets of brochures. One set of the colorful brochures contains information in German and is handed out by a Swiss German-speaking law student; the second, in Italian, by an Italian-speaking student. The brochure in Italian is entitled 'Facoltà di Giurisprudenza' (English translation: Faculty of Law), thus explicitly addressing potential law students from the Italian-speaking Ticino. The cover displays a smiling female student wearing a grey hooded sweater with the English lettering 'UCS' across her chest. In her hands, she is holding the very same brochure on which her portrait is recognizable below the Italian title. In the background, we can make out the most famous landmark of central Switzerland, the wooden Chapel Bridge.

On opening the brochure, we come across an introductory paragraph that outlines the intention of the brochure, i.e. to give a brief description about the faculty of law and to mention that the local staff is always available for personal consultation. The faculty of law is further depicted as providing a warm welcome to anyone coming to study in central Switzerland, 'la regione più mediterranea della Svizzera tedesca' (English translation: the most Mediterranean region in German-speaking Switzerland). As Southern Ticino is commonly discursively framed as the sunniest region in Switzerland, this rather unusual cross-reference between the two regions, inferring Mediterranean sunshine and *savoir-vivre*, (supposedly) serves to emphasize ties and similarities between the two regions. It is no coincidence that the brochure further stresses the geographical proximity, arguing that, from the Ticino, UCS is easily and quickly reachable due to its central location in the 'heart of Switzerland'.

Throughout the brochure, further advantageous points on the faculty of law are listed. Most importantly, these points are underlined with short portraits of students or professors, either from the Italian-speaking Ticino or from Italy, hence creating a setting of familiarity. Along these lines, it is highlighted that the professorate includes several Italian speakers, followed by a list of Italian-sounding names, which the students have the possibility to consult with in Italian, especially in case of linguistic difficulties. Most importantly, however, it is stressed that students from the Ticino will benefit from special regulations for exams in German: They have more time available in written exams, in which they may even use the legal texts in Italian in addition to a German-Italian dictionary. Further advantages are advertised that relate to language, for example introductory courses in Italian as well as German lessons with a focus on legal terminology. Finally, the faculty states in the brochure that it recognizes the difficulties the Ticinesi students might encounter at the beginning of their studies due to language obstacles – and thus offers them the institutional support necessary. Next to this statement, we find a photograph of a young male law student, depicted in a black jumper over a white shirt. His testimonial confirms that the introductory courses were of invaluable help: 'Nella nostra Facoltà gli student ticinesi sono facilitate nel superamento della barriera linguistica del Tedesco grazie a ottimi corsi di introduzione' (English translation: 'Our faculty helps the students from the Ticino to overcome linguistic difficulties in German by offering introductory courses').

It can be argued that the special regulations for exams and the exceptional introductory courses are presented as offering the students better conditions for acquiring the necessary skills to become competitive and, finally, to succeed. This accommodation, however, is only needed (or possible) when presupposing that Italian-speaking students wish to increase their own capital in completing their studies at a German-speaking university. At the same time, the proposed accommodation implies that the choice of studying at a German-speaking university is linked to risks – most importantly, the risk of failing one's studies because of lacking competence in the German language. As any choice can be seen as an engagement with risk (cf. Forsey, 2014), could the university thus claim to offer risk-minimizing help to its Italian-speaking students? In offering language-related help, the faculty of law at UCS indeed distinguishes itself from faculties at other universities that do not accommodate Italian-speaking students in this way. By distinguishing itself, the faculty in turn tries to become competitive by attracting students – even presenting itself in the language of the specific target student body. Against this background, the question emerges regarding whose interest these practices serve: Is it the students' interest or is it the university's interest?

An Analytical Account of the Experience of Italian-Speaking Students at the German-Speaking Faculty

In the course of the ethnography, Martina engaged in several conversations and interviews both with enrolled and future students from the Ticino, a number of which were recorded and transcribed. In the following, a few particularly illuminating extracts of these interviews will be presented in their English translation from the Italian original. These extracts shed light on the questions (1) of how students experience their choice of studying in a linguistically different environment, (2) of the role of language as a marker of distinction and (3) of whether the institutional language regulation presents a win-win situation for the students. The interview with Ilaria, a young woman from the Ticino studying law at UCS in her first year, was revealing regarding her choice of studying in central Switzerland.[2]

ILA: In the end, I was convinced to come here because it is a small university, we are about 1260 students compared to other universities where they are three times as much, if not more.

INT: Yes, ok.

ILA: And in any case it's smaller, this means that we are in closer contact, also with the professors.

INT: Yes.

ILA: And I liked that

INT: Yes.

ILA: That aspect.

INT: Yes, does that mean that you have come to UCS right after college?

ILA: Yes. I have finished my 'matura' (British equivalent: A-Levels) and then

[...]

INT: And how come you have chosen to study law at UCS? You could have gone to other places.

ILA: I said to myself, law can be studied in different places also in the French-speaking part of Switzerland, e.g. Lausanne and Fribourg if I am not wrong.

INT: Yes.

ILA: From the very beginning, I excluded the French-speaking part because I said to myself my French is more or less ok.

INT: Yes.

ILA: It is similar to Italian and therefore let's say, I can learn it in little time. German however is much more important and spoken by three quarters of Switzerland. And I am still struggling with German, thus, I prefer studying in German, so that my German gets better and I'll have advantages for the future.

INT: Yes.

ILA: That's why I chose German at UCS and this delegation came and the university is small and also quite close to the Ticino but this, I did not, I did not, I would also have gone to Basel, I don't know.

INT: Yes.

ILA: Other places would have been fine for me too. But the fact that it's small and closely supervised was more convincing for me. (Cafeteria UCS, November 2012; our translation)

In this first extract, we can observe Ilaria reproducing a series of the marketing arguments as put forward by the university in the information brochure described above: She mentions the small size of the university as well as the institutional promise of close supervision ('this means that we are in closer contact, also with the professors'). Closer contact in this sense seems to imply better access to knowledge for students, especially the Italian-speaking ones. Furthermore, she makes an explicit link between the possibility to improve her German and better her chances for the future ('I prefer studying in German, so that my German gets better and I'll have advantages for the future'), thus rationalizing her choice and presenting herself as a responsible self, while at the same time dismissing studying in French arguing that she already has competency in this language, not least because of its similarity to Italian. Doubting that the geographical proximity was an influential factor leading to her decision to come to central Switzerland, she muses that a further distance would have been acceptable as well ('I would also have gone to Basel', which is about an hour further away). In the end, she insists that she had been striving for the best place, defined in her eyes as the smallest and most closely supervised institution, as UCS had presented itself. Later in the interview, she goes on to list different aspects that had spoken in favor of UCS and thereby explicitly refers to the language regulations that would allow Italian-speaking students more time for exams and the possibility to use an Italian dictionary, while also mentioning that it is convenient to be home on time.

Ilaria's account appears consistent with the points proposed in the brochure produced by the faculty of law. The arguments put forward serve both students as well as universities when highlighting the advantage of a specific institution. We cannot know if Ilaria draws on promotional arguments at hand or on 'common sense', but we argue that this is not of primary importance – the sheer fact that she uses similar or even the same argument could point to the power of common sense for promotional purposes on an institutional and individual level. It seems even more likely, however, that this consistency stems from Ilaria's need to legitimize her choice for UCS: she has internalized the 'official', i.e. institutional, discourse that in itself offers an explanation why UCS was the choice that had to be made and reproduces the neoliberal dogma of rational choice. In the end, Ilaria's account confirms research results that indicate that a variety of factors (individual, cognitive, institutional, etc.) play a role in the process of choosing a subject and location of study (cf. Bieri *et al.* [2008] for the Swiss context). As this choice is not always merely 'rational', it appears to be justified in retrospect for which reasons at hand are used. In a way then, Ilaria adopts the official marketization of UCS as her own self-marketization, in which she explicitly highlights the advantages of choosing *this* university rather than another. Yet, is this consistency (that does not challenge the institutional marketization) sufficient to conclude that students actually profit from the specific language regulation provided by the university, which, in turn, benefits from the thus attracted student body? Or in short: Can we, in reality, speak of a 'win-win' situation? There are at least two reasons that lead us to contradict this. First, difficulties and failure among Italian-speaking students despite the specific regulations and language accommodation allow us to question the sustainable effect of these measures. Second, the sheer existence of Italian-speaking student associations being described as fundamental by students from the Ticino cast doubt on the sufficiency of support provided by the faculty of law at UCS.

In all of the four encounters with Ilaria, she emphasizes the help that is provided for Ticinese students by the faculty of law. At the same time, she points out the difficulties she is confronted with in her studies due to the German language. Stefano, one of her peers from the Ticino, refers to such difficulties in the following extract from an interview with him.

INT: And how was it for you in the beginning?
STE: It was terribly difficult. I spent the evenings reading just one page without getting anything. Some days at university, I would not have had a clue what the lecture was about, I would go home and start reading in a book and still not understand what it was about. It was very difficult.
INT: Um
STE: You have to be studious and keep going.
INT: Um
STE: You have to persevere, you have to do some reading after every lesson, and after some time, you will improve by consequence. (UCS, Winter 2014; our translation)

Ilaria not only confirms these difficulties herself, but she also mentions that she had failed most of the exams. Yet, even if she never challenges the institutional back-up provided by the university, she admits to at times feeling depressed, as she studies really hard but still feels as if her understanding of the study matter is not comparable with that of her Swiss-German peers. She also complains that it takes her a considerable amount of time to read the required chapters, as she still needs to look up words in order to comprehend the texts, similar to Stefano's account. According to her, she had never struggled to get good grades at high school; her experience at UCS, however, impacts on her self-confidence and has raised doubts about her suitability for law studies. After the first year at the law faculty, she finds herself repeating the majority of the courses together with other unsuccessful students and newcomers. Of course, Ilaria's failure and problems cannot simply be reduced to her linguistic difficulties; there are other students who have to repeat exams, among which are also speakers of German.[3] However, we can conclude that, in any case, the language regulations and language accommodation measures, as provided by the faculty of law, are far from guaranteeing success to the students.

As mentioned above, there is yet another reason for questioning the win-win conception. In the brochure described, the faculty of law gives room and voice to one specific student association. It is the association of Italian-speaking students, which organizes cultural and entertainment events and offers students the opportunity to help each other on a personal level, e.g. in the context of academic studies. This student association is not only referred to in the official brochure, but it is also, in reality, frequented by students such as Ilaria. In the following, she explains the activities of this association.

> **ILA**: We organize events and dinner parties. It is a group of Ticinese students and of students from Italy, in any case for all Italian-speaking students
>
> **INT**: Yes
>
> **ILA**: Living in central Switzerland.
>
> **INT**: And what are you doing?
>
> **ILA**: Well, we organize activities in order to unite ourselves but it is also a point of reference in the case someone would have problems to find an apartment. A place to stay. The association can offer some help. And maybe I don't know for example second-hand books. And in any case they support the Ticinese who feels disoriented. It is a point of reference. (Cafeteria UCS, Spring 2012; our translation)

Students, as responsible subjects, have thus organized themselves and created an association that gives newcomers like Ilaria access to a pre-existing network, to informal and constant help and to an Italian-speaking environment. This network facilitates new acquaintances in a linguistically foreign environment, in which Italian-speaking students from the Ticino would not be able to draw on pre-established social bonds. At the same time, however, the association in a way exempts the university from taking on obligations that would go beyond the relatively basic support in place. In a strategic move, then, the faculty of law dedicates a certain amount of space in its official information brochure to the presentation of this association. In a similar vein, the faculty invited the association's president to welcome potential newcomers at the information day; an opportunity not given to any other student association. We argue that the faculty's presentation of this pre-existing assistance embodied in the student association presents a veritable strategy of outsourcing. This strategy is also made use of in everyday university life. Despite the possibility to ask questions and get answers in Italian thanks to the Italian-speaking staff (as indeed promoted in the brochure), Ilaria mentioned how dependent she is on the association. For instance, when Ilaria emailed one of the Italian-speaking assistants in order to ask for further explanations on a topic discussed in a lecture, quite ironically, he invited her to approach her peers instead. This is relevant insofar as the faculty of law had actually, in its brochure, advertised the personal contact and exchange that would be possible for Italian-speaking Ticinesi students with their professors and assistants. However, it is the association that becomes the main point of reference, which can be read as an emblematic trend in neoliberal policies: Intermediate and personal networks are promoted and celebrated as individual initiatives, while systemic and state-sponsored programs are rolled back (e.g. Giddens, 1988). The association in turn grants Ilaria the required support: she can ask for help in Italian and acquire the skills that she might be missing due to lacking competence in German. This practice not only allows the Italian-speaking students to support each other but also gives them the responsibility in their endeavor to become competitive actors.

Win Some, Lose Some: Concluding Remarks on the Institutional Marketization Strategy

The practices mobilized on the information day and materialized in the Italian information brochure touch upon the fundamental question of how language is invoked as a marker of distinction in order to become a competitive actor on the market, as neoliberal policies demand of institutions of higher education. In this context, Bourdieu's (1979) marker of distinction becomes a helpful analytical tool if we read these language regulations by the faculty of law as aiming to distinguish this faculty from other, comparable German-speaking law faculties in Switzerland – exactly as accommodating its Italian-speaking students. As we have seen in the brochure, a certain closeness between central Switzerland and the Ticino was carefully and discursively constructed as tying in with an existing tradition – again, this 'closeness' is a discursive strategy and marketization from which UCS can profit by attracting additional students.

The discursively marketed geographical proximity between central Switzerland and the Ticino can be read in a similar light: Defining central Switzerland as the counterpart of the Ticino – at least for the German-speaking part of Switzerland – becomes a marker to increase the competitiveness of UCS through the very creation of a niche that targets the Italian-speaking students. In turn, the students and professors portrayed or listed in the brochure were carefully chosen on the basis of their potential for marketization, thus becoming objects of commodification for the sake of competition. On the one hand, the young female student, pictured on the brochure cover as holding her own picture, is presented as a 'real' student who identifies herself with UCS (hence the hooded sweater), with the faculty of law and with its local Italian-speaking student population. The listed Italian-speaking professors, on the other hand, can be commodified as experts of language for a specific target group in need, namely the Ticinesi. Yet, mentioning their names and the possibility of personal consultations also highlights another marker of distinction: the familiar dimension of the university, hence, its manageable scale, and the personal atmosphere of the faculty both allow for face-to-face interactions between staff and students. What is most important, however, is that Italian can be used (e.g. in consultations) in the process of acquiring the skills needed to succeed in the studies of law.

Summing up, the special regulations in place are supposed to allow the students to be competitive and to bring them onto the same level with students not confronted with a linguistic barrier. The university thus recognizes differences between the German-speaking and the Ticinese students in terms of linguistic prerequisites. Among the Ticinese students, however, potential (linguistic and social) differences are erased, i.e. they are treated as homogeneous by the administration, not least as there is only one kind of language regulation in place. In a sense then, the institution profits from marking the student body hailing from the Ticino as heterogeneous, as long as it remains a homogeneous heterogeneity compared to the German-speaking student body. This trend is exactly what we can observe in other neoliberal spaces, in which diversity is superficially celebrated while being used as a means for distinction (e.g. in branding a space as inclusive, open or tolerant). Yet, any celebration has its limits, also in this context. For example, no comparable services are offered to speakers of other languages, e.g. of French, which, after all, is also an official Swiss language. It is also remarkable that, apart from the promised facilitation for Italian-speaking students outlined in this brochure, the Italian language is not present in the syllabus. It thus loses its worth for capitalization for the students themselves as soon as they enroll at the university, which, in turn, had addressed them in Italian. However, nearly all the courses are in German, the scripts are in German and papers and exams have to be written in German (cf. Shohamy [2006] on the power of the language of an exam). Finally, then, the value of the Italian language appears to be recognized only for the purpose and in the process of attracting Italian-speaking students. The advertised linguistic accommodation presents itself as an effective marketing strategy for UCS with Italian gaining a highly contextualized and only temporary value. Italian-speaking students, in return, feel the constant pressure of self-improvement and self-responsibility – with regard to their language competency and *vis-à-vis* their German-speaking peers. Quite often, as has been recounted in interviews and conversations with Ticinesi students, the only environment in which Italian, their home language, is valorized is in interactions within the student association. Nevertheless, the view toward institutional practices held by targeted Italian-speaking students remains uncritical. They do not see themselves as part of a neoliberal ideology but are thankful for the supposedly facilitating measures provided.

We are not the first to argue that students have understood the neoliberal need to optimize their 'bundle of skills' which is valued for its potential for productivity (Seaman, 2005). As we have seen, universities capitalize on this need which also finds expression in the will for the right choice – of university and study. In multilingual Switzerland, however, we observe an additional dimension: Even if all official languages are equal on paper, the economic, political and cultural centers are in German-speaking cities. Learning German therefore promises to increase one's chances in the market – in German-speaking Switzerland, but also in the other regions that stand in economic and political relations with the center. Studying in a German-speaking region thus becomes a strategy to improve German competency and, as a consequence, to improve one's chances in the labor market. Tertiary institutions such as UCS therefore try to augment their student body in addressing this very need and in offering remedies to ease the linguistic transit from one language region to another. Yet, as we have mentioned several times in this contribution, these offers of language accommodation have to be read in the perspective of universities as profit oriented and in need of customers, i.e. students, in order to attain a competitive status. In this context, language becomes a temporary benefit, used explicitly to attract students speaking specific languages and implemented to increase the competitiveness of the university – just as the university makes use of a variety of discourses and marketization strategies that invoke tradition, closeness and familiarity. Consequentially, language is only used for initial accommodation, whereas additional support is outsourced and handed over to the student body – marking them as mainly responsible for their success and failure.[4] Students have to come to terms with this and while some may win additional skills, others might lose in failing their exams due to lacking language competency. The focus on the students' challenges shows that the neoliberal strategies fail insofar as they fall short of the student's expectations and constrain them to compensate lacking support with an informal student association. The university, on the other hand, keeps on winning as long as the linguistically divided power structure in Switzerland remains the same, pushing Italian-speaking students to acquire German.

As we have shown in our contribution, the neoliberal marketization of universities leads to a myopic implementation of 'language' as capital, increasing student numbers on the basis of undifferentiated and unsustainable language accommodation programs, leaving unsuccessful students out in the cold. Thereby, their failure is even acerbated since this faculty actually offers language accommodation in contrast to other faculties and universities, which in the end gives increased responsibility to the Italian-speaking students. On the other hand, if they succeed in their studies, the university can lay claim to this success on the basis of its accommodation program. In a way then, the students really just lose rather than win, no matter what the costs.

Acknowledgments

We would like to thank the Sinergia-Project of the Swiss National Science Foundation no. 130457 (2010–2013) and the Departement of Linguistics at the University of Bern (Switzerland) for financial support during this study. We have greatly benefited from discussions with many people while preparing this chapter. Particular thanks go to Aneta Pavlenko (Temple University), Luisa Martin Rojo (Universidad Autónoma de Madrid) and Sari Pietikäinen (University of Jyväskylä); the editors of this volume; all the active contributors present at the conference of the American Association of Applied Linguistics in Dallas in March 2013 where the idea for this chapter was born; and to all the participants who patiently answered questions and allowed Martina to accompany them for her ethnography. It goes without saying that no one except the authors of this chapter is responsible for the errors or misinterpretations present in this work.

Notes

(1) A map of Switzerland showing the distribution of the national languages can be found online: http://www.bfs.admin.ch/bfs/portal/en/index/regionen/thematische_karten/maps/bevoelkerung/sprachen_religionen.NewWindow. parsys.0002.3.Preview.html (accessed 28 January 2015).

(2) The participants are systematically anonymized.

(3) Official figures of failure rates at the university are not publicly accessible.

(4) Park (2011; this volume) shows very similar results demystifying the simplistic picture of English as a language guaranteeing social and economic advancement in South Korea.

References

Altermatt, U. (2009) *Die Universität Freiburg auf der Suche nach Identität: Essays zur Kultur- und Sozialgeschichte der Universität Freiburg im 19. und 20. Jahrhundert.* Fribourg: Academic Press.

Andres, M., Horn, K., Barjak, F., Glas, A., Leukens, A. and Niederer, R. (2005) *Fremdsprachen in Schweizer Betrieben. Eine Studie zur Verwendung von Fremdsprachen in der Schweizer Wirtschaft und deren Ansichten zu Sprachenpolitik und schulischer Fremdsprachenausbildung.* Olten: Fachhochschule Solothurn Nordwestschweiz.

Biebricher, T. (2012) *Neoliberalismus zur Einführung.* Hamburg: Junius Verlag.

Bieri, C., Buschor, S. and Keck, A. (2008) *Forschungsbericht Berufs- und Studienwahl von Maturanden und Maturandinnen.* Zürich: Pädagogische Hochschule Zürich.

Bourdieu, P. (1979) *La distinction. Critique sociale du jugement.* Paris: Les Editions de Minuit.

Bourdieu, P. (1998) 'What is neoliberalism? A programme for destroying collective structures which may impede the pure market logic'. In *Le Monde diplomatique* (Jeremy J. Shapiro, trans.). See http://mondediplo.com/1998/12/08bourdieu& (accessed 12 August 2015).

Boutet, J. (2008) *La vie verbale au travail, des manufactures aux centres d'appel.* Toulouse: Octarès.

Bowles, S. and Gintis, H. (1976) *Schooling into Capitalist America: Educational Reform and the Contradictions of Economic Life.* New York: Basic Books.

Brown, W. (2015) *Undoing the Demos: Neoliberalism's Stealth Revolution.* New York: Zone Books.

Bundesgesetz über die Förderung der Universitäten und über die Zusammenarbeit im Hochschulbereich (Universitätsförderungsgesetz, UFG) vom 8. Oktober 1999 (Stand am 1. Januar 2013). See https://www.admin.ch/opc/de/classified-compilation/19995354/index.html (accessed 6 December 2016).

Cameron, D. (2000) *Good to Talk? Living and Working in a Communication Culture.* London: Sage.

Carbonazzi, G.A. (1845) *Estratto con analisi delle relazioni di accompagnamento del progetto di massima per l'apertura di strade ferrate nel Cantone Ticino.* Lugano: Tipografia del Verbano.

Ceschi, R. and Mittler, M. (2003) *Geschichte des Kantons Tessin.* Frauenfeld: Huber.

Denzler, S. and Wolter, S.C. (2010) *Wenn das Nächstgelegene die erste Wahl ist. Der Einfluss der geographischen Mobilität der Studierenden auf die Hochschullandschaft Schweiz.* Staff Paper 2 der Schweizerischen Koordinationsstelle für Bildungsforschung.

Dubach, P. and Schmidlin, S. (2005) *Studentische Mobilität an den Schweizer Hochschulen. Ergebnisse der Absolventenbefragungen 1991 bis 2003*. Neuchâtel: Bundesamt für Statistik.

Duchêne, A. and Heller, M. (eds) (2012) *Language in Late Capitalism: Pride and Profit*. New York: Routledge.

Federal Statistical Office (2014) 'Languages'. See https://www.bfs.admin.ch/bfs/de/home/statistiken/bevoelkerung/sprachen-religionen/sprachen.html (accessed 12 December 2016).

Forsey, M. (2014) Learning to stay? Mobile modernity and the sociology of choice. *Mobilities* 10 (5), 1–21.

Foster, J.B. (2011) Education and the structural crisis of capital. *Monthly Review* 63 (3). See http://monthlyreview.org/2011/07/01/education-and-the-structural-crisis-of-capital/ (accessed 11 November 2015).

Foucault, M. (1988) Technologies of the self. In L.H. Martin, H. Gutman and P.H. Hutton (eds) *Technologies of the Self: A Seminar with Michel Foucault* (pp. 16–49). Amherst, MA: University of Massachusetts Press.

Fritschi, T. and Spycher, S. (2003) *Evaluation der Investitionsbeiträge des Bundes an die Universitäten*. Bern: Büro für arbeits- und sozialpolitische Studien.

Gerbert, A.J. (1971) *Hat das Hochschulförderungsgesetz (HFG) die Erwartungen erfüllt?* Zürich: Schweizerische Hochschulkonferenz.

Gershon, I. (2011) Neoliberal agency. *Current Anthropology* 52 (4), 537–555.

Giddens, A. (1988) *The Third Way: The Renewal of Social Democracy*. Cambridge: Polity Press.

Giroux, H.A. (2013) 'Public intellectuals against the neoliberal university'. *Truthout*. Blog post 29 October. See http://www.truth-out.org/opinion/item/19654-public-intellectuals-against-the-neoliberal-university (accessed 22 January 2016).

Gonon, P. (1997) Schule im Spannungsfeld zwischen Arbeit, elementarer Bildung und Beruf. In H. Badertscher and H.-U. Grunder (eds) *Geschichte der Erziehung und Schule in der Schweiz im 19. und 20. Jahrhundert* (pp. 58–88). Bern: Haupt.

Grin, F. (1999) *Compétences et récompenses. La valeur des langues en Suisse*. Programme National de Recherche 33. Fribourg: Editions Universitaires Fribourg Suisse.

Harvey, D. (2005) *A Brief History of Neoliberalism*. Oxford: Oxford University Press.

Heller, M. (2003) Globalization, the new economy, and the commodification of language and identity. *Journal of Sociolinguistics* 7 (4), 473–492.

Heller, M. (2010) The commodification of language. *Annual Review of Anthropology* 39, 101–114.

Herren, M. (2008) Die nationale Hochschul- und Forschungspolitik in den 1960er- und 1970-er Jahren. In L. Criblez (ed.) *Bildungsraum Schweiz. Historische Entwicklungen und aktuelle Herausforderungen* (pp. 219–250). Bern: Haupt.

Hill, D. (2003) Global neo-liberalism, the deformation of education and resistance. *The Journal of Critical Education Policy Studies* 1 (1), 1–28.

Hill, D. and Kumar, R. (2009) *Global Neoliberalism and Education and its Consequences. Routledge Studies in Education and Neoliberalism* (Vol. 3). Routledge: London.

Holborow, M. (2012a) What is neoliberalism? Discourse, ideology and the real world. In D. Block, J. Gry and M. Holborow (eds) *Neoliberalism and Applied Linguistics* (pp. 14–32). London: Routledge.

Holborow, M. (2012b) Neoliberalism, human capital and the skills agenda in education: The Irish case. *Journal for Critical Education Policy Studies* 1 (10), 93–111.

Kellermann, P. (2009) Geschäft versus Wissenschaft, Ausbildung versus Studium: Zur Instrumentalisierung von Hochschulbildung und Universität. In P. Kellermann, M. Boni and E. Meyer-Renschhausen (eds) *Zur Kritik europäischer Hochschulpolitik. Forschung und Lehre unter Kuratel betriebswirtschaftlicher Denkmuster* (pp. 47–64). Wiesbaden: Verlag für Sozialwissenschaften.

Kelly-Holmes, H. (2006) Multilingualism and commercial language practices on the Internet. *Journal of Sociolinguistics* 10 (4), 507–519.

Lemke, T. (2001) 'The birth of bio-politics': Michel Foucault's lecture at the College de France on neo-liberal governmentality. *Economy and Society* 30, 190–207.

Lessenich, S. (2008) *Die Neuerfindung des Sozialen: Der Sozialstaat im flexiblen Kapitalismus.* Bielefeld: Transcript.

Lüdi, G. and Werlen, I. (eds) (2005) *Sprachenlandschaft in der Schweiz.* Neuchâtel: Bundesamt für Statistik.

Marginson, S. (2004) Competition and markets in higher education: A 'glonacal' analysis. *Policy Futures in Education* 2 (2), 175–244.

Marx, K. and Engels, F. (1974) *The German Ideology*, C.J. Arthur (ed.). London: Lawrence and Wishart.

Mattioli, A. and Ries, M. (2000) *'Eine höhere Bildung thut in unserem Vaterlande Noth'. Der steinige Wege vom Jesuitenkollegium zur Hochschule Luzern.* Zürich: Chronos Verlag.

Metzger, F. (2010) *Religion, Geschichte, Nation. Katholische Geschichtsschreibung in der Schweiz im 19. und 20. Jahrhundert – kommunikationstheoretische Perspektiven.* Stuttgart: Kohlhammer.

Mok, K.H. and Tan, J. (2004) *Globalization and Marketization in Education: A Comparative Analysis of Hong Kong and Singapore.* Cheltenham: Edward Elgar.

OECD (2004) *Examen der nationalen Bildungspolitiken: Die tertiäre Bildung in der Schweiz.* Paris: OECD Publishing.

Olssen, M. and Peters, M.A. (2005) Neoliberalism, higher education and the knowledge economy: From the free market to knowledge capitalism. *Journal of Educational Policy* 20 (3), 313–345.

Piller, I. (2001) Identity constructions in multilingual advertising. *Language in Society* 30, 153–186.

Polanyi, K. (1944) *The Great Transformation: The Political and Economic Origins of Our Time.* Boston, MA: Beacon Press.

Rossiter, N. (2003) Processual media theory. *Symploke* 11 (1–2), 104–131.

Saunders, D.B. (2010) Neoliberal ideology and public higher education in the United States. *Journal for Critical Education Policy Studies* 8 (1), 41–77.

Seaman, B. (2005) *Binge: What Your College Student Won't Tell You: Campus Life in an Age of Disconnection and Excess.* Hoboken, NJ: John Wiley and Sons.

Shohamy, E. (2006) *Language Policy: Hidden Agendas and New Approaches.* London: Routledge.

Sparke, M. (2017) *Introducing Globalization: Ties, Tensions and Uneven Integration* (2nd edn). New York: Wiley Blackwell.

Spilker, N. (2010) *Die Regierung der Prekarität: Zur neoliberalen Konzeption unsicherer Arbeitsverhältnisse.* Duisburg: Edition DISS.

Spring, J. (1998) *Education and the Rise of the Global Economy.* Mahwah, NJ: Lawrence Erlbaum.

Streckeisen, U. (1996) Die Mobilität der CH-Unimobil-Studierenden und Schweizer Erasmus-Studierenden. Eine Untersuchung zu Motiven und Erfahrungen. In U. Streckeisen (ed.) *Akademische Mobilität aus der Sicht der Studierenden*

(Begleitforschung zu den Mobilitätsförderungsprogrammen) (pp. 11–67). Bern: Bundesamt für Statistik.

Torres, C.A. and Schugurensky, D. (2002) The political economy of higher education in the era of neoliberal globalization: Latin America in comparative perspective. *Higher Education* 43 (4), 429–455.

Urciuoli, B. (2003) Excellence, leadership, skills, diversity: Marketing liberal arts education. *Language and Communication* 23, 385–408.

Urciuoli, B. (2008) Skills and selves in the new workplace. *American Ethnologist* 35, 211–228.

Urciuoli, B. (2010) Neoliberal education: Preparing the student for the new workplace. In C. Greenhouse (ed.) *Politics, Publics, Personhood: Ethnography at the Limits of Neoliberalism* (pp. 162–176). Philadelphia, PA: University of Pennsylvania Press.

Urciuoli, B. (2014) The semiotic production of the good student: A Peircian look at the commodification of liberal arts education. *Signs and Society* 2 (1), 56–83.

Wilkins, A. (2010) Citizens and/or consumers: Mutations in the construction of concepts and practices of school choice. *Journal of Education Policy* 25 (2), 171–189.

Wilkins, A. (2012) Commodifying diversity: Education and governance in the era of neoliberalism. *Human Affairs* 22 (2), 122–130.

Wilkins, A. (2014) School governance and neoliberal political rationality: What has democracy got to do with it? Conference paper, University of Vic – Universitat Central de Catalunya (Barcelona).

Zimmermann, M. (2014) Ticinità mobile. Von der variablen Konstruktion der Legitimität. *Bulletin de la VALS/ASLA – Bulletin suisse de linguistique appliquée* 99, 97–114.

Zimmermann, M. (2017) Researching student mobility in multilingual Switzerland: Reflections on multi-sited ethnography. In M. Martin-Jones and D. Martin (eds) *Researching Multilingualism: Critical and Ethnographic Approaches* (pp. 73–86). London: Routledge.

12 Neoliberal Reforms in Language Education: Major Trends, Uneven Outcomes, Open Questions

Mary McGroarty

Introduction

The chapters in this volume provide a range of current examples, provocative interpretations and insights into the multiple effects of neoliberal reforms in language education. We may view many of the neoliberal reforms discussed here as apotheoses of the European/North American political and economic consensus promoted by liberal (in European terms) and conservative (in US terms) economists and commentators that coalesced after World War II and has grown in influence since the 1980s and 1990s (Holborow, 2015; Mirowski & Plehwe, 2009). There are many approaches to neoliberal policies, but all reflect to some extent an acceptance of the need for government and business to work together, the value of competition, and expectations that the operation of market forces in most arenas of social life will produce benefits. These core principles are further influenced by a country's history, current realities and cultural traditions (Yergin & Stanislaw, 1998). Taken as a whole, these chapters illustrate three major trends affecting language education, encourage caution in uncritical acceptance of neoliberal rhetoric, and indicate crucial directions for further research and ongoing theoretical debate into the dynamics of language education in multiple sites. Furthermore, in a post-Brexit era, they evoke multiple questions about the pedagogical adequacy and moral legitimacy of the aggressive promotion of English and other neoliberal educational reforms going forward. It is far too soon to appreciate the effects of the British vote to leave the European Union; there will be different effects in various parts of Britain and outside it (Ip, 2016; Yardley *et al.*, 2016). At minimum, this event makes it an opportune moment to reflect on the economic and political underpinnings and current manifestations of neoliberal theory, particularly the innovations it has inspired in language education, the topic of this volume.

Three trends, a kind of new 'three Rs', stand out in the cases recounted here. They are (1) language as a recruiting tool, a tool to help institutions maintain and increase student numbers, as well as a tool to help countries validate their membership in the modern socio-economic community that uses English in the commercial sphere; (2) the restructuring, deregulation and privatization of language instruction as a way to achieve greater institutional flexibility; and (3) language learning as self-realization, often directed toward professional or occupational ends, but admitting selected other goals in some circumstances. Reviewing each of these in turn helps us to appreciate both the pervasiveness of neoliberal ideology and attendant practices and some of its gaps and internal contradictions.

Language as a Recruiting Tool

Particular forms of language education, whether dual immersion programs in the US (Flores) or English-medium courses in Korea (Park), Canada (Luke) or China (Gao) have long served as recruiting tools that enable institutions to increase student numbers. Indeed, related developments have preceded to some extent the neoliberal era. International students have been coming to Great Britain and the US to study in large numbers since the end of World War II, and Canada and Australia have actively sought international enrollees as well. The chapters by Gao and Park attest to the proliferation of English-medium courses, including entire degree programs, in Asia. Such programs are assumed to indicate a university's and a country's international competitiveness. Concurrently, and of interest with respect to matters of shifting patterns of enrollment around the globe, the rapid growth in English-medium degree programs in other such locations as Europe (Brenn-White & Faethe, 2013) and Japan (Hadley, this volume; Taguchi, 2012), among others, suggests that we may be entering an era of the diminution of the domination of inner-circle English countries as providers of academic English as university students seek to build their English skills and pursue academic training not in the US, the UK or other anglophone countries, but elsewhere, including their home countries, that now offer possibilities to develop academic English and even receive advanced degrees in an English-medium environment.

While most cases here and internationally reflect the attraction of English as a medium of instruction in higher education settings, English is not the only target language to serve as a recruiting tool. Particular local and national situations may inspire the use of other target languages to recruit students. China's Confucius Institute provides low-cost materials and, in some locations, teachers to spread the knowledge of Mandarin, the national standard, and good will for the country (Gao). Intriguingly, these efforts have sparked unease with traditional expectations for perfect mastery of grammatical and literary forms associated with conventional instruction in Chinese. It is as if the need to recruit and retain students in the study of Chinese demands relaxation of expectations, an attitude that is distasteful to the usual linguistic authorities. Yet another illustration of language used strategically to recruit students comes from Switzerland, where a relatively new, fairly small German-medium university recruits Italian speakers from another part of the country to enroll for law degrees in a German-medium faculty (Zimmermann and Flubacher). The Italophone law students are allowed extra time on exams given in German but few other institutional concessions or sources of academic assistance, and often turn to fellow Italian-speaking classmates for strategic and personal support.

In the US elementary and secondary system where English is assumed as the main language of instruction, it is the combination of English with another language, often Spanish but including other major languages such as Chinese, in a dual immersion model that has been promoted to keep students enrolled in public schools, rather than allowing them to move into charter or private schools (Flores). This chapter raises the possibility that dual immersion models are too often oversold as the solution to the many systemic problems in American education. Flores holds that they favor a superficial multiculturalism that leaves untouched the considerable structural and socio-economic disparities among student groups who differ in ethnicity, cultural capital, and native languages.

Restructuring of Language Education; Altering the Public/Private Mix

Global enthusiasm for learning English has led to a proliferation of private providers of instruction and pedagogical materials, many operating entirely outside the ambit of any of the traditional authorities such as Ministries of Education, local or state departments of education, teachers' organizations or university researchers, who would traditionally monitor quality. The originator of the 'New Oriental' method in China (see Gao's chapter) has been hailed by the government and official press for large student enrollments and great commercial success each year, achieving the capital needed to be listed on the New York Stock Exchange in 2006. This is not the only unusual proprietary method to arise and thrive in China, where potential for very large enrollments has drawn many entrepreneurs, with and without expertise in language teaching and education, into English instruction. An account of workers' lives in Dongguan, a large industrial city in South China, describes 'assembly line English', which omits teachers entirely, compels learners to copy unrelated lists of words and say them aloud as quickly as possible and defers any study of grammar until a learner can write 600 English sentences in an hour (Chang, 2009). Within more traditional educational environments such as those found in Japanese universities, Hadley's chapter shows that the drive to provide more English to more students more efficiently in Japan has given rise to a new category of practitioner/administrator, the blended English for academic purposes professional (called, tongue in cheek, a BLEAP), situated between teachers and administration. The task of such individuals is to manage the teachers who provide direct language instruction and keep prospecting for new students and new programs that can boost revenues while keeping costs to a minimum.

Reliance on private providers of curricula and materials for language instruction and sometimes other skills is a major current in deregulated educational environments. In the US, the provisions in the No Child Left Behind Act for particularly stringent accountability measures and provisions for hiring private tutoring for students experiencing difficulty created an opening for many providers of educational materials that promised, sometimes even guaranteed, student progress, again absent actual data (Glass, 2008; Ravitch, 2010). Koyama's chapter shows that some school administrators, desperate to improve a school's ranking, were easy marks for promotion of such materials; only the resistance of parents and community members who generated alternative activities and locations in which to provide their own types of tutorials for refugee students spared students from what a teacher called the 'drill and kill' approach the commercial materials reflected.

Sometimes non-traditional providers from the non-profit or private sectors are hired to develop special programs combining language instruction with particular occupational tasks, as in the US-sponsored English proficiency program for college graduates at a university in Mindanao, in the southern Philippines, a region marked by political instability and presence of a Muslim minority (Tabiola and Lorente). This program subsidized purchase of a special curriculum and materials from a US company to be used to develop the level of English needed to work in business process outsourcing, or call centers. Students using these English improvement materials were required to be present in a dedicated language laboratory that was, not coincidentally, air-conditioned, another draw in a hot climate. Also notable here is that those targeted by the program were already university graduates; thus this project was premised on giving workers who were already among the educational elites of their locality more specific language skills to match them with a global market operating mainly in English.

Educational materials generated by outside contractors along with a related training program were also part of the migrant training for entrepreneurship in Italian agriculture described by Del Percio and Van Hoof. Participants in this program were neither university students nor graduates, but adult migrants, many with prior experience of farming in their home countries (Peru, Chile, Ecuador, sub-Saharan Africa, the Mahgreb) or in the south Italian tomato industry. Levels of Italian mastery, in literacy and in oral skills, were extremely varied. Despite the heterogeneous levels of prior education and second language skill in the group, the training was quite theoretically oriented, partly because of the constraints of EU funding. It included development of technical vocabulary related to agricultural products and processes, development of a statement of personal and family goals, a business plan and role plays simulating sales and other consumer interactions. Ultimately, however, there were no funds, public or private, to support the business plans that had been generated, nor was it possible to rent, lease or find a donor to provide the land needed for growing agricultural products for the program's participants. Many expressed satisfaction at learning how to produce a business plan, but still complained about the difficult job market.

Language as Part of the Re-Invention of a Successful Self

A final theme worthy of focus is the promotion of language skills as part of a successful adult self. Most of the chapters in this volume deal only or mainly with language study in higher education, a level of education in which, even in prosperous countries, a minority of young people participate. A recent summary of educational participation in the G-20 countries representing two-thirds of the world's population and 75% to 80% of world trade shows that, for 20- to 29-year-olds, these countries have an educational participation rate of between 20% and 30% (Stephens et al., 2015: 12). In the present volume, all chapters dealing with language in higher education reflect G-20 countries except for those treating language programs in Switzerland and the Philippines, which are not G-20 members. In the tertiary level cases included here, the language linked with success has most often meant the mastery of some level of English thought to both demonstrate and facilitate ability to engage in entrepreneurial behavior, to become 'enterprising' in the literal sense. So, for example, Luke (chapter 6) describes how university students from Brazil were specifically sought for participation in a program that promised to advance their credentials in science and technology through study of scientific fields and related internships in Canada. Although the internships never materialized, and students' initial low levels of English limited their access to classes in more specialized fields, many expressed satisfaction that they had acquired enough English to distinguish themselves from other similarly qualified graduates without English in the Brazilian labor market. Their situation was thus not unlike the Italian law students who decided to pursue law degrees in German, the most important commercial language in Switzerland (Zimmermann and Flubacher). In Mindanao, the Job Enabling English Proficiency (JEEP) project promised a relatively quick pathway to more focused English skills to individuals who were already university graduates, already holding university degrees, who, on completion of the program, would then qualify to work in the call centers jointly sponsored by the US Agency for International Development and the Philippine government (Tabiola and Lorente).

In the academic environments profiled here, nearly all of them related to tertiary education, increased mastery of English is promoted as an indicator of individual competitiveness as well as institutional and national prestige. The chapters by Gao and Park imply that, for university faculty and students in China and Korea, the ability to lecture or attend lectures in English and profit from such instruction serves as a way to build individual capabilities to publish in English, thereby enhancing individual and institutional reputations and each country's international standing. This is a salutary effect at the institutional and national level. Nonetheless, it may be tempered somewhat by individual hesitance in using English in interaction. A recent study (Vasilopoulos, 2015) indicates that Korean young adults who were successful and fluent bilinguals showed reluctance to display their advanced English proficiency in public, finding ways to disguise their oral skills around interlocutors whose English level was unknown or less advanced.

Determination of the types of language skills characteristic of a successful self looks different when considered at the elementary level. Most often, one of the main tasks of universal education is the achievement of literacy in a country's principal language. In the US, as Koyama's chapter explains, the unusually stringent requirements regarding minimum acceptable annual progress in English literacy that were part of the No Child Left Behind (NCLB) regime made achievement of higher levels on an obligatory English test a high bar for many of the refugee children enrolled in middle school. Thus, 'progress' was operationally defined in a highly reductionist way, as movement from one level, 2 to the next, 3, in a 4-category system. However, another chapter in this volume reminds us that English literacy skills are not the only language abilities valued by some younger learners and their families. De Korne's chapter on the re-valorization of Isthmus Zapotec shows that, despite historical and contemporary ambivalence regarding the importance of this language, some members of this indigenous community in Mexico are beginning to appreciate and aspire to continue to use that language and even achieve literacy in it. Sometimes this interest reflects awareness that the language has value in the local, literal market; sometimes youngsters and their teachers see it linked to opportunities for designated scholarships; sometimes they see it as part of their connection to a distinctive local community, a connection perceived as meaningful beyond commercial or business applications. This investigation attests to the many motivations that can influence retention, re-vitalization and broader learning of native languages. The chapter will, let us hope, inspire others to look at younger language users and trace the intra-community variation over time.

Uneven Outcomes and Open Questions

The cases here show that the varieties of neoliberal reforms implemented to date have often had uneven outcomes (if, indeed, outcomes have been specifically identified for study, and students followed long enough to see what happens; neither of these can be assumed for many, if not most, educational innovations, including those linked with neoliberalism). Despite the strong rhetorical claims in neoliberal socio-economic theory between the benefit of competition, the impartial and beneficial operation of market forces, and the value of entrepreneurial activity, results observed in the settings described are neither uniform nor always positive. Government projects constructed in bursts of enthusiasm often run short of funding; the crucial experiences of internships in actual businesses or academic departments somehow disappear for various reasons before students can actually participate; and the use of competition across schools as an engine of increased achievement has been shown to be sorely deficient.

What can we learn from these instructive cases, and what kind of research is indicated to further evaluate neoliberal reforms in language and education? There is much to be done. For at least 30 years, educational philosophers have made efforts to describe options for post-liberal language policies in education (e.g. Petrovic [2015] for a summary). I now turn to some of the many types of research that could usefully build on these cases and advance general understanding of the effects and limitations of various approaches to educational reform and social change, including but not limited to the various neoliberal reforms discussed here. My focus is on the US because that is the educational policy world I know best. Readers can judge the degree to which similar research efforts may make sense in their own policy environments.

We continue to need economists to provide careful documentation of the economic value of language skills. Grin (2008, 2015) shows that, assuming the availability of sufficiently detailed statistics on individual educational trajectories, there are accepted econometric methods that can be used to determine the impact of language skills on earning power. While few countries even in Europe, let alone elsewhere, have such data, it is not to be disregarded. Chiswick (2009) described such studies for immigrants to the US, noting that such research rests on inferences about the links between second language abilities and income levels. While statistics at the national level have some uses, even more vital for theory and for assessing differential impacts are the more fine-grained examinations of the impact of bilingual skills on particular professions in similar locations in the same political unit (e.g. Alarcón et al., 2014). In the US and elsewhere, studies with comparable levels of detail and comparison groups are desirable.

Because many of the projects reported here represent relatively short-term efforts funded by governments and other policy actors or groups using scarce funds to advance policy objectives, it is essential to use the tools of political science to examine the implementation of reforms more systematically than has been done in the past. McDonnell and Weatherford (2016) make a strong case for investigations in educational policy to move beyond the focus on policy enactment that has so far dominated related models, to encompass research on policy implementation, a far more complicated matter. Policy implementation generally includes a larger number of different actors and agencies operating in disparate locations across different time spans. Using the enactment of Common Core curricular standards in the US as an example, they show what relevant research on implementation could include.

One of the hallmarks of neoliberal reforms in American education, specifically the detailed approach to identifying annual progress in reading and math, has been the creation of space for non-traditional providers of curricular materials and assessments. It has been suggested that there has also been a strong commercial motive to provide such pre-packaged lessons and assessments (Glass, 2008; Ravitch, 2010). At the very least, the No Child Left Behind (NCLB) approach to accountability opened up opportunities for many different individuals and groups to sell goods and services, from annual tests all the way through charter school models, to public entities such as school boards and state departments of education (McGroarty, 2013). At a minimum, such costs should be identified in the interest of good public management and for consistency with a paradigm that promotes efficiency. Yet, within the current regime of American elementary and secondary education, clear and current cost information regarding, for example, charter schools has not always been available, nor is it always readily accessible in a reporting format that can be used by school boards, legislators or other political leaders (Baker & Miron, 2015).

But costs are only one aspect of accountability in education. Equally, perhaps even more crucial, is the deep-seated concern that an educational model that specifies a certain amount of required annual improvement is ill-suited to assess educational efforts comprehensively (Rothstein *et al.*, 2008). NCLB was intended to work in part by punishing children, their teachers and school leaders for insufficient progress, a step that countermanded the US constitutional tradition of state and local control. Even panels of technical experts associated with advanced psychometric approaches have noted that those within the educational system respond more positively to rewards than to negative sanctions for test-based incentives (though even that effect is relatively small, when examined across the entire country; National Research Council, 2011). This group, along with a range of other scholars, urges a much wider range of accountability indicators be identified and documented regularly including evidence in areas such as opportunity-to-learn standards and factors related to the lived experiences of learners and teachers. Other types of accountability, such as ensuring that all schools within a state enjoy generally similar resource levels and students and their teachers have comparably safe physical environments and manageable class sizes, both far more relevant to the day-to-day experience of education, were not even suggested in the original formulation of accountability regimes such as NCLB, and must be recognized and taken into account (Firestone, 2014).

In fact, the logical mismatch between the perceived difficulties of American public education – low achievement and poorer social outcomes, especially by learners affected by poverty or belonging to disadvantaged groups – has been noted for over a decade by well-established critics with long experience in education (Noddings, 2007; Sahlberg, 2015). Noddings observes that the kind of 'choice' embodied in NCLB was invariably parent choice of schools for their children; this is only one aspect of what is relevant to learning and teaching, and ignores issues related to student choice of an appropriate, interesting curriculum, a scope greatly reduced by NCLB's mandatory concentration on instruction in subjects that would be assessed. Sahlberg (2015: 142) too remarks that, partly in reaction to overemphasis on knowledge-based teaching and test-based accountability, very much a part of the Global Educational Reform Movement (or GERM), educational authorities worldwide are now working to develop 'more dynamic forms of curriculum', including new approaches to accountability and leadership, to encourage greater flexibility, networking and creativity – the social skills that have been entirely left out of the US test-driven regime. If these skills are a key to a successful self and an effective community, they cannot be ignored or neglected at any level of education. Social science research shows that, in the US, educational outcomes are shaped as much by out-of-school factors, particularly the nature of neighborhoods and family resources – as in-school factors (Duncan & Murnane, 2011).

Finally, for all countries, and for citizens of all ages, the matter of what constitutes an appropriate education and the language skills that contribute to it is as much a philosophical and moral matter as an economic one. These dimensions cannot be ignored. Much scholarship on neoliberal reforms in education and in language has concentrated on the use of incentives and analogies drawn from the economic aspects of neoliberal theory; such analysis is important, but partial. It is now time to articulate political connections and their implications for education in comparable detail. This effort is particularly urgent at this moment, after the UK has voted to leave the European Union. What, if anything, might this mean for English, for other parts of the UK, for other anglophone countries, for countries in Europe and for countries elsewhere? Will the vote have any impact at all on the learning of English or the popularity of English-medium instruction? British liberalism, a predecessor of the neoliberal consensus, had assumed that political freedom was a necessary precondition for economic freedom; over decades, subsequent neoliberal consensus reversed this, presenting economic freedom as a prerequisite for the relative political freedom of (limited) individual choice (Mirowski & Plehwe, 2009: 28). The individual and social choices represented by language use and language education and training need to be further interrogated from the perspective of their relationship to personal and political freedom, not only economic opportunity. Chapters like those in this volume can serve as a starting point for further investigation of the personal and social futures in which language skills are embedded. Education, including language education, is multi-faceted, can continue over decades and has stops and starts. Language may constitute an intensive focus at one point, less of an emphasis later, only to be picked up again and renewed and diversified. Life changes may bring about the need to use languages never envisioned as essential during the years of universal schooling.

The emphasis on language as part of personal reinvention, often automatically applied to English skills for entrepreneurship in many neoliberal projects, with an echo effect of allowing or encouraging other languages where they may have local, internal, national or regional commercial relevance, underrepresents the many reasons for learning and using two or more languages. If a dominant language such as English is part of the picture, concentrating only on its assumed economic relevance can appear to endorse language uniformity without acknowledging the political values associated with diversity (Grin, 2015). Bilingual and multilingual skills may indeed connect an individual to a larger market of exchange, commercial or academic; they may connect speakers with local communities valued for their personal relevance; they may also simply reflect enhanced ability to adapt to different environments, a life skill of perennial relevance (Heath, 2012). What this means now and in the future for users, learners and teachers of English and the other languages included in this volume is being worked out daily around the globe. Let us hope that future scholarship will build on these chapters and complement attention to the economic impacts of language use and language study with attention to their personal, social and political valences as well.

References

Alarcón, A., Di Paolo, A., Heyman, J. and Morales, M.C. (2014) Returns to Spanish-English bilingualism in the new information economy: The health and criminal justice sectors in the Texas border and Dallas-Tarrant Counties. In R. Callahan and P. Gándara (eds) *The Bilingual Advantage: Language, Literacy, and the US Labor Market* (pp. 138–159). Bristol: Multilingual Matters.

Baker, B. and Miron, G. (2015) *The Business of Charter Schooling: Understanding the Policies that Charter Operators Use for Financial Benefit.* Boulder, CO: National Education Policy Center. See http://nepc.colorado.edu/publication/charter-revenue (accessed 22 June 2016).

Brenn-White, M. and Faethe, E. (2013) *English-Taught Master's Programs in Europe: A 2013 Update.* New York: Institute of International Education. See www.iie.org/mobility (accessed 19 June 2016).

Chang, L.T. (2009) *Factory Girls: From Village to City in a Changing China.* New York: Spiegel and Grau.

Chiswick, B. (2009) The economics of language for immigrants: An introduction and overview. In T. Wiley, J.S. Lee and R. Rumberger (eds) *The Education of Language Minority Immigrants in the United States* (pp. 72–92). Bristol: Multilingual Matters.

Duncan, G. and Murnane, R. (eds) (2011) *Whither Opportunity? Rising Inequality, Schools, and Children's Life Chances.* New York: Russell Sage Foundation.

Firestone, W.A. (2014) Teacher evaluation policy and conflicting theories of motivation. *Educational Researcher* 43 (2), 100–107.

Glass, G.V. (2008) *Fertilizer, Pills, and Magnetic Strips: The Fate of Public Education in America.* Charlotte, NC: Information Age Publishing.

Grin, F. (2008) The economics of language education. In S. May and N. Hornberger (eds) *The Encyclopedia of Language and Education,* (2nd edn; Vol. 1) *Language Policy and Political Issues in Education* (pp. 83–93). New York: Springer.

Grin, F. (2015) The economics of English in Europe. In T. Ricento (ed.) *Language Policy and Political Economy* (pp. 119–144). Oxford: Oxford University Press.

Heath, S.B. (2012) *Words at Work and Play: Three Decades in Family and Community Life.* New York: Cambridge University Press.

Holborow, M. (2015) *Language and Neoliberalism.* New York: Routledge/Taylor & Francis.

Ip, G. (2016) Nationalism vies with economics to drive politics. *The Wall Street Journal,* 27 June, p. A6.

McDonnell, L.M. and Weatherford, M.S. (2016) Recognizing the political in implementation research. *Educational Researcher* 45 (4), 233–242.

McGroarty, M. (2013) Multiple actors and arenas in evolving language policies. In J.W. Tollefson (ed.) *Language Policies in Education: Critical Issues* (pp. 35–58). New York: Routledge/Taylor & Francis.

Mirowski, P. and Plehwe, D. (2009) *The Road from Mont Pèlerin: The Making of the Neoliberal Thought Collective.* Cambridge, MA: Harvard University Press.

National Research Council (2011) *Incentives and Test-Based Accountability in Education.* Committee on incentives and test-based accountability in public education, M. Hout and S.W. Elliott (eds) Board on Testing and Assessment, Division of Behavioral and Social Sciences in Education. Washington, DC: The National Academies Press.

Noddings, N. (2007) *When School Reform Goes Wrong.* New York: Teachers College Press.

Petrovic, J. (2015) *A Post-Liberal Approach to Language Policy in Education.* Bristol: Multilingual Matters.

Ravitch, D. (2010) *The Death and Life of the Great American School System.* New York: Basic Books.

Rothstein, R., Jacobsen, R. and Wilder, T. (2008) *Grading Education: Getting Accountability Right.* Washington, DC: Economic Policy Institute and Teachers College Press.

Sahlberg, P. (2015) *Finnish Lessons 2.0: What Can the World Learn from Educational Change in Finland?* New York: Teachers College Press.

Stephens, M., Warren, L., Harner, A. and Owen, E. (2015) Comparative indicators of education in the United States and other G-20 countries: 2015 (NCES 2016-100). US Department of Education, National Center for Education Statistics. Washington, DC: US Government Printing Office. See http://nces.ed.gov/pubs2016/2016100.pdf (accessed 27 June 2016).

Taguchi, N. (2012) *Context, Individual Differences, and Pragmatic Competence.* Bristol: Multilingual Matters.

Vasilopoulos, G. (2015) Language learner investment and identity negotiation in the Korean EFL context. *Journal of Language, Identity, and Education* 14 (2), 61–79.

Yardley, J., Smale, A., Perlez, J. and Hubbard, B. (2016) A caustic postwar unraveling: A test of Western alliances and institutions. *The New York Times*, 26 June, pp. A1, A8.

Yergin, D. and Stanislaw, J. (1998) *The Commanding Heights: The Battle Between Government and the Marketplace that is Remaking the Modern World.* New York: Simon & Schuster.

Index